# The Good

## Memoirs of an Int

### by

### Jan Kurzke

With an Introduction by Richard Baxell
and an Afterword by Charlotte Kurzke

The Clapton Press

First published 2021 by:
THE CLAPTON PRESS LTD,
38 Thistlewaite Road, London E5

ISBN: 978-1-913693-06-0

# Contents

# Dedication

To the memory of William (Bill) McGuire (1917-2009).
Without him this book would never have seen the light of day.[1]

*Publisher's spoiler alert: the end notes provide mini-biographies of some of the main characters, including in some cases when and where they were killed.*

# List of Illustrations

All photographs courtesy of Charlotte Kurzke, with the exception of
*International Brigaders inside the Faculty of Philosophy & Letters;
Approach to the Plaza Mayor, Madrid;* and *The Palace Hotel, Madrid.*

# Introduction by Richard Baxell

In November 1936, during the first few months of the Spanish Civil War, a handful of English students were holed up in the Department of Philosophy and Letters, in Madrid's University City. They were part of a desperate and last-ditch effort by the Republican government's forces to hold back Franco's Nationalist troops who were advancing ominously on the Spanish capital. The group of students were reduced to taking pot-shots at the occupants of the adjacent buildings, 'firing from behind barricades of philosophy books.' The piles of dense volumes of Indian metaphysics and early nineteenth-century German philosophy, they discovered, gave highly effective protection against enemy small arms fire. Given that the Republican government had made vigorous efforts to promote education and raise Spain's shameful literacy levels, while the leader of Franco's Foreign Legion had been accused of yelling 'long live death' and 'death to intellectuals', it's difficult not to see the skirmish as a metaphor for a much wider struggle.

The group of young students were members of the now legendary International Brigades, made up of volunteers from around the world who were determined to fight for the Spanish government against the forces of General Franco and his German and Italian backers. The majority were from Britain, though one was from Germany, a refugee from the Nazi regime. He was, wrote one of his fellow volunteers, 'a very handsome young man, with aristocratic looks and manners . . . [a] very quiet, cultured chap . . . and a talented artist.' His name was Jan Kurzke.

Born in 1905 to a German father and Danish mother, Hans Robert Kurzke, known as Jan, hailed from a modest background, leaving school at fourteen. However, having shown promise as a portrait artist, two years later he was awarded a scholarship to art school. During the 1920s under Germany's progressive Weimar Republic he became interested in left-wing politics and worked for a time for a Socialist newspaper. In the early 1930s, with Hitler's Nazi Party becoming increasingly powerful and violently attacking its opponents, Kurzke prudently fled into exile, travelling through North Africa before ending up in Spain.

Kurzke's account of his experiences in Spain, published here, was written while the civil war was still raging. It's a common media trope to talk of 'long-lost memoirs' being 'discovered' but this is often down to journalistic license (as archivists and historians will confirm). This is not the case here either, for the typescript has resided for some time in the International Institute of Social History in Amsterdam. However, despite a number of previous efforts to see it published – including one by Bernard Knox, a friend of Kurzke's from Spain, who went on to become a well-respected Professor of Hellenic Studies at Harvard – it has remained tucked away for years, read only by a small number of specialist historians.

Kurzke's record forms roughly half of a wider memoir that was co-written with his girlfriend, the artist, model and journalist, Kate Mangan (formerly Katherine Prideaux Foster). The two accounts were originally combined into one volume, though it's pretty clear that Kurzke always intended for his account to stand alone. Now disentangled from each other, the two memoirs have been published separately; Jan's under the full memoir's original title, *The Good Comrade* and Kate Mangan's as *Never More Alive: Inside the Spanish Republic*. While the two occasionally overlap, they are very different, both in subject matter and in tone. Kate worked in the Spanish Republic's Press Office for a time and her account dazzles with descriptions of celebrities such as W.H. Auden, Stephen Spender, Ernest Hemingway, Martha Gelhorn, Gerda Taro and Robert Capa. Kurzke's memoir, on the other hand, is a soldier's tale, focusing on his personal experience of combat. He frequently resorts to short, sometimes even terse, sentences, which read much like a series of diary entries, helping to create a real sense of immediacy. It's notably anti-heroic and a generally honest appraisal, laying bare his own faults and errors, as well as those of his comrades and the Republican army itself. He has a keen eye - he was, after all, an artist – and the account is littered with well-observed descriptions of Spain, its people in the 1930s and the civil war.

While personal accounts are by their very nature subjective and not always reliable, Kurzke's does chime with other accounts, by both contemporaries and historians. When his friend Bernard Knox first read the memoir, many years after the war, he was astonished by Kurzke's extraordinary power of recall and the ability to bring back memories of people and events long forgotten, often capturing the particular linguistic idiosyncrasies of his comrades. He wrote with genuine admiration of Kurzke's account of the fighting in Madrid, how he 'catches the reality, the tone, the feel of those terrifying and exhilarating few weeks.'

Kurzke did have a distinct advantage over many other foreign commentators on the civil war, in that, having travelled extensively through the country, he spoke enough Spanish to be able to have some understanding of its history, culture and politics. This allowed him insight into areas such as the rivalries between the political factions on the Republican side that bewildered so many foreigners. Nevertheless, in contrast with some memoirs by protagonists, Kurzke does not over-labour the political lessons to be drawn. There is wry humour too, with no attempt to soft-soap the chaos and confusion that is often part and parcel of a foot soldier's lot. His description of one morning in Madrid is typical:

> The sun rose. We still marched. It was nearly eight o'clock when we reached a village. We halted and received a cup of coffee, a little brandy and a piece of bread. We waited again. Somebody said the attack was off. Somebody always says something. We told him to get stuffed.

Kurzke's memoir actually begins two years before the civil war, in 1934, as he takes leave from Barcelona, his girlfriend and most of his belongings, which had been stolen from his hotel. His colourful description of tramping from Alicante to Málaga, a trek of nearly 500km, gives a personal and poignant insight into the appalling levels of poverty and inequality in early twentieth century Spain. Unlike the winsome Laurie Lee, Kurzke had no violin with which to charm the locals, though his ability to draw a likeness and speak English provided him with the occasional peseta. In Granada he encountered a group of busking German emigres who asked Kurzke if he would like to join them, despite his lack of musical prowess. His decision to accept was due, in no small part, to the presence of a 'beautifully built' young blonde. 'I am Putz', she informed him. The leader of the German troop, Walter, informed Kurzke that he could join them under one condition: 'You mustn't fall in love with her.' Of course not, he promised.

The first section of his memoir ends, somewhat abruptly, in Granada, before picking up again in Cádiz in late summer, with the depiction of a rather dismal bullfight, where the bull, which hadn't been killed cleanly, 'had to be finished off with a knife.' At this point, the narrative pauses once again. Though we don't hear it from him, Kurzke bid a no doubt emotional farewell to the admirable Putz – who, of course, he had fallen for, and made his way to Mallorca, where he fell in with a crowd of English holidaymakers who took him back to Britain with them. At a party in London he met Kate Mangan, who was recently separated from her husband (the Irish-American writer, Sherry Mangan), and the two soon fell in love.

Early in 1936 the couple travelled to Mallorca and then on to Portugal, where they heard the dramatic news that a military coup had been launched in Spain against the democratically elected government. Jan immediately wanted to go to Spain to volunteer, but with the frontier closed, the pair were forced to linger in Portugal, reading newspaper reports of the rising with growing alarm. Both were horrified to find that a massacre of 4000 Republican defenders at Badajoz, just over the border, 'was greeted with open rejoicing, the newspapers gloated over the massacres and boasted that the streets were running with blood.' Kate later speculated that Jan's loathing of Franco's *Nacionales* was bolstered by seeing a propaganda film about the Spanish Foreign Legion called *La Bandera*. It featured an officer with one arm and an eye-patch, clearly based on the Legion's infamous commander, General 'long live death' Millán Astray:

> It was not that it inspired him with animosity against the men of
> the Legion but it made him want to lead such a life, and perhaps

death, of hardship and comradeship in a cause he believed in.

While Kate approved in principle of Jan's wish to volunteer, she was understandably anxious about what might happen to him. However, deeply troubled by the prospect that Madrid might not be able to resist against Franco's army, he was utterly determined to go. His desire became even more urgent when he heard of the failed Catalan attempt to capture Mallorca in mid-August and the fall of Irún in northern Spain the following month. Jan and Kate returned to London and having sensibly obtained a typhoid inoculation, Kurzke secretly set out for Spain in October.

Like the majority of volunteers who left from Britain for Spain, Kurzke made his way to Paris, where the Communist Party headquarters in La Place du Combat (now La Place du Colonel Fabien) was acting as the central recruiting point for the International Brigades. He then joined other international volunteers on a boat and was smuggled into Republican Spain:

> In less than an hour we should be in Alicante. I say 'we' now, because I am not alone and the ship is much bigger than the one I came on before. We are six hundred men, Germans, Poles, French and English and we know what to do and where we are going.

Kurzke was one of many volunteers for the International Brigades to see the fight against Franco as part of the same struggle they had been waging throughout Europe. French Socialists, Polish exiles, Germans and Italian antifascists, all hoped that victory in Spain would be a first step towards achieving the same in their homelands: '*oggi in Spagna domani in Italia*', wrote one Italian volunteer, 'today in Spain, tomorrow in Italy'.

Kurzke paints a colourful picture of travelling through Republican Spain on trains that rarely increased their speed above walking pace, of railway stations bedecked with banners defiantly parading their solidarity with the Spanish Republic. Kurzke's unpretentious prose movingly recreates the powerful emotions that many volunteers remembered, inspired by the welcoming crowds, waving flags and chanting *¡Viva la República! ¡Viva la democracia!* 'Spain had come to greet us' he wrote proudly. His account, like those of many others, illustrates, contrary to Francoist propaganda, just how welcome these foreigners really were.

Most volunteers for the International Brigades served with their national compatriots, partly because of the common language. Kurzke, however, chose to fight alongside the group of young English volunteers he had met travelling to Spain. At this point in the war there were not yet enough English-speaking volunteers to form a battalion, so Kurzke and his comrades were assigned to a French unit, part of the 11th International Brigade. Officially called the Commune de Paris Battalion, it was known by all as the Dumont, after its popular commander, a former French army officer and long-standing Communist. The English group that Kurzke joined was led by a handsome, charismatic and brilliant former Cambridge student called John Cornford. He had originally intended to write about the conflict, but decided that 'a journalist without a word of Spanish was just useless' and had taken the decision to actively join the fight. Alongside Cornford was a friend of his from Cambridge, the classics scholar Bernard Knox, and a writer called John Sommerfield. Other students to join the group were a young Jewish east-ender and Archaeology undergraduate, Manny 'Sam' Lesser and a Rear-Admiral's son and Edinburgh medical student, David Mackenzie. All were, like Cornford, members of the Communist Party. Despite their undeniably scholarly and bourgeois backgrounds, it would be a mistake to assume that the members of the International Brigades were mainly intellectuals. In fact, the students were a small minority and, as Kurzke describes, most were working-class, political activists:

> There was Fred, twenty-nine years old from London and his inseparable friend Steve, a small cockney with a big nose and blond hair. There was Jock, a Scot, who had done a prison term for mutiny, he later rose to the rank of colonel. There was Joe, an ex-fighter from the Red Army in China. There was George, a pale, thin young man with a red beard which made him look like Christ

and Pat a young Irishman.

Kurzke's portrayals of his comrades are generally unsentimental but affectionate and occasionally reveal his dry amusement. The bewilderment of their French comrades at the two John's precocious pipe-smoking habit and their vain attempts to mimic Jock's impenetrable Scottish accent 'by making strangled sounds' provide a brief respite of comic relief. Though the group clearly seems to have formed a strong bond, Kurzke hints that they were not immune to the misunderstandings and differences that could develop between the middle class students on one hand and the working class activists and former soldiers on the other. As Winston Churchill's nephew Esmond Romilly also recounts in his own memoir, *Boadilla*, some of the 'old sweats' harboured grave doubts about the younger volunteers' lack of military experience, and were fearful that they might unwittingly put themselves or their comrades in danger.

Any doubts were unlikely to be assuaged by the standard of military instruction given in Spain. Kurzke's experiences of a rather brief and chaotic period of training echo that of other accounts. In the International Brigades orders were usually given in the dominant language of the unit, which for the German Kurzke and his British friends, meant French:

> Every morning we trained in the wood just outside the town with many Spaniards looking on. They mimicked Marcel's 'un, deux, un deux.' They had every reason to be amused. When Marcel said 'à gauche' some went to the left, others to the right.

Uniforms were anything but uniform and the mishmash of different outfits led to the first of the International Brigades becoming portrayed as 'the army in overalls.'

> The next day we were issued with uniforms consisting of dark blue skiing pants and jackets which looked like those worn by the *serenos* or night watchmen. They were of thick blue cloth with black braid. They were made for smaller people and did not fit at all ... our company looked a fantastic sight. The berets and the

short jackets made us look like a bunch of artists from Montmartre.

The arms issued were similarly hotchpotch, consisting of numerous different makes and calibres. Many were in poor condition, some were antiquated and obsolete. Kurzke was appalled to discover that his rifle was an American Remington from the First World War. Many were even older. Kurzke's account amply demonstrates how the western powers' policy of non-intervention in the Spanish war, which severely limited the Republic's opportunity to purchase arms, actually played out on the ground.

Like soldiers of time immemorial, Kurzke writes about the misery of being exhausted, hungry, thirsty, wet, and freezing cold; 'war is bloody' wrote George Orwell famously. The food was dreadful and stomach upsets endemic, 'nobody slept much [and] the cold was terrible', consequently 'some men got colds and infected everybody else and soon most of us were coughing and spitting.' As Kurzke and his comrades learned, though Madrid is often warm during the day, the city's altitude means it can get surprisingly cold at night. This rather came as a distinct shock to many of the volunteers from Britain, as the correspondent for the Communist *Daily Worker*, Claud Cockburn, sneeringly related:

> They had all got the impression they were going to sunny Spain, they'd all seen the posters. And the main source of discontent and grumbling ... [was] the feeling that somehow they'd been swindled by the weather.

Understandably, many men became disenchanted and drunkenness very quickly became common, causing serious discipline problems, as Kurzke admits:

> Our Jock was one of them; when he was drunk he started slugging everybody. We wanted to send him back to England but he would not go and he became a great nuisance.

It's not difficult to understand why such pessimism was rife. In many ways, November 1936 was not so much a time of heroism and glory, as one of trepidation. Few doubted that it was a time of great peril for the Spanish Republic. Franco's forces had effortlessly brushed aside any opposition on their advance on Madrid. Now the enemy was very much at the gates; 'everything looked grey, dirty and hopeless,' confessed Kurzke.

Widespread rumours that Foreign Legionaries and Moroccan *Regulares* had been seen moving into the western suburbs of Madrid had aroused terror and panic among the city's population. The wholesale slaughter of the Republican defenders at Badajoz ensured that *madrileños* were in no doubt of their fate, should Franco's forces prevail. And very few doubted that they would, not least the members of the Republican government, who had decamped to Valencia, leaving the city under the command of a military defence junta. Franco's field commander, General Varela, was supremely confident that his elite force of Spanish Legionaries and Moroccan mercenaries would encounter no more resistance than they had over the previous four months. However, to the astonishment of the representatives of the world's media, some of whom had already filed stories of the capital's fall, the population were determined to resist. 'Madrid will be the tomb of fascism', declared its grimly determined defenders: 'They Shall Not Pass!' The battle for Madrid, the central epic of the Spanish conflict, was about to begin. 'Spain was the heart of the fight against fascism,' wrote a supporter of the Spanish Republicans, paraphrasing W.H. Auden's famous poem, *Spain*, 'and Madrid was the heart of the heart.'

On 7 November 1936, Kurzke was among the first of the International Brigades to arrive in the capital to take their place alongside the Spanish defenders. While many *madrileños* assumed that they were Russians, the 1900 volunteers were in fact mainly French, Germans and central Europeans. But, as the Madrid correspondent for the English newspaper, the *News Chronicle* Geoffrey Cox, reported, 'Madrid was not worrying who these troops were. They knew that they looked like business, that they were well armed, and that they were on their side. That was enough.' As Arturo Barea, who worked for the Republican Foreign Ministry's Press Office recounted in his magnificent autobiography, *The Forging of a Rebel*, the defending Spanish Republicans were jubilant:

> *Milicianos* [militiamen] cheered each other and themselves in the bars, drunk with tiredness and wine, letting loose their pent-up fear and excitement in their drinking bouts before going back to their street corner and their improvised barricades. On that Sunday, the endless November the 8th, a formation of foreigners in uniform, equipped with modern arms, paraded through the centre of the town: the legendary International Column which had been training in Albacete had come to the help of Madrid. After the nights of the 6th and 7th, when Madrid had been utterly alone in its resistance, the arrival of those anti-Fascists from abroad was an incredible relief . . . We all hoped that now, through the defence of Madrid, the world would awaken to the meaning of our fight.

Despite their inexperience and lack of meaningful training, the International Brigades were nevertheless among the Republic's best troops. Consequently Kurzke's battalion was thrown into combat, first in the Casa de Campo, the large park to the west of Madrid, then as part of a 'great flanking attack on the Fascist lines at Aravaca', just to the north of the park, before moving to occupy the shell-pocked buildings of University City. His description of the devastation wrought on Madrid is depressingly familiar, no surprise given that the civil war was clearly a forerunner of what was to be unleashed across Europe, and beyond:

> There was a great house with only the outer walls standing and the interior blown completely out like a piece of scenery for a film. Through the windows one could see into the empty space strewn with débris and blackened by fire. Other houses were cut in half with furniture hanging from the blackened ruins.

Kurzke's descriptions of the frontline fighting evocatively portrays the moments of terror interspersed with hours of boredom that soldiers endure, and he captures the confusion, the blunders, and the disasters that are an inevitable consequence of warfare. His account of the accidental death of the groups' commander, a former soldier from London called H. Fred Jones, is very moving, though just as harrowing is his description of a group of Polish volunteers who had been hit by shellfire:

> They all looked strangely alike; their faces pale, waxen, yellow, their eyes dark and still with the expression of surprise and horror of the terrible moment when the shell had burst upon them. Their hair was full of sand as if they had been buried. I fumbled for a cigarette and lit one. One of the wounded was talking to me in Polish and I could not understand what he said. He looked at my cigarette and I put it in his mouth. He sucked it greedily and then died, the smoke still trickling from his mouth.

Fully aware that they were pitted against the best troops of Franco's army, it must have seemed miraculous to Kurzke that the hastily-assembled forces defending Madrid managed to throw back Franco's forces. Yet throw them back they did. However it was only a temporary setback for, the following month, Franco launched a new offensive, hoping to encircle the Republican capital to the north. Consequently Kurzke's unit in the 11th International Brigade was moved up to help stem an attack on the village of Boadilla del Monte, fifteen kilometres west of Madrid.

It was to be, Bernard Knox believed, 'the biggest offensive the Fascists had yet launched.' Occupying a defensive position in Boadilla, the defending Republican forces quickly found themselves hopelessly outgunned and outnumbered. Kurzke's group were forced to retreat through the village, crawling on their stomachs to avoid the murderous hail of bullets. Bernard Knox was hit in the throat and he later described eloquently how he was consumed with a furious, violent rage: 'Why me?' he wrote,

> I was just 21 and had barely begun living my life. Why should I have to die? It was unjust. And, as I felt my whole being sliding into nothingness, I cursed. I cursed God and the world and everyone in it as the darkness fell.

Shortly afterwards, Kurzke was also wounded, briefly losing consciousness after suffering 'a fearful blow' to his right leg. Both

Knox and Kurzke were fortunate to survive. Two days later, another small group of British and Irish volunteers, part of the German 12th International Brigade, were not so lucky. The group, of whom Churchill's nephew Esmond Romilly was part, were virtually wiped out trying vainly to recapture the village that Kurzke and his comrades had fought so hard to defend.

Kurzke's painful journey to hospital in Madrid and his subsequent convalescence in Murcia and Valencia comprise the final part of his memoir. His recovery was a long, slow process and reveals not just the critical lack of resources in Republican medical facilities, but also the personal toll it took on Kurzke. At one point, unable to sleep due to an agonising pain in his damaged foot, he pleaded to be given a painkilling injection: 'A strong one,' he begged the nurse. 'I don't want to wake up any more.'

Eventually, however, Kurzke did recover and he was safely repatriated to the UK. But the story of Kurzke's convalescence holds a puzzle that goes right to the very heart of this memoir. That is, what is missing from his account and why. Clearly, as in any first-hand account, there is much that has been left out: there's very little on Kurzke's life before arriving in Spain in 1934, apart from what comes out in conversations with people he meets on the road. There is also the missing period between tramping around Spain in 1934 and his return to the fight for the government two years later. Did he ever write about this time, or did he later decide to edit it out? And what about the story of his life after leaving Spain?

Yet the most significant absence from the book only becomes clear if you have read the account written by his girlfriend, Kate Mangan (and I strongly recommend that you do). She was with him in Portugal when news of the military coup began to trickle out and she travelled to Spain to find him after he volunteered. After he was wounded, she tracked him down to his hospital in Murcia, no mean feat given the chaotic nature of record-keeping in Republican hospitals. And when he was transferred to the Pasionaria hospital in Valencia in April 1937, she devotedly followed him there. She essentially nursed him back to health and almost single-handedly got him out of Spain, accompanying him on the train to Barcelona and over the frontier to Perpignan, Cerbère and Paris. And she got him back to England, despite him being essentially a stateless refugee. Yet Kurzke makes no mention of her at all.

This is problematic because, as Bernard Knox acknowledged, her glaring absence potentially raises questions about Kurzke's reliability as a witness:

> The real difficulty most readers will face is ... the total exclusion in Jan's account of Kate from his narrative – not only the meeting with him in Madrid before Boadilla which ended with the night they spent in a hotel (he substitutes a night in a hotel with a girl he picks up) but also of her many visits to him in hospital and even of her company on the train leaving Spain for France. Coupled with her very moving accounts of her efforts to trace him and her devotion to him once found it presents a real problem both morally and artistically. For one thing the reader cannot help feeling that he is capable of *suppressio veri* in such a vital matter, he may be also capable of *suggestio falsi*.

How Kate must have felt about being written out of her lover's account is not known, but she must have been hurt. It's hard not to agree with the words of a French fellow patient of Jan's who remarked, *'Il a de chance le bougre, d'avoir sa femme ici!* (He's a lucky bugger, having his wife here!) Still, perhaps she was slightly mollified to discover that other individuals had also been excised, such as the American Kitty Bowler, who visited Jan in the Palace Hotel in Madrid, and Kate's long-term friend, the journalist Hugh Slater, who visited Kurzke in hospital in Murcia. Why Jan cut Kate out is not entirely clear, though when she tracked him down in Spain and asked why he hadn't answered any of her letters, Kurzke told her that:

> his life now was too different from anything I could imagine. He did not want to see girls or maintain any links with what to him was another world. He talked as if he were already dead.

One possible explanation for Kurzke's equivocation might lie with his previous episode in Spain and infatuation with the beautiful young German woman, Putz. It seems highly likely that Kurzke's decision to go to Spain was driven, in part at least, by a desire to find Putz. Certainly that was the impression gained by Bernard Knox and other comrades of Jan in Spain. In fact, in his memoir Kurzke describes meeting up with Walter (the leader of the German group of musicians) in Madrid and asking where he might find her, only to be told that she had been killed three months earlier. His poignant description of his feelings for Putz reveal an emotional numbness, even existential despair, amid the realisation that all too soon he will also exist only in memories:

> I felt very tired. I wanted to think of Putz, but I could not. There was a blank every time I thought of her. There was some mistake, surely, it could not be and yet I knew it was true, but something kept on saying, 'there must be a mistake – people are often reported dead and it proves false.' I had to find out, but when and where and how? I knew she was dead. It was no good pretending it was not so. It did not hurt much. It was unreal, like anything else in the war. A bad dream. After one wakes up, it is all over and past. What did it matter? How long is one going to live? A few days, perhaps a few weeks.

Readers, perhaps, should not be too hard on Kurzke. He was by no means the only veteran of the war in Spain to be deeply scarred by his experiences. Rose Kerrigan, wife of the senior British Political Commissar in Spain, described how she found her husband altered almost beyond recognition on his return:

> There was a terrible change in him, he was quite morose and he seemed very within himself. He was really going grey and this was because he'd seen all the people who had died in Spain.

After all, Kurzke had willingly and selflessly volunteered to put his life on the line for the Spanish Republic. He was lucky to survive the war at all; many didn't. Of almost 2500 men and women to go to Spain from Britain, one fifth never returned. The psychological effects of combat and the death of many of those he served alongside – then known as 'shell-shock', but now referred to as PTSD – can be profound and enduring. Certainly

Kate found him to be 'very melancholy [and] despairing' when he was in hospital and understood that 'a man cannot be left alone in bed for months thinking and be the same as he was before.'

Spain provided a salutary lesson for the antifascists and supporters of the Spanish Republic, many of whom never got over their shock and heartbreak. Their feelings of desolation and despair were admirably summed up by the French writer and philosopher Albert Camus in his preface to *Espagne Libre*:

> In Spain [my generation] learned that one can be right and yet be beaten, that force can vanquish spirit, that there are times when courage is not its own recompense.

The International Brigaders had warned that defeat in Spain would bring war not peace, yet the democracies had remained unmoved. 'The writing on the wall would not be read, not even if it were written in flaming letters,' raged Kurzke. It soon would be. On 1 September 1939, as Hitler's Wehrmacht forces swept across the border into Poland, the Western powers could hardly claim that they had not been warned.

# PART 1 : RAMBLING IN SPAIN

## Chapter 1 — Barcelona to Alicante

It was nine o'clock in the evening when I took María to the boat. She did not want to go but I managed to persuade her. She had been offered a good position somewhere else and, after I lost my job, it was not possible to keep the house or even a room and I wanted to move on. I had been in Barcelona for more than six months and I could not stand it any longer. I had waited for the winter to end in order to try my luck somewhere else.

We walked along the Rambla for the last time. We had a drink sitting in front of the little kiosk below the statue of Columbus. What do people say when they part? We wished each other the best of luck and promised to write often, though I had no address and did not know where I was going. She cried a little. I said there was no reason to cry as we would see each other very soon. I knew we would probably never meet again but one says that sort of thing in such a situation. I heard the first blast of the steamer's whistle. I got up and took her suitcase and I was glad it was over.

I stood on the quay looking up to where she stood at the railing but the light was behind her and I could not see her face. We waved goodbye from time to time. There was nothing else to do because we would have had to shout, so we said nothing and just looked at each other. At last the boat was moving away. After it had turned it moved fast and silently over the black water. I stood where I was for a long time. I could only see the lights of the boat but I knew María would be able to see me as I was standing under the lamps of the quay. I have gone away myself many times and I know how it is.

I went back to the kiosk. The chairs were made of straw and very comfortable. I had another drink and I could see both the Rambla, with its row of plane trees, and the sea. The bootblacks did not annoy me any more because, by now, they knew I did not wear shoes but *alpargatas*. Not even a Barcelona bootblack can shine *alpargatas*. The next day I would leave this town myself. I thought I would be better off further south, but the sky there could not be deeper and bluer than it was on this night. I saw the brightly lit funnels of steamships over the warehouses and, a little to the left over the old port, the black masts of many sailing ships.

I could have sat the whole night watching, but the old *camarero* hovered over me to make me go away because he wanted to close up, so I paid my bill and went. I passed the huge yellow walls of the bug-ridden barracks on the port on my way to the *barrio chino*. I heard the music and the sad *flamencos* outside La Criolla² and other night spots and I was sorry I did not have enough money for another drink. I went through narrow streets full of beggars and whores and I lingered a moment before the poster for the Easter bullfight.

Ortega was going to fight but I would not be there to see him. I went to my hotel room and found that most of my things had been stolen. It was no good protesting and I did not mind really except for the loss of an old but warm sweater. The *portero* was very apologetic and I was sure he had stolen them. I cut him short; I was tired and I did not really care. What the hell, I thought. What difference does it make now?

I woke up late in the morning. I took my suitcase with me when I went out to have breakfast. I was not taking any chances. It was too early to go to the port so I bought a paper and sat for an hour over my coffee. I walked to the port and found the boat to Alicante lying close to the post office. They were still loading her and it was nearly two hours until sailing time. I went about and watched them loading. They seemed to have a lot of chickens in wooden cages which smelled dreadful and a few motor cars and other odds and ends.

It was warm in the sun and the water was calm with a light blue-green colour. I had never seen the town look so beautiful. The houses showed silvery-white and the hills in the distance were a silver-blue; there was no cloud in the sky.

A few people came aboard with parcels and suitcases. Like me they were travelling *cubierto*. This meant we had no cabins and would have to stay on deck during the voyage. I lay on the hatch which was covered with a clean, white tarpaulin until the boat sailed. As soon as we were on our way everybody started eating.

Most of the time we were in sight of land. It got much cooler in the afternoon and I hired a blanket and bought a bottle of white wine. I had found a sheltered spot and slept the whole night without waking once.

The boat arrived at Alicante at seven in the morning. It was grey and damp and very warm. One could not see more than the fortress high above the town and the houses and palm trees on the port. I had to walk through the town until the cafés and hotels were open. I found a cheap room and left my suitcase. The streets were still empty and everything looked clean in the sun. A water-cart drawn by a tired mule sprayed the streets, which changed from a dusty white to a wet black but dried very quickly.

I had a *café expreso* and then a *café con leche* and some sweet buns. There was nobody else at the kiosk. The waiter washing the chairs and tables joked with me about being so early and I told him I had just arrived. I liked this town. I hoped I would be able to stay here for some time but my money would last for only two days and I had to find a job. I was glad it was Sunday. It gave me an excuse to laze around. I would have plenty of time to chase after a job tomorrow. I went back to the port and sunbathed, for the first time this year, next to the *playa*. I only took off my shirt as I had no bathing trunks. It was a good place for a holiday; it was a great pity I could not afford one just now.

I had a glass of vermouth on my way back to my room and slept during the afternoon to save paying for lunch. I went to a small cinema outside the town but the projector light broke down right at the beginning and I got my money back. I found a cheap eating place. For a few pence I had a thick soup of beans, a piece of bread and some wine. In the evening I walked up and down the *paseo* among the swells of the town. They were all well dressed and the girls looked very pretty.

On Monday I went round the town asking for jobs but I had no luck. A man in a shipping office gave me the address of a German who might be able to help me and I found his place with great difficulty. I saw only the secretary, a sour looking woman, who asked me a lot of silly questions and advised me to go back to Germany as everybody was getting jobs under Hitler. I said I was not sure about that as when I left the jobs had already been handed out and I was not much good at bashing people's heads in anyway. She threw me out.

I passed a smart hotel and ran into a man I knew. I could not remember where I had met him or what his name was. He pretended to be pleased to see me and bragged about the swell people he knew, the swell car he had and the swell places he was going to. He invited me to a drink and asked me what I was doing there. I wanted to say I was just having a grand holiday but it seemed too silly so I said I was broke and looking for a job. His face fell; he was afraid probably that I would touch him for some money. He left me in a hurry saying he would call for me the next day but, of course, he never showed up. He did not pay for my drink either.

I spent the afternoon trying to find work but in the evening I gave it up as hopeless. I did not even try on Tuesday. Sitting in the shade on a bench on the Paseo, I watched the water. Twice a tramp passed me. He looked as if he wanted to ask me for some money but he finally walked on without speaking to me. I do not know what was the matter with me, I should have bought him a drink. Tomorrow I would be in his shoes and it would have been good to get some expert advice on the tramping business, but I just sat there and said nothing. I was angry with myself. I had more drinks. My room was paid for and I did not want to hang on to my three pesetas. I blew it all. I wanted to make a clean start, with nothing.

I went to a cinema in the afternoon. I forget what I saw. It was hot and full of noisy children chewing monkey nuts. Every fifteen minutes there was an interval and it was hours before I came out.

I was in a better mood after the show. I had two portions of bean soup and more wine. I was down to my last fifty cents. I was sorry it was not five pesetas; I would have liked to see a girl. I spent the fifty cents on a vermouth near the port, and hung around for a time with the silly idea that perhaps something would happen which would change everything. Nothing did happen so I walked back to my hotel room and went to bed.

# Chapter 2 — Alicante to Lorca

When I woke up it was dawn. I got up and slowly started to dress. I put my spare trousers, shirts and razor in a towel and rolled it all up in my trench coat. I tied both ends with string so that I could hang the roll on my shoulder. The empty suitcase I shoved under the bed and, after a last look round, I left the room and went down the stairs quietly so as to wake nobody and, after opening the heavy door, I stepped out into the street.

Just around the corner I came upon the waterfront. It was still very quiet and the air felt fresh and a little cool and damp from the night. The sea was grey, heavy looking and smooth like a mirror. The wind stirred the leaves of the palm trees but already the sun was colouring the tops with a soft yellow light.

I went down to the seafront and then crossed one of those small, pathetic-looking Spanish *plazas* with flowers and trees, carefully tended and watered, and one or two benches made of white and blue tiles and a statue of some forlorn-looking, forgotten man. Stopping for a moment to consult the map for the last time, I found I was on the right road. I walked on. First I passed a long row of small houses, a garage and barracks which looked like a high fortress and then I left the town behind. I soon came upon a sign pointing out my way and read: Murcia, 60 kilometres.

The sun was out now and it was already very warm so I took off my wind-cheater and put it over the bundle on my shoulder. I walked on along the road which was glistening with tar and seemed endless without a tree or shadow.

I was not a tramp yet. My trousers were dirty and full of nettles and bits of grass and my shoes would not last much longer but I still wore a tie, God knows why, and a battered, grey felt hat. I thought I might look more respectable that way and less dangerous but it seemed to frighten people more. They could recognise a tramp, with his stick and blanket, but my outfit must have been that of a cut-throat. I had shaved, which I later seldom did for lack of water, but I needed a haircut badly.

It was about midday, judging by the position of the sun. I was walking more slowly now and the heat was softening the tar on the road and little bits of sharp stone stuck to the soles of my shoes and made a crunching noise at every step.

My shadow, behind which I had walked all morning, had now shrunk to the size of a dwarf. It was very quiet save for the tramping of my feet and I just looked straight ahead with my hat pulled down over my eyes to protect them from the glare.

I had not noticed the landscape very much for some time when I came into the shade of a cliff on the edge of which a few small farms were resting their crumbling walls. The earth was yellow, the rocks a dull brown, and a few date palms stood upon their fan-shaped shadows.

After leaving the ravine I saw, suddenly, the town of Elche in front of me, looking like an oasis in the desert with its hundreds of date palms and clean white houses.

In the first street I saw the sign of a barber's shop and walked in. I sat down to wait as the barber, a little man with curly black hair, was busy shaving a peasant. They both stared at me for some time in astonishment. Then the barber said, without stopping his noisy work, '*¿De dónde viene?*'

'Alicante,' I said.

'*¿Adónde va?*'

'*A Málaga*.' I said.

'*Hombre*,' he said, waving his long razor before the nose of the man in the chair, '*Está muy lejos.*'

'Yes,' I agreed, 'it's a long way.'

'*¿A pie?*' he asked, looking a bit bewildered.

'Yes, I'm walking all the way.'

He swore softly to himself and scraped away at his peasant and they both gabbled so quickly that they sounded like drums and I could not understand what they said.

'Are you a refugee?' the barber asked.

I replied that I was and wondered why he did not ask me first whether I was German. Both men talked again and I heard the word *socialista* and the peasant did not look very pleased but he suddenly gave me a small paper bag containing a black bread and bacon sandwich and said, '*Come, hombre, es muy bueno.*' I thanked him and started eating. Presently he got up, paid and went out.

I took out of my pocket a small leather purse which I had hardly used and which was no good to me any more and asked the barber whether he would take it for a hair cut. He took the purse and shoved it indignantly back into my jacket pocket and pressed me into a chair and started cutting my hair. 'Go on eating,' he said, and he talked rapidly all the time as he worked. He fired questions at me and lectured me about the working class and *la lucha final* and old Karl Marx and a great deal more besides. I hardly understood half of what he said because I felt tired and drowsy. I watched the flies crawling over the dirty mirror and I could see my face, dimly, rather burned and red and getting more and more German-looking as my hair came off.

'Finished,' the barber said and waved a mirror around my face so that I could see the back of my head. I said that it was fine and he smiled and said, 'Just wait a minute.' He disappeared into a back room and came back to show me, with a proud gesture, a membership card of the Communist Party of Spain.

'My name is Carlos,' the little man said and we shook hands. 'I wish I could be of some help to you but I have a large family and I'm very poor.'

I thanked him again but he could only stammer, '*Nada, hombre, nada.*'

I put my hat on and we shook hands again and there was a tear in his eye when he said, '*Adios, camarada, buena suerte.*'

'*Salud, camarada,*' I said and went out into the street.

I walked a little way and passed a gay-looking bandstand and a couple of roundabouts covered with grey cloths, standing in the little *plaza* which was empty apart from a group of men who were having lunch under the trees. I crossed a bridge and walked along a lane with date palms on both sides and I decided to rest in their shade during the middle of the day. The long grass was warm and a little damp. A small stream murmured along between the trees and the road. When I drank the water it tasted sweet and cool.

In the afternoon, towards dusk, I came to a small village and I asked a man in the street whether he would put me up for the night but he said he could not as he lived with his wife, children and parents in only two rooms. When I asked him if, perhaps, he knew a neighbour who would let me sleep in a stable, he said it was no good trying because nobody would do that. When I asked him why he just shrugged his shoulders. It was clear he was frightened and, at the same time, a little ashamed to have to refuse my request, but I did not mind very much.

It had been a warm day and it would be all right sleeping in the open. I went through my pockets to search for a cigarette and I found thirty *céntimos* which must have been stuck in the lining of my coat. When I saw an inn, not far from the village, I went in to get some wine. The inn was big, like a barn, with whitewashed walls and black beams across the ceiling. It had a huge door which stood open and benches around the walls with a few clumsy tables in front of them. At the far end stood a little bar with bottles and glasses and some barrels. A few men stood drinking around the bar and two little children were playing on the earth floor with a dog which disappeared at once when I came in.

I put my money on the table and asked for some *vino tinto* and the innkeeper gave me a half-full jug and a glass which I took with me to a bench. It was good wine, dark and thick, tasting a little bitter. After the second glass I felt that life was not so bad. After the third glass life seemed very good indeed and everything was fine. If only the people were more friendly. I saw them looking at me with suspicion from the far corner and I started to feel a little angry. The innkeeper looked a mean and sour fellow but I was getting drunk and suddenly I heard myself bawling at him, '*Oiga, señor.*' He came over rather reluctantly and I gave him a hard luck story which would have softened the hardest citizen. I never thought I would be any good at this because every time I had to ask for bread I had to swallow my pride and could hardly find words when someone opened a door to me. But here I was getting very good indeed. 'I am a poor man,' I said, 'with no work and nowhere to go. How about one on the house?' He looked at me without speaking and I saw that he would have liked to throw me out and all the time I was grinning at him. I took out my leather purse and gave it to him saying, 'I'll have some wine for this.' He fingered it and I saw that he liked the thing. To my astonishment he came back with more wine and then he went to fetch some green olives and a piece of dry bread. It was a fine meal and when I left, much to the relief of the innkeeper, I was ready to walk to Africa if necessary but, only a few hundred yards from the inn, I left the road and went to sleep in a field.

After a few hours I woke up. It was still dark so that I could not see the road from where I lay and I knew it was not yet midnight. A wet, icy cold rose from the ground. I wished I had a blanket. I took off my jacket and covered myself with it; it seemed a little warmer for a while. Then I thought of sleeping on the road, which was a few feet higher than the field, but I was afraid of being hit by a car and I was too tired to get up and look for a better place. It was a long night which became unbearable towards morning but after daybreak I felt better and when the sun came out I slept for a few hours.

That day I walked thirty kilometres, feeling tired and hot towards evening. I slept on a little hill near Murcia, overlooking the road and other hills. I found one of those small huts made for shepherds and, before lying down, I smoked my last cigarette which I had begged from a peasant in the last village I had passed.

There were some old, dusty straw mats which I used as covers to keep myself warm. The hut had only three walls, being open in front, and I could see down in the valley the endless white road with vineyards further back and orange groves already showing small, pale yellow fruits. It was getting dark but the dusky blue and pink twilight would linger for a moment until it changed into a deeper blue and black.

From the road came, occasionally, the creak of the high-wheeled, covered wagons loaded with enormous wine barrels and the quick step of donkey hooves and the long wailing shout of the driver, '*Arre, arre, burro!*' The cigarette was burning down to my finger tips and I took a piece of straw which I pushed into the butt to make it last a little longer.

I was dreaming about the sailing ship I was going to catch in Málaga, about the odd looking Spaniard I met in Barcelona who offered to take me along on his schooner, the *Goa*. I had not decided at once because I did not believe his story, but a friend of mine wrote from Alicante telling me he had got a job as an engineer on the ship and that they were going to Málaga and would stay there a week. But Málaga was still a long way off and I was afraid I would not be there in time even if I walked thirty kilometres a day, which was not bad considering the little food I ate and the fact that my shoes were already falling to pieces. A white, pale mist was rising from the valley and the stars were glittering in an inky sky when I fell asleep.

When I woke up the moon had risen, moving slowly across the sky. From time to time I opened my eyes and looked at the lights and shadows of the huge cacti which grew in masses on the hill which, in the moonlight, wandered and moved, looking like crouching men and other threatening forms. I was a little afraid and had to laugh at myself because I knew nobody would wander round these parts at night. I woke often because it became bitterly cold and twice I had to get up and walk about because my heart seemed to stop.

Towards morning a drenching rain began to fall; it did not stop for a day and a night. I walked on to Murcia, meeting on my way a number of peasants going to market. At one of the first houses on the outskirts I begged a piece of bread from a poor and care-worn looking woman. She looked very frightened when she saw me and kissed the bread and made the sign of the cross over it before she gave it to me. I did not ask for shelter because I knew she would refuse me. I went to another house soon after to ask for more bread but the woman had none and gave me a penny instead with which I bought a glass of wine.

In the middle of the town was a small park and under an open bandstand I ate my bread and waited for the rain to cease, but it never stopped. Rivers of water flooded the streets and finally I walked on. The doors and windows of the houses were shut and nobody was about. The streets were long and winding and led me out to the other side of the town. Before I came to the edge of the town I saw a newly built brick house, not quite finished, in which I took shelter. At first it was good to be out of the rain. I tried to light some wood shavings to make a little fire but they were too damp and I wasted nearly all my matches. An icy wind was blowing through the door and window frames and I felt I could not stay there without becoming ill, but I did not want to leave either. My clothes never dried out but only grew more cold and clammy every minute so, in spite of the rain which was coming down in torrents, I had to walk on again to get warm. The rain was soaking me to the skin and water welled up out of my shoes at every step. When I saw a small inn a little way off the road, surrounded by puddles of water, I just walked in determined not to be thrown out if I could help it.

The inn was small and dark but a fire was burning and a few brown, unshaven shepherds in corduroys and strangely shaped leather leggings sat at a table playing cards. An old man with white hair came over and I asked him if I might rest a bit until the rain stopped. '*Sí, amigo,*' the old man said. He told me that I could sit by the door as long as I liked. For hours I sat there having smoked my last cigarette, drowsy and tired, watching the card players. I would have liked to ask them for a drink but they never took any notice of me and I was afraid the old man would then try to get rid of me. It was dark when he came up to me again. 'Friend, I will let you sleep in the stable but you must give me your matches.' This I gladly did and followed the old man to a barn across a courtyard. He pointed to a loft. I mounted the ladder and found heaps of straw into which I crept and felt warm at once. The straw tickled a bit, mice were running about and an owl was hooting outside in the dark. While I was listening to these noises and the monotonous drumming of the rain I fell asleep.

Nothing much happened the next day. When I woke I saw that the rain had stopped and the sun shone through the roof of the barn. A hen was cackling away when I left the inn and I took her egg with me and drank it on the way. Towards midday I rested in the courtyard of a farm where I got some bread and water. I spent the night in the open. The next morning I walked on and the weather continued to be fine.

I was not far from Lorca but I did not want to reach it before the next morning because people were easily frightened in the dark and would not even open the door when I asked for food.

One day I had asked a Spanish tramp just outside a village why he did not go into it instead of camping in a field. I thought that the people were only afraid of me because I was a foreigner. '*No, hombre*,' he said. 'Never go into a town at night. Go in the morning when it's light and men are not afraid and you will always get something. You can also see the *Guardia Civil* before they see you,' he added as an afterthought. He had looked around so as to make sure that nobody could see him and his face was suddenly full of hate. He spat and repeated, 'Those *guardias civiles*, they are bad men, *hombre*, you had better keep out of their way.' I had said I was not afraid but he did not believe me. I really was not but every time I saw them a feeling I cannot describe came over me. With their black, shiny tricorn hats and full cloaks they were like something from another age, like hooded men, sinister and inhuman.

I had gone a few paces after having wished the tramp *buenas noches* when I remembered that I had forgotten to ask him a question.

'Listen,' I called back, 'why is everybody afraid around here?' I could not see him and there was silence for a moment, then out from the dark, at some distance as he must have been walking away from me, he said, '*Hombre*, there are bad men around here who cut people's throats.'

'Blast you!' I thought as I walked on. Blast your throat-cutting and the whole lot of you. What a country! Everybody is afraid of everything. Surely there was less crime here than in any other country. But then I remembered the dark, solemn churches, the black priests, the *Guardia Civil* with the right to shoot to kill and the gruesome prisons full of vermin in this grim and hard country and I understood. It was annoying though and very depressing and I felt like a man walking through a hostile country.

That afternoon I was only two miles from Lorca and I slowed down. There were a few houses along the road and I went up to one of them to ask for a drink. It was not an inn but a place where they sold wine and lemonade. A woman gave me a glass of water and I noticed two men who were arguing in loud voices over a jug of wine. I went out but I heard them coming after me.

One was a ratty little man with an iron bar and the other, younger looking with long black hair, was very drunk. Both had blankets and I saw they were tramps. I thought at first they were going to attack me and I was ready for them when the drunk came up and threw his arms around me. I had to hold him up to prevent him from falling.

'*Amigo*,' he sobbed, '*amigo mío*.' He was looking at me with affectionate, glassy eyes and he stank of wine and garlic. 'You mustn't drink water,' he said reproachfully, 'it's bad. You must have a glass of wine with us.' He waved to the rat who stood in the background.

'I haven't any money,' I said just to make sure.

'We're comrades,' he roared, 'aren't we?'

'Of course,' I said.

His friend came up and we took hold of the drunk and walked along. We did not go back to the woman and I thought they were just fooling me but the rat said there was a good inn just ahead of us.

'I must sing,' said the drunk. 'Are you with me?'

'We are,' I replied. 'You just start us off.'

'A flamenco,' he said.

'A flamenco it is,' I said.

'But you must begin,' persisted the drunk.

'I don't know the words,' I said. 'I can only sing in German.'

He did not seem to grasp this and stared at me. Suddenly he began, with a frightful howl, '*Ni madre, ni padre, ni casa, ni familia*,' and we had to hold him up while he lamented and nearly split my eardrums. We reached the inn and sat down at a table outside the door. A few girls, who had been preparing vegetables, fled hurriedly. The innkeeper came out and the rat ordered wine and olives and was asked for the money in advance. We ate and the drunk fished a piece of bread out of his sack and tried to feed me.

'We're poor, aren't we?' he shouted.

'We are,' I agreed.

His friend tried to get him to pipe down but he would not listen.

'Where are you from and where are you going,' I asked him.

He pointed towards the hills not far away.

'From over there,' he said. 'We're going home now. We left our *pueblo* to find some work but there wasn't any. *Ni padre, ni madre,*' he sang again.

The innkeeper came out and tried to shut him up. I got angry at this and swore at him in English.

'You're my friend,' sobbed the drunk on my shoulder. '*Amigo mío,* where have you been?'

I said that I had been around all the time and he seemed satisfied. We had another jug of wine and I must have cowed the innkeeper because he did not ask for the money in advance. We got pretty drunk. Peasants on donkeys and carts who passed by looked up in alarm when they saw us three in front of the inn howling like wolves. I now knew all the words and we must have sung the song twenty times. 'No mother, no father,' we lamented. 'No family, no house, nothing,' we howled, and tears were streaming down the face of the drunk and we had some more wine. I tried to start *With the Gitanos to Sevilla* but he did not like it. '*Amigo,*' he cried from time to time, 'where have you been?'

Two pretty girls were peering at us from behind a window with frightened faces. The rat got amorous all of a sudden and he called out with deep sighs, '*Ay morena, ay*, you beautiful one.'

We had finished our wine and the olives, and the innkeeper came to collect the money. The drunk was fumbling in his pockets and could not find anything. Now we can add 'no money either' to our song I thought, and watched the innkeeper looking round for help. I went through the pockets of my '*amigo*' and found, after a long search, a five peseta piece, which infuriated the rat for some reason. We paid and staggered along the street wailing our mournful song.

The rat was in a bad temper and he was arguing with his friend about something or other. He brandished his iron bar and nearly brained the drunk, who was sobering up a bit. They made an infernal noise and I thought it better to move on before the police appeared. An old, white-haired man stood before us suddenly and tried to make peace between the friends, who were chasing each other over a field. It looked very funny. The old man was hobbling after them with his coat-tails flying. I was still laughing when I was already a long way off. I left the road and found a place to sleep amongst strangely shaped rocks just under a mountain. I was drunk and dead tired.

It was early in the morning, near Lorca, when I met the German. I had just come from the hills where I had slept and, passing a farm, I tried to get some water, but two big dogs growled and barked at me and I had to beat it. After crossing a few fields I struck the main road from whence I could see the town. A man was sitting in a ditch not far off and I knew he was a German from the map he was studying. A Spanish tramp does not mind where he goes or what the distance is between one place and another, but Germans are more methodical. They always have a plan, or make one; they like to have an objective, they like to know the country they are tramping through. I found it helped me a lot, especially when resting, and I studied the names of places and mountains, towns and villages, and I would pencil off the roads already covered and measure the distance to the next town.

The man looked up when I approached and I saw that he was much older than me. His face was very brown as if it had been exposed to the sun for many years; his clothes were shabby, he wore an old overcoat and a little blue beret. I greeted him in German and sat down next to him. I asked him where he was bound for and he told me he was going to Sevilla. It was the second time he had gone round the whole of Spain and he knew every place.

'It's cold up north,' he said, 'I always like to be in the south in the springtime.' It sounded as if a wealthy man was talking about going to Monte Carlo. I told him I was going south too and I suggested we might go together, but he did not seem enthusiastic about this idea. He mumbled something about having to know me first and I thought, OK sourpuss, and started to get up. 'You haven't been on the road very long?' he asked. I admitted that he was right, thinking of my tie, and I saw with envy that he carried a blanket like a real tramp.

'Sit down,' he invited me, 'It's too early to go into town, anyway.'

I asked him what he meant and he explained that the women were still in church and it was better to wait until they came out.

'When they've prayed they always feel happier and they feel like doing a good deed, and they won't refuse a gift to a poor man,' the tramp said.

I listened carefully as here was something to be learned. He went on, 'When they come out you wait a bit until they've reached home, which is about fifteen minutes because they like to chat a while with neighbours. That's the time to start working.'

I was not quite sure what he meant by that but I did not like to ask.

'We'd better split this town,' he said. 'It won't bring much otherwise.'

I was glad to stay with him because I liked talking to him and I would have hated to part with this fountain of knowledge and wisdom.

'How much will it bring?' I asked him, remembering his last remark and thinking he was talking about food. He looked at the town, squinting his light blue eyes, and after some silent calculation he said, 'Not more than three pesetas.'

I marvelled at this, feeling small and dumb like a pupil in the presence of a master. He looked at me and asked me whether I had a razor. I said I had. 'You'd better have a shave first,' he said, viewing my chin with disapproving eyes, 'you look like a lousy bum.'

He fished out of his sack a small mirror and I began to shave with the help of a cupful of water which he fetched for me out of the ditch. While I was shaving the tramp was lecturing me in his quiet, kind voice.

'You may think that if you look like a scarecrow people will take pity upon you and help you,' he said. 'Well, you're wrong. They'll just be afraid of you. They'll slam the door in your face, or they probably won't open it at all. Then what? You pipe through the door and they can't hear what you say and if you raise your voice it only sounds ridiculous. Imagine me standing at a closed door hollering away at nobody, what would you think?'

I did not know what to think.

'You would think,' he went on, with slight indignation in his voice, 'you would think I was just a lousy bum making a row in the street.'

Here the lecturer scratched himself absent-mindedly and when he saw I was a little worried he smiled. 'I've got a few lice,' he said, apologising. 'I can't seem to get rid of them. It's the warmth, you know. You'll soon have them too,' he said with great satisfaction. 'You can't help it. It's this sleeping around in *posadas* and dirty inns where you pick them up. These Spanish bums are just a lousy, dirty lot,' he added with disgust. 'I wash frequently,' he said, 'I always carry soap around and I hope you've got some too.'

I said that I kept myself as clean as possible and that, just the other day, I had washed myself from head to foot in an ice-cold stream and could hardly get warm again afterwards.

'Ah,' he said, looking at me for the first time with respect, 'I only wash my hands and face, that's in winter. In summer I take a bath frequently in the sea. I always carry my swimming pants about,' and he showed me a mouldy green garment which did not seem to have been in contact with the sea for a very long time. Suddenly he said, 'I don't mind if we walk a little way together.'

He introduced himself and said his name was Hermann. We shook hands with formality and the church bells of Lorca started to ring just to give the final touch to the solemn moment.

'Hear the bells,' my new friend was saying, 'we'd better get ready to go.'

He was screwing up his face again as he watched the black-clad women of Lorca filing out of the church and walking, singly or in groups, along the street. Like a bird of prey he watched them. We started moving slowly towards the town. When we came near it looked much smaller than it had first appeared. 'We'll each take one side of the street,' said Hermann, 'and for God's sake, take your hat off.'

I knocked at the first door and, when it opened, I mumbled something. The door closed and nothing happened. I saw Hermann, on the other side of the road, put something in his pocket. When he saw me looking he came over and I told him I had not had any luck.

'You watch me,' he said, 'I'll show you how it's done.'

He knocked at the next door very politely and, with his head cocked to one side, he listened closely, and presently the door was opened by an old woman. Now I witnessed an amazing transformation. My friend took off his cap and, in a quiet, shaking voice, he broke into a litany, a sort of wailing sing-song which went like this: '*Soy un alemán, sin trabajo*, mumble mumble, I'm a German, I've no work, mumble mumble, *por favor*, if you could spare a little change mumble mumble, *una limosna*.' As he rattled this off he seemed to shrink and look pale and ill. I looked at him with alarm. He could hardly hold himself upright, he shrank, he stood with his hand to his head and I probably would have thrown a penny at him myself if I'd had one to throw. He had finished and he waited at the door with his head bowed. A hand appeared with bread and something else and he mumbled, '*Muchas gracias*.' He came back to me, healthy and well again. He showed me fifteen *céntimos* and, with triumph in his voice, he asked me how it was, and I said that it was wonderful. I said I would never be as good as he was. I felt discouraged because I knew I could not perform this mummery, even after a thousand years on the road. He said that was nonsense and we worked our way along the street and along many other streets. I was not doing too badly. By about eleven o'clock we had been everywhere. We counted the pennies, which came to two pesetas and seventy cents.

'A little less than I thought, still it's better than nothing. You're quite good,' he praised me, 'but remember that a poor man has to lie about his being poor. You say "I'm poor, give me something" but you don't get anything. Now you lie, you invent a story. You say you've been in hospital, your wife has died, or you have twelve kids. They give you something, see what I mean?' I said it was clear as daylight.

'It's sad, you know,' he said, shaking his head. 'It's really tragic.' However, he soon brightened up. 'We'd better buy some food, tobacco and perhaps a glass of wine, but not here, in the next place,' the imperturbable Hermann lectured again, 'because it wouldn't do to show how much you've got. Even though it isn't much it may be less should one ever come back here again.'

We left the town and ate some bread along the way. About an hour later we reached an inn and went in to have a glass of wine. A young man served us and the place looked better and cleaner than most inns I had seen. He told us he had just taken it over and hoped to do good business. Only the other day a car had stopped there with three Englishmen who had lunch and advised him to put a sign on the road to attract customers. I am sure they must have been kidding him because it was a lonely road with hardly any traffic apart from a lot of donkey carts on market day. However, the young man was very excited and he wanted the whole place done up, but the paint had not arrived yet. I said I was sorry about that because my friend and I were born decorators and would do the job for a small sum. He replied that the paint would not arrive for a week but he asked me to paint him a sign in English. I wrote on a big piece of cardboard in black letters, 'STOP HERE FOR A GOOD LUNCH. THE BEST FOOD AND THE BEST WINE.' When I translated this the innkeeper was very pleased and he cooked us a huge *arroz con carne*. Hermann seemed to be quite happy now that he had taken me along and he dreamt already of a big sign-writing business which we would establish one day.

I surprised our host by drawing his portrait on a piece of brown paper. He was delighted with his *foto* and, when we parted, he presented us with a bottle of wine and four eggs. I hope my sign brought him a lot of *ingleses* but I doubt it very much.

# Chapter 3 — Lorca to Granada

From Lorca there were two ways to the south. The big *ruta nacional* went to the left down to Cartagena and rolled along by the sea as far as Cádiz. Hermann and I decided to choose the second road which was hardly used by anyone as it went through small, unknown places and, finally, over the Sierra Nevada down to Granada. We chose this way because the main road to the sea was crowded with beggars and families of tinkers who sent their masses of children into the houses, left and right, and we had little chance of getting anything. The police too were guarding that road more carefully and we thought it better to avoid them as far as possible.

We had been on the road for some time. It began to look more and more desolate and fewer farms were to be seen, though there were one or two dotted here and there in the distance, far from the road. We talked a lot and then walked in silence again for hours. I could not find out at first who my friend really was or what he did before he started tramping and I regarded him as just a bum. When I chaffed him about the act he had put on in Lorca and said how badly I felt about taking money from these poor people he agreed. He said he had felt the same when he started out two years ago but one had to do a lot of unpleasant things if one wanted to stay alive. I said that this was true. He went on to explain that these halfpennies and pennies would not make the people much poorer and, after all, it was not our fault that they had so little.

'We can't afford to be sentimental or, at least, we can't afford to show it and in a short while you'll see it isn't quite as simple, because today we just had luck. Don't let it fool you. When I went through Extremadura I ate grass and leaves and the people looked so poor that, for days, I didn't dare to ask for anything, because with these shabby clothes of mine I looked like a rich man compared with most of them.'

I liked him better now. He was really kind and soft-hearted and a little naïve. I liked the way he noticed small things around him, a bird, a flower or a strange-looking building. Everything interested him and, before we went to sleep at night, he used to take out a bundle of worn and dirty-looking postcards and write down, in his very small handwriting, everything he had seen during the day. I asked him what he did it for and he said that he was writing to his wife in Germany.

The day before that we had visited a silk-worm farm and Hermann was looking at everything, seeing everything and asking a thousand questions of a man who kindly showed us round. He was writing it all down and filled three postcards. He said that his wife would enjoy reading all about it. I asked him about his wife and why he had left her and he said he had had bad luck in a small business and had come to Spain to look for work. He was lying, of course. I knew he was a refugee like myself because he avoided all questions about politics and Hitler's coming to power. I found out later on that I was right; he probably wanted to be careful because his wife was still in Germany and I had not told him much about myself. It is very funny that we should have walked side by side for such a long time without telling each other that we were both anti-fascists. Only people who had been hunted by the Gestapo and saved their skins would understand why we did not talk openly. I think he must have been a Social Democrat; a mild revolutionary, probably a small party official with a good income. Once I saw his passport, when we were held up by the *Guardia Civil*, and I saw the picture of a very fat man (he was quite thin now) in a fur coat. I told him that I would not have liked him then. He smiled and said he had not liked himself. I admired the way he faced his new situation without complaining or harking back to the good old times, a habit which tends to make refugees into a bunch of complaining, useless snobs.

His Spanish was quite good but he carried a little dictionary. He wanted me to teach him English but we gave it up as we mixed the three languages into a frightful muddle.

We had not seen a house for nearly ten miles and no drinking water was to be found but, as night was falling, we looked round for a place to sleep. We had a beautiful view down a valley. The great heat was leaving the earth and a mist was slowly creeping out of the hollows over the fields. The moon was bright in the sky and it was going to be cold. We found odd-looking holes on the crest of a slope, about ten feet long with small entrances. They went into the earth and we could not think why they had been made or for what purpose. We gathered branches of tough scrub, which grew in abundance, to cover ourselves. Hermann slept down at the bottom of a cave while I lay with my head sticking out. It was not very comfortable as I kept slipping down but I woke only once, when the bright, cold moon shone into my face and I heard a dog barking and wondered why we had not seen a house or a village.

We found some water the next day and washed and shaved. I went up to a farm, in spite of two fierce dogs, and a tall, gaunt peasant gave me a piece of bread which was as hard as the rocks over which we stumbled.

The sun shone every day although the nights remained cool. A strong wind was blowing over the plains we crossed and the earth looked more and more dry and brown. The wind blew down from the *sierra* – still far away – and blew dust into our eyes. As the wind blasted straight at us we made slow progress. We saw very few people. Every ten miles there was a road-mender's house. These were mostly empty. Sometimes, if we knocked on the door, we could see somebody watching us through the heavy, barred door. The wind blew every day; it blows here the whole year round, and we got burned inside and out as we tramped thirstily behind our shadows. The wind swept down at us, hot and dry, and rattled through the poor-looking corn fields, driving clouds of dust before it in which bushes and pieces of straw floated like clumsy, misshapen birds.

We did not talk much. Every time we opened our mouths the wind blew a funny melody through our ears. It was like going through No Man's Land. We walked along roads cut through rocks. It was even hotter here and we were powdered white like millers. We saw big caves cut into these rocks, as large as a good-sized room. We thought of resting in them but they were dirty and smelly and Hermann swore about the unclean habits of Spanish tramps and we walked on. We had to climb most of the way and, in the evening, we reached an oasis with trees and bushes. We saw a few lights down in a deep valley. We thought this was perhaps a small village but it was already too dark to approach it. We prepared to go to sleep under a tree but, after a while, Hermann said he would go down to get some bread and water as we had not eaten for twenty-four hours.

I must have fallen asleep and I woke with a start. I heard voices and saw three figures coming towards me. It was Hermann, followed by two Spaniards whose faces I could not see. He had gone down and found a group of socialists at a meeting and he said he had never seen anyone as poor as they were. Between them they had collected just enough to buy half a loaf for us.

'Wait until you see the place,' Hermann said to me. 'You won't believe your eyes.'

The Spaniards asked us to come along as they wanted to find us a place to sleep and they seemed to be uncomfortable and frightened. We crept through the dark and suddenly the moon rose and, in its blue light, I saw a fantastic scene. Before us lay a deep valley. At the bottom I could see a few houses and a church a little higher up. The cliffs round the valley were full of black holes as if gigantic rabbits had burrowed in them. In some of them I saw lights and, when I passed one of these caves, I saw people and shadows and a donkey's head in a flickering oil light. It was a picture like one of Goya's bad dreams. We moved along behind our guides in single file and they warned us to be careful. We crept over narrow stone paths along steep walls until we reached the other side of the valley where our guides directed us to a vacant cave. They asked us to be quiet and not to show a light because the people of the town had already heard about the two strangers. I asked the Spaniard what he meant by town and he said that this was Guadix, a town of eight thousand people.

I could not believe it at first. Eight thousand people living in caves. After a thousand years of so-called progress people were back where they started from, or perhaps they had never left. Even the oil lamps were the same as those used in ancient times. The only difference was the schoolhouse built of brick and, of course, the church. If people are so poor they cannot afford houses there is always enough money squeezed out of them to build a big church. The other gift of civilisation was a white square in the market place which I later saw was a cinema screen. They had a cinema once a week in the open air where they could see, for a penny, old and blurred films.

We lay down to rest although we would rather have slept out of doors because the place stank and I was sure it was verminous. We were woken shortly afterwards by a voice from the mouth of the cave. I saw dark figures and a flashlight was pointed at us. Somebody said, 'Hands up,' and I could see a revolver. We got up and the voice asked whether we carried guns and we said no. We stepped out of the cave with our hands above our heads and two men, in blue uniforms and caps but wearing canvas shoes, searched us. The revolvers were shaking in their hands but they gathered more courage when they saw we were unarmed. They asked us to follow them to the *jefe de policía* and we trotted behind them, followed by many shadows. At the bottom of the valley we entered a house and I saw the *jefe de policía* sitting at a table. He asked us a lot of questions and he said we should have come straight to him instead of frightening people out of their wits. He was not unkind but said we had to sleep in the prison until the next morning. We did not mind where we slept and were locked in a stable which apparently was the prison. There was a lot of straw lying around and we slept beautifully. A uniformed policeman and the *sereno* guarded the door the whole night.

The next morning we washed and shaved outside the stable and our keepers were now unafraid and quite friendly. They said we should wait until the mayor arrived as he would like to talk to us. We waited in the little square on a bench. There were a few trees trying to grow out of holes and, surrounding the square, were the schoolhouse, the *farmacia*, two other business premises, the church and the town hall. While we were waiting and wondering what the mayor wanted of us the *jefe de policía* crossed the square and said, '*Buenos días, señores*, have you slept well?'

'*Buenos días, señor*,' we replied, lifting our hats gravely. I would like somebody to show me another country where a police chief greets a tramp with such politeness.

While we sat around, dozing in the sun, a sad procession was winding down the slopes towards us. First came two boys, one with a cross, the other with a bell which he rang at intervals. Following them was a fat priest who was trying to pray with both hands and holding up his gown at the same time so as to see where he was stepping. Then came a tall man in a black suit. He had an El Greco face, haggard, long, with deep set black eyes. He wore no hat. In his hands he carried before him the small coffin of a child and, staring straight in front of him, he came down the path, slow but sure-footed. He was followed by his wife and neighbours, all in black, the men bare-headed, the women black-veiled. He came down to the church and I have never seen anything so dignified and tragic as this father carrying his child with an unmoved face. He was carrying this coffin like a piece of evidence and I wondered whether he was going to church to pray or to accuse.

From the town hall one of our keepers waved to us to come over and, through the cool hall, we marched to the office of the mayor. He was a small healthy looking peasant wearing a cap. He said, 'Keep your hats on, *señores*,' and after many questions he gave us five pesetas and wished us luck. He said, however, that we had to leave the town immediately and we thanked him and went on our way. The police saw us to the main road and watched us for a while as I kept on looking back to get a last glimpse of the caves.

The landscape was the same as before: miles of grey-brown desert with hardly a farm or a tree. The weather was changing as we climbed higher and though the sun was still out it shone through a white film of mist which made its light even more glaring. We saw swarms of big yellow grasshoppers crossing the road and many of them lay dead, struck by some passing car. Sometimes we found a dead dog or the skeleton of a donkey. It looked as if a plague had struck this country, with swarms of locusts eating the last dry vegetation. The plague of poverty and backwardness, a plague as disastrous as cholera or pestilence, had written its sign for ever on these parts. Had it not been for the fairly new road we would have thought there was no way out of this wind-swept desert. We squashed a few of the grasshoppers and picked them up. Looking at them closely they took on the appearance of enormous, greedy dragons.

We had not seen a house all day but Hermann said that we would come to one very shortly. He remembered having been there before and he said the people had been very nice and had given him a soup made with milk and bread. He did not remember quite where it was but we found it in the afternoon.

It was an old farm built of grey stone but it stood alone, with no human habitation for miles around, and it had no garden and no trees. A woman was sitting in the doorway. She immediately recognised my friend and asked us to come in. We went into the dark kitchen, where lots of pots and pans were boiling over the fire, and were greeted by another woman, a girl and a young man. The women wore black clothes, had black hair and ivory-coloured faces. They were good-looking though only the girl was young. There was an atmosphere of gloom and sadness; everybody seemed to be uncomfortable and ill at ease. I soon found out the reason. While the women made us a soup the young man, who had been sitting in a dark corner, came up to us and I have never seen a more beautiful face. He had a pale, olive skin and his eyes were dark and shiny. His forehead and nose were straight like a Greek statue, but he wore a small, black beard, unusual for a Spaniard, especially as he was not more than twenty-five. With his long black hair he could have been a Christ in a Giotto painting. He smiled at us but I felt he was not really seeing us and he insisted on shaking hands again.

'You are fond of music, friends?' he asked us.

I said I was. He seemed very happy about this and rambled on, 'I'm a great musician. I'm writing my own music and I play it with my own instrument. Would you like to hear it?'

I said I would be delighted, and all the time the women were watching me anxiously. The young man went back to his dark corner and came out with an iron triangle and a short iron rod. He seated himself and, for a while, he seemed to listen to something and then he said, '*Señores*, I'm now going to play my first symphony.'

After this announcement he rattled his iron rod on the triangle producing a thin, awful sound and while he did this his face showed an unearthly delight and I knew the man was mad. I watched him with a straight face as the women kept on looking at me. When he had finished I went over to him and shook his hand and said this was the best music I had ever heard, which was not even a lie as he made his music with his face rather than his instrument. The madman gave me a grateful look and he talked excitedly and fast. He kept on saying, 'I knew it, I knew it. You can appreciate good music, I knew that the first moment I saw you. I've been in Paris, I've seen something of the world. I've studied for years. I've learned everything there is to learn. *Gracias María. Ah, señores*, this is the best day of my life. My head is full of music.'

Here he put his long hands to his forehead as if it hurt him.

'Somehow I can't write it down, but I don't have to. I'm full of melodies and symphonies. I'm a writer of music. I'm a maker of music. You must hear my second symphony, *señores*.'

Now he played with a whole orchestra of pots and pans as well as his triangle, making a hellish din while we ate our soup. He had forgotten us, apparently, and we got up to be on our way. We thanked our hosts and I went over to the young man to say good-bye.

'Who are you?' he asked me with mild surprise.

I did not know what to say, so I said I wanted to be a maker of music too and I had come all the way to see him as I had heard of his fame. He smiled at this compliment; it was a sad smile and it said, 'You're lying,' and I was ashamed of myself. He rattled on his triangle and we heard him for some time after we had left the house and the women were waving goodbye to us. When they closed the door I knew they would pray and weep and worry, for God had punished them heavily.

'Repent,' the triangle was yelling at them every day, 'repent for the sins which made me a maker of music.'

We camped out again in an open field the next night, but it was getting too cold and uncomfortable so we decided not to risk it again if we could help it. After walking the whole day, rather tired and silent, we came upon another cave-dwelling in the evening. A labourer, working in a field, gave us directions. He was sitting near the road having his lunch and he said, 'Sit down and eat with me,' as is the custom in Spain and we replied, 'Thanks, but we've eaten already,' as is also the custom.

We nearly missed the village because we could see nothing in the dark but fields with deep, winding ditches like trenches. Only when we saw smoke pouring out at various places did we gather that this must be the village. To make sure, Hermann left me to find out and when he came back he led me to a cave where he had found a family willing to put us up for the night. The cave consisted of two rooms divided by an earthern pillar and was lit by candles. A donkey was chewing something in a corner and I saw six people huddled round a wooden box on which the crockery and pots and pans stood. It was airy and clean. A fire was burning in a hearth made of earth under a hole cut into the ceiling to let the smoke out.

The family consisted of an elderly man and woman with their four grown-up sons and, though they were poor, they looked healthier than other people I had met in those parts. They gave us each a hand-carved wooden spoon and we all scooped up a thin soup out of a big pot. It tasted good to us as we were very hungry. After the meal was finished we rolled cigarettes, which I never learned how to do properly, and the old man finally helped me when he saw me struggling with the short, crumbling tobacco.

We asked them how much they earned and the old man said that he and one of his sons were working on an estate for three pesetas a day each. However, this was only in the summer. In the winter they had hardly anything to eat and they had to save a little for the time when they were not earning anything. He told me, to my astonishment, that they had to pay rent for living in the caves, but he said they were more comfortable than a cheap house: cool in summer and warm in winter. One of the sons caught sight of my shoes and said, 'Look, he's wearing leather boots.' Though my shoes were made of leather they were torn and held together by pieces of string and the soles were worn through on both feet, but still everybody seemed to stare with admiration at my awful footwear. I had the uncomfortable feeling that I was really better off than they were.

Soon we all retired to bed, which consisted of a square block of earth about two feet high and, with a blanket and the fire still glowing, we slept well. I dreamt about a pretty girl with the face of the madman minus his beard and she wore long plaits and we kissed each other long and passionately, but she suddenly started to blow into my face. I woke up and saw the big head of a donkey bending over me; it was probably testing to see if I was edible.

We parted with many good wishes the next morning, after breakfasting on warm goat's milk diluted with water. The sun was out again when we set out, and burned from the blue sky. We passed through a small town where we begged a few pennies but we had to give up before long, when the police arrived and drove us away. Shortly afterwards, after an exhausting climb, we entered a small village and looked for an inn for a rest and a glass of wine. The village consisted of only a few houses with high, grey walls and hardly a window. The streets looked desolate, hot and shadeless. We found an inn and sat in front of the door in a strip of shadow. After some knocking and shouting a man came slouching out and took our order but he gave us an angry, unfriendly look.

We drank our wine slowly, hoping to wait there until the midday heat had passed, but we soon had to leave. A few men had appeared, apparently from nowhere, and settled down on the other side of the street, although it was in the heat of the sun. They were cadaverous looking fellows, unshaven, with big hats, barefooted, and some were carrying old shotguns. They squatted on their heels and eyed us fiercely and it was plain that they did not like us. I called out, 'Hola, paisanos,' but they did not answer. The wine did not taste so good any more and Hermann said that he did not like the look of the locals. I said, 'These must be the hillbillies out for some rough shooting.'

No women were to be seen. They were probably locked up and, when some especially crazy-looking fellows started to load their rifles with what looked like good-sized shells, we got up and left in a hurry. The posse followed us for some time until we were clear of the village, and I hope that since then they have wiped each other out with their blunderbusses and are buried and gone for ever.

The evening was very beautiful, thanks to the sunset and the magnificent landscape, and thanks to an old woman who gave us two eggs and a piece of bread and did not seem to be afraid, although she lived alone in an isolated house. We found a sand hole still warm from the sun and dry grass to cover us. We laughed and joked about the shooting party and watched the sun go down over a huge plain of rock and fissures which the night filled with blue shadows. It looked as if an earthquake or a terrible bombardment had moulded the surface. Behind it, not far away, towered the Sierra Nevada, its snowy crests dazzling white against a pale sky. We saw the road we had just come along flanked by cypresses. It was very beautiful and we watched until the first stars appeared and we fell asleep.

We were in the *sierra*. We had left the plain behind us and from then on we moved high above the earth and went up to more than nine thousand feet. Although the sun was shining over most parts of Spain, winter still had its grip upon the mountains. They looked dark and brown with trees which still carried last year's black leaves. Patches of mists covered our way and sometimes cold, drizzling rain fell, although so fine that one could not see it falling. Through the misty clouds we caught a glimpse of the valley.

The road was winding along steep precipices or sometimes it was cut through cliffs which gave sudden protection and warmth. The road had been built quite recently and the black belt of tar shone in the wet. We climbed steadily but the *sierra* was towering on our left, out of reach, and its sombre black and white crown looked down on us with pity as we wormed our way around its feet. Sometimes we could hear goats above us among the rocks but they were difficult to see.

We met a goatherd once. He was thin and tall, like many Andalusians, and he wore green corduroy breeches and jacket and leather leggings elaborately bound with red strings. He seemed unafraid when we approached him. I asked him about his job and said it must be difficult to climb after the goats at such a height, but he said it was very simple. To show us, he took out a leather sling from his jacket, picked up a stone as big as a fist, and hurled it with deadly accuracy just above a goat which jumped down towards us, startled.

'I could hit the goat if I wanted to,' explained our David, proudly, 'but, of course, it wouldn't do, and I only drive them.'

Hermann tried his hand with the sling but nearly knocked his head off as the stone refused to part with it. He wrote a long story letter on one of his postcards.

We walked on through a grey and gloomy day and Hermann was wondering whether 'David', who we could see just below us, could have hit Goliath at this distance, and it was all I could do to prevent him from abusing the stone-thrower just for the sake of an experiment.

It rained in the evening and we reached a town at nightfall. It was a quaint old town with beautiful sandstone buildings. I would have liked to wander about its streets but we were wet, cold and penniless. It was too dark to try begging so we decided to be arrested for the night. I asked a man in the street the way to the police station but he did not seem to understand. I think he was one of those who just assume a foreigner must be speaking another language. I was bawling at him, '*¡A la policía, hombre!*' but he just stared at us.

After some searching we found the police station and tried hard to be thrown into prison, which was not as easy as we thought. As a matter of fact we did not succeed, and we had a long palaver with the two bewildered policemen. It is funny that one only lands in prison when one does not want to. It was too bad a night to sleep outside and we haggled away with the police but they only shrugged their shoulders and said they could not put us in prison as we had not done anything wrong. We offered to go out and do something if that would help but they did not see the joke and got very angry. To get rid of us they finally gave us fifty *céntimos* to sleep in a *posada*, but the people there threw us out and we had to go back and fetch the police, who told them off.

The next night we had the same trouble but it was much worse. Snow was falling heavily and, by the afternoon, we looked like walking snowmen. We came to a village more desolate and melancholy than any we had seen. After some argument with the *jefe de policía*, whom we dragged out of a café, he gave us one peseta and we bought a place at the Posada de la Sierra. We had to wait a long time before they showed us our quarters as it was only four o'clock. The *posada* was like an enormous barn with a little kitchen at the back and it was full of donkeys, wagons and peasants who were marooned by the sudden snowfall. We sat around a fire, steam rising from everybody's clothes, and we watched a group of peasants eating a delicious *arroz*, but they did not offer us anything. We got some tobacco, however, and a drop of wine out of a leather bottle from a young man next to me. I was glad when the innkeeper showed us to a loft full of straw where we slept until very late the next morning.

It took us three days to reach the highest point of the road and after that the going was easy as it was downhill all the way to Granada. I liked the walk among the mountains and, had it not been for the cold and hunger, I would have liked to stay longer. With the rivers rushing through deep gorges, the snow shining through the mist and brown eagles circling above, it was melancholy, lonely but beautiful wandering.

Every hour now it seemed to get warmer and, in the afternoon, the sky was clear and before us lay the warm, fertile valley of Granada. Over the town we could see the square towers of the Alhambra. We were held up by two *guardias civiles* who demanded to see our passports, but they let us go and we wound our way down to Granada with the afternoon sun warming our backs. We made two pesetas and we felt our troubles were over for the time being.

# Chapter 4 — Granada

It was good to see trees again and well tended gardens and friendly houses and crowded streets. It was evening, people were going home from work, children were playing and men sat in front of cafés.

After walking through a long suburb we came to a *plaza* near the centre of the town, with benches and plane trees, and we stopped at an old *posada*. The big, heavy doors were open and inside, on the left, was a small box-like room from which a man watched the comings and goings like a concierge in a big hotel.

We rented two beds and waited, sitting on a bench just inside the porch from which we could observe the street. Opposite us was a kitchen and a small dining room with chairs and tables and a bullfight poster on the wall. A woman was putting wine bottles and glasses on the tables but dinner was not ready yet. We were too tired to go out to have a look at the town. I asked Hermann if he would come to Málaga with me but his heart was set on Sevilla and he talked of taking the inland road via Jaén. I wanted to see the sea again and, though my schooner had probably sailed a long time ago, there were other ships. I suddenly could not bear the thought of having to walk for years up and down Spain. We did not want to part and Hermann said he would think it over but I knew he preferred this life and he was too old to risk a start in a new and unknown country.

While we talked we saw two girls entering the *posada* but they did not see us as we were sitting behind the door. We only caught a glimpse of them walking up the stairs. Both wore the same light blue full skirts, darker blue short jackets and sandals. '*Wandervögel*, I bet,' I said and Hermann laughed. The man in the cubby hole popped out and asked if we had seen the *señoritas alemanas*. He repeated again and again that they were Germans also, and we laughed because nobody could have mistaken them for anything else. The man babbled on, '*Señoritas alemanas, sí, sí señores,*' because he thought we did not believe him.

The oil lamp was lit in the dining room and we went in and ordered beans, which cost twenty-five céntimos each, and for the rest of the pesetas some wine. The room was soon filled with workmen, poor travellers and a few tramps. We had our soup, which was good, and drank our wine. Hermann scraped a few shreds of tobacco out of a tin and rolled us a cigarette. A man gave us a handful of his tobacco when he saw we did not have enough. We stayed on after the diners had disappeared, too lazy to move and tired from the food and wine on an empty stomach. I had my hat pulled over my eyes and Hermann half lay with his feet on a chair and we stared at the poster with its matador in gold and black, with his gory cloak and the bleeding black bull.

'Hello boys,' said a voice, and we both looked up and saw a girl standing at our table.

'Hello,' we said. She was one of the girls we had seen before. She was small with black eyes, black hair, which she wore in plaits round her ears, and she could have been Spanish or Italian but for her dress. She said the doorkeeper had told her there were some Germans down here and she thought we might have been friends of theirs.

'We've just arrived,' said Hermann, quite unnecessarily. He was a bit flustered and took off his cap and wriggled on his chair. I thought he would get up, make a bow and introduce himself. The girl only looked at me, but I said nothing.

'Take your hat off. Not bad,' she said, eyeing me critically after I had removed it. 'Not bad at all.' I did not know what the answer was to that so I put my hat on again.

'Why do you wear that awful thing?' she asked. I replied that I did not have a better one and I did not think it was so bad anyway. She smiled at me rather coldly and I felt myself getting angry.

'Do you play anything?' she asked. When I did not understand she said she meant a musical instrument and she wanted to know whether we were singing or what we were doing for a living. This was Hermann's opportunity, and he delivered one of his lectures on the art of begging. The girl asked us whether we had any money. When we replied we had not she put a handful of coppers on the table. 'Take it,' she said, 'you may need it.'

I said that we were all right and she would need it herself, but she said I should not be so proud, after all we were comrades. She said that she and her friend and a boy, who was upstairs with a cold, made enough money by singing and playing instruments. She left the money and said goodnight. After she had gone Hermann went out to buy some more tobacco.

While I was waiting for him the second girl came in. She was tall and big and she walked with a long stride. Though I could not see her well in the bad light, I saw that she was young and blonde, not more than seventeen. She came to my table and, without saying anything, took my hat off and flung it on the table.

'You look very nice,' she said, and I wondered why both girls did and said the same thing. 'I'll throw it away for you if you will let me,' she said, and she laughed at me, like children do, with her wide open mouth showing lovely white teeth.

'Why do you wear a tie? You must give it to me as a present.'

I did not think it was so funny but she roared with laughter and the old man popped his head out of his cubby hole.

'Oh boy,' she said, 'what a sight you are. I've never seen a tramp in such a get-up. Oh God, you look like a real bum.'

I said that I did not just look like one but I was one. At that moment Hermann came in and she shrieked with laughter when she saw him. I must confess that we could have scared birds away from many a field. We rolled cigarettes and the girl said it was disgusting to drink and smoke. We told her to run along like a good little girl because her uncles were too tired. She invited us to go with her to their room because Walter, the boy upstairs, wanted to see us.

We followed her up to a large room with three beds. It was very untidy with a lot of clothes and musical instruments lying about. The boy was in one of the beds and looked feverish. He was about twenty-five with long blond hair which fell over one side of his forehead. We greeted him and sat down while the dark girl made a hot lemonade for him and the blonde girl took off her clothes and started to wash herself. She was beautifully built with broad hips and breasts, a little too large and womanly, firm and round. She made Hermann extremely uncomfortable. He did not know where to look and I saw that he was shocked, which struck me as very funny. The girl went to bed and looked at us with her arms folded behind her head.

'How are you feeling?' I asked the boy. He croaked that he was all right and expected to be up the next day. We talked about this and that and the longer I looked at him the more I felt I had seen him somewhere before.

'I'm sure I've seen you before,' I said. 'Did you ever live in Berlin?'

He replied that he had, and when I saw a camera lying on the table beside his bed I knew who he was.

'Your name is Walter,' I said and I told him mine and asked him whether he had ever heard of me. He sat up in surprise and said that of course he had. I told him that we had worked on the same paper, and he remembered me now although we had only seen each other once or twice. We shook hands and Walter said he had not recognised me because my hair was cropped so short.[3]

'I am Putz,' said the blonde girl from the bed.[4] The dark girl came over and said that she was glad to meet me and that her name was Fatima.[5]

'That's a strange name,' I said. 'Are you from Arabia?'

'No,' she answered, 'but not very far from there.'

We had much to tell each other and it grew very late. Hermann listened to us rather sad and isolated.

We said goodnight at last and promised to see each other in the morning. Our room was awful and dirty with eight beds in which men slept, mostly fully dressed, and it was close and stinking. I opened the shutters. The sheet was grey and crawling with bugs. I threw it on the floor. I did not dare take my clothes off and slept badly.

Walter woke us the next morning and asked us to breakfast. The pigsty we slept in made him shudder. I went into the courtyard to wash and shave and I smartened myself up with my spare blue shirt. I left my hat with the bundle in Walter's room.

It was Sunday. The *churro* baker stood in the square and we watched him pressing the dough through a tin shaped like a trumpet, cutting it off in five-inch lengths and dropping it into boiling oil. The *churros* came out brown and crisp after a minute and he wrapped them in brown paper. We bought some and went to a café where we ate them with plenty of *café con leche*.

After breakfast Hermann went away to look up somebody he knew in a village outside Granada. Walter fetched the guitar and mandolin and I walked with them to the Paseo – a wide street with a promenade in the middle flanked by shady trees and benches. On Sunday mornings or weekday evenings people, young and old, walked up and down to meet friends, to talk or to flirt. The girls were mostly in rows of three or four or, if they were alone, well chaperoned by relatives. The young men also walked in groups, in smart grey and black suits, with fancy shoes, jackets a bit too square on the shoulders and too short and narrow on the hips, their hair well oiled, reeking of cheap *eau de cologne*. The girls were very beautiful when young, with shining black eyes and a peach-like bloom.

Walter and the girls did not feel much like work but they needed some money so, after tuning their instruments, they started. Walter and Fatima played and sang while Putz collected the money in a black cap. They sang old German folk songs and they sang them well. I walked beside them and then they asked me to sing with them. I protested that I did not know the songs but they insisted. I did not like it. People were staring at us, some collected in groups, and we had difficulty in getting through them. We walked along while we sang and I did not know where to put my hands from embarrassment, so I put them in my pockets and tried to look as if I were singing voluntarily. However, in a very short time we had more than ten pesetas together and we stopped.

We sat on a bench and talked to two little gypsy girls and we gave them a little money because they were trying to sell flowers and we had spoiled it for them. They were very nice and asked us to visit them at the *ciudad de los gitanos*. Putz took the instruments to the *posada*, as they did not want to work any more that day, while I stayed with Walter and Fatima. They asked me how I liked the singing and I explained how bad I felt about it but they laughed at me and said that they had felt the same for quite a long time when they began. They asked me about my plans and I

59

said that I did not know what I was going to do and did not really care. They wanted me to come along with them.

Walter asked me how I liked Putz and I said I liked her very much.

'If you want to come with us,' he said, 'we must make one condition. You mustn't fall in love with her.'

I was a bit astonished until they explained that they had just parted with another German, who they had met and taken along, and he had fallen in love with Putz. He had made things difficult by making scenes and threatening suicide. I promised what they asked and so took up my new career.

Putz came back with Hermann and I told him that I was staying with Walter and the girls. He said that it was all right but we all felt sorry for him. We took new rooms in another *posada* opposite the first one, which were much cleaner and had a lovely view over the *plaza*. I had one to myself. We lunched together and spent the afternoon in a café.

In the evening, after dinner, I strolled round the town with Hermann but we had little to say, as is often the case when one wants to say a lot. When we got back to the inn I said goodbye to him because he wanted to get up before sunrise the next morning to start on his way. I could not help feeling that I had let him down although we would have parted anyway since he was taking the route to Sevilla.

'I am glad you've found friends,' he said – which made me feel more miserable – 'I don't think we shall ever see each other again.' I said that I hoped we would, but we never did.

'I wonder what will become of us all,' he said and I was thinking the same. Much later I was looking for him among the German volunteers but I did not find him.

'Goodbye Hermann,' I said, 'and the best of luck to you.'

We shook hands for the last time and I watched him as he walked away with his long, old coat which he always wore, although it was very warm, and his little blue cap. His walk was rather bent and tired.

When I got to my room Walter and the girls were still up and waiting for me. He said they were going out for a while. They told me later that they had seen Hermann and given him some money.

I had a bottle of wine by myself sitting on the open balcony, watching the dark square and the light of the café opposite, listening to the steps and scraps of conversation of passers-by. I was thinking about Alicante and how I had wondered where I would go – and here I was. It seemed only hours since I had left it yet my room was just the same as the one from which I had started out. It was really very simple. It always is afterwards.

The next morning we sang and played for over two hours in the narrow streets near the Convento de Gracia. We left the main streets for the afternoon when they would be more crowded. I liked singing in the suburbs; the people were more friendly and responsive. They always had a penny to spare and did not mob us but followed at a distance to hear the same songs over and over again.

We wanted to visit the Alhambra in the afternoon but it was too hot at midday so we had lunch and rested until it became cooler. We went up the steep Calle de Gomérez, from the Plaza

*Putz, Fatima and three Gypsy girls, Granada 1934*

61

Nueva with its old, beautiful houses, until we came to the gates of the Alhambra. It was like coming into a cool, dark church, the trees were so thick and high. Small water channels ran along beside the paths. We rested at a well and took our sandals off to cool our feet. We all had well-shaped feet, straight and broad, from walking without shoes. Walter said that he had made his sandals himself. They were just two thick soles with two leather straps.

A few guides and two old beggars were waiting at the Gate of Justice. We gave a few pennies to the beggars. One of the guides, a pot-bellied young Spaniard, offered to show us round. We refused but he said he knew we were not tourists as he had seen us singing in the streets and there was no business at the moment anyway since it was too early for the English, who were all having their tea. He was slightly drunk. He wore a short pair of trousers and a short jacket out of which his belly stuck like a melon.

'You are Germans,' he said. 'I can hear it. I can speak the language myself, or at least,' he modified, 'I know some words. *Kartoffelbauch*,' he said, slapping his belly. 'That's me.' We laughed so much that we could not stop. The guide was pleased that we understood. He rattled off a lot of words, '*Kartoffelbauch, Schweinefleisch, Fraulein, sehr hübsch, Guten Morgen, schlafen sie mache.*'

It was very funny but, unfortunately, after exhausting his German, he remembered that he was a guide. He took his hat off and pointed with it rapidly left and right and upwards and began his lecture.

'You see here the Puerta de la Justicia – erected by Yusuf I in 1348 – that the Moors called the *Bab al-Sharia* or the Gate of Justice. Sixty-seven feet high and forty-eight feet wide.'

He was well meaning but he was spoiling everything with his rambling speech, which he must have made a thousand times so that he could fire it off without stopping, in an endless monotone. He was soon boring us and insisted on showing us things we did not want to see.

Looking back towards the Puerta de la Justicia, I fortunately noticed a party of old English ladies approaching. They were thin and very old and wore high collars, flapping hats, heavy shoes and carried coats and sticks. I told our guide not to bother about us and thanked him for his kindness. I said we did not want to stand in the way of his earning something and we would not mind if he left us. But, like a true Spaniard, he protested, saying it did not matter, what was money after all? It was a great pleasure for him to show us round for nothing. All the time he watched the approaching party out of the corner of his eye and backed away from us towards the gate.

'If you insist,' he said, by now almost running. 'If you insist, then I must go. But I don't like to,' he shouted back from the gate. 'I would rather have stayed with you.' We saw him pouncing on the party with the other guides. We left hurriedly in case they did not take him and he came back.

Later on we met him again near the garden of the Caliphate, with two ladies who hurried behind him with Spanish diction-aries in their hands. It seemed the guide knew some English as well. After every explanation we heard him saying, 'Wonderful, no? Very good, no?' He winked at us when we passed but looked rather exhausted and depressed. I could see he was not having much fun because he could not show off the rest of his vocabulary. 'Good morning, nice girl, did you sleep well? Pig meat, potato belly.'

We went to the ruins of Silla del Moro, the highest hill above the Alhambra. We sat down, leaning against the stones. Parapets had crumbled away and there was nothing to obstruct the view as far as the Sierra Nevada.

'We must come back tomorrow and every day,' I said.

'Yes,' said Walter. 'As long as we are here. We'll have left this town in a week. But there are other places like this. We have never been in the south – Málaga, Cádiz, Sevilla, Córdoba.'

'And after that?'

'I don't know,' he said, 'we'll have to go back to Madrid in the autumn. It will be too difficult in the winter. In the spring we'll start again.'

I did not want to go to Madrid but I did not say so. It was May; the summer was only just beginning. We would go south; that was where I wanted to go but I did not want to come back. I was looking for a cigarette and my passport fell out of my pocket. Fatima picked it up and opened it. They laughed at my photo. It was as bad as only passport photos can be. I was depicted in a leather coat and a white scarf looking stern and forbidding.

'I can't recognise you,' said Fatima, 'you must have changed a lot.'

'It's five years ago.'

'I'm sure I wouldn't have liked you then.'

'That's what I said to Hermann when I saw his picture. He wore a fur coat and was as fat as a pig. I haven't changed much.'

They said I had and that I looked much better now.

'The only thing I like is that you wore your hair longer,' said Putz. 'Who gave you that Prussian haircut?'

'A barber in Elche cut it for me when I had no money. He was a communist.'

'He was a bad barber.'

'I told him to cut it short because I didn't know when I would be able to get it cut again.'

Fatima looked at my age. It was my birthday.

'Why didn't you tell us?' said Walter. 'We must celebrate.'

'I forgot about it.'

'We'll go to a café tonight and have lots of ices and cakes,' said Fatima.

'I wish you'd told us. We could have bought you a present.'

'You'd probably rather have a drink,' said Putz. Walter laughed.

'You can have as much as you like, but only today, because it's your birthday.'

'Tell us about your last one,' said Fatima, 'we don't know anything about you.'

I did not want to.

'Not here,' I said. 'Let's talk in the café. A life story is always dreary. Let's just sit and look. It's getting dark and we'll have to go back soon.'

When we went down the gates were just closing. A lot of people were round the little stalls in the Plaza Nueva. Lights had just been lit and burned dimly in the twilight. Little boys with big, gruff voices were calling out the evening newspapers. After dinner we went to the café on our *plaza*. It was modern, with a long bar, painted in horrible colours: green, red and cream. The lamps were of surrealistic design, reflected a hundred times in the mirrors. The bar was crowded but nobody was sitting at the tables. We took a corner seat on a sofa. I ordered brandy while the others had coffee and cakes.

*Jan's narrative breaks off at this point. Inevitably he did become infatuated with Putz and the party continued to travel westwards. By the late summer they arrived in Cádiz.*

*Left to Right: Fatima, Jan and Putz, Granada, 1934*

# Chapter 5 — Bullfight in Cádiz

Coming out of the glaring sun it was dark and cool in the passage which ran under the seats of the amphitheatre. Like a church it looked, with its great pillars and tall, narrow windows in the thick walls of the tower. In front of the windows were the iron stairs which led to the upper tiers. The stables were empty as the horses had not yet arrived. A little old man who was cleaning the stables stopped working and showed us round. He wore blue overalls, a bright red handkerchief tied round his head. I asked him about the fight.

'No good,' he said. 'The fighters are only locals and the bulls are small.'

'What about García?" I asked.

'His trick with the *banderillas* isn't bad,' he said, 'but it's only a trick. He can't fight and he can't kill. They're only locals.' There was a great contempt in his voice. 'They couldn't kill a bull with a gun.'

'Are you from Madrid?' I asked him. It was clear that he was not Andalusian. I just named the first place I could think of.

'Yes,' he said, with a sad smile. 'I'm from Madrid, how did you guess?'

'It's the most beautiful city in Spain,' I said to please him, though I had never been there. He kept on asking if I had seen this or that and Walter and the girls had to help me out.

We climbed up to the seats and looked over the arena. It was like a smooth, round yellow disc, very hot, very desolate and still. The sun was high above the ring and there was no shade as there is in the afternoon when the fight takes place; two glaring discs, one enormous, below, the other small, high above.

We looked at the fighters' dressing rooms. They were small and simply furnished with only a few chairs and a row of hooks to hang their clothes on. Next to an old, beautifully printed poster was the head of a black bull. The rest of the walls were plastered with photos of fights and fighters. Our guide pointed out the famous people who had fought here. Most of them were dead. 'Ah, you should have seen them,' he said, blowing a smacking kiss on his fingers. 'This one here, and that one.'

He used the pet names that Spaniards give to their heroes, Joselito for José, Angelito for Ángel. He talked about them passionately, like a lover raving about his mistress. 'What wonderful *verónicas*, what marvellous *mariposas*! Ah, what beautiful killers they were! You should have seen them as I saw them,' he said, with a sob in his voice. 'We shall never see their equals again, there will never be another one like this and this one!' And he pointed left and right, sobbing, calling, praising, mourning, bereaved and inconsolable.

Next to the dressing room was the infirmary, a bright white room with big windows and built-in cupboards. The operating table stood in the middle covered with a dust sheet. We passed the chapel which was windowless. The floor was of coloured tiles forming a cross in the middle with a black outline and many rays. Candles burned on the altar which was covered with red silk and lace. The statue of María holding her child stood in the middle, between the candles, a low chair in front of it to kneel on.

We climbed a small flight of stairs which led to a balcony from which one could see the yellow fields, the gates of the town and beyond that the white town itself, a silver plate on a sea of blue. Below us were the pens divided into triangles. The bulls were lying on the ground or standing in the narrow shadow of the high walls and they looked small and harmless. Our guide asked us if we were coming to the fight. We said that we were and he promised to show us round to see the preparations if we came early. I offered him some money but he would not take it so we thanked him and left.

* * * * *

I left early for the ring. Before I took the tram I had a coffee and some brandy at a kiosk. Outside the gate of the town the main road was filled with a huge, black procession of people walking slowly towards the bull ring. The sky was overcast, the atmosphere was close and a cloud of dust hung over the road and the procession.

I bought a cheap seat and went to look for our guide of the day before. I found him in front of the stables. The *picadores* had already mounted the big, cadaverous-looking horses which had Mexican saddles with stirrups like large iron boots. The horses were thickly padded on one side. The *picadores* were strong and tough-looking men. They wore yellow trousers, black elaborately embroidered jackets and wide-brimmed, round felt hats with a red pom-pom on the side. I wanted to look at the dressing rooms, infirmary and chapel again before the fight started but I could not get permission.

I took my seat which was high up in the unshaded, cheaper side of the arena, but there was no sun and no shadow and only a white, hot glare. People streamed in from all sides, crawling up and down like a swarm of ants before they settled down. I sat next to a crowd of gypsies who had brought bottles of wine, but they were already drunk. They sang, clapped their hands and stamped their feet. One of them tried to dance on the small, stone seat and kept falling off.

A shiny, modern water cart drove into the ring and sprayed the sand. The driver was an artist. He drove round the ring at terrific speed in smaller and smaller circles until he ended up exactly in the middle. The crowd cheered him. The musicians had taken their places and were testing their instruments. The excitement grew. At five minutes to four half a dozen fat, middle-aged men in black suits and hats appeared in the box. They acknowledged the cheers of the crowd and settled down behind the red-draped balcony. One could just see their heads and they looked like pale, unripe melons on a red tablecloth.

At exactly four o'clock the door opposite the box was thrown open and a man in sixteenth century costume with a plumed hat rode out across the ring. He halted under the box, saluted, and the key was thrown down to him. He caught it in his hat, which brought applause from all sides, and galloped back to the entrance where the bullfighters were lined up. He swung his horse round, the band struck up a *pasodoble* and they marched across the ring towards the box, where the fighters saluted and discarded their parade capes for the plainer fighting ones.

The first *matador* was a fat, oldish man in tight, brilliant purple trousers and jacket and pink stockings. He waited. After a trumpet signal the doors opened. The crowds yelled and cheered but the bull only showed his head and refused to come out. The *matador* went to the door and banged on it with his fist and the bull suddenly shot out sending him and his men scrambling over the barrier. The crowd laughed and cheered the bull which stopped, bewildered, in the middle of the ring and then trotted back to the door. The exit was closed and he banged on the door with his horns and bellowed. He turned round, saw the cape and charged but stopped dead whenever it was taken away or did not move.

The *picadores* came out and the crowd booed and hissed. The bull was brought to the horse and charged. His horns were under the horse which reared and kicked, and he tore and banged it against the barrier and finally threw it. The *picador* had managed to free himself but limped badly when he was helped out. The crowd yelled and hissed. The horse was kicking amongst its entrails and somebody killed it and covered it with a cloth. The bull did not want to leave that corner. When they brought him to the middle again they placed the *banderillas* in his neck and he bellowed and pawed the sand. He was tired and the blood flowed freely from under the gaily striped *banderillas*. He charged feebly at the last stage with his head close to the cloth and was easily killed. There was great applause for the fat man who ran around the ring with the bull's tail in one hand and his sword in the other. He was bald and short-winded.

The next *matador*, a tiny, bow-legged man, was greeted with a storm of applause. He was García, a man famed for his tricks with the *banderillas*. His bull came out lively and strong and eager to fight. He went for the cape and tore it and chased García round the ring and over the barrier. After some chasing round, the bull always behind the man, the *picadores* came out. The bull charged the horse but did not throw it or hurt it much and it was taken out. García tried a *verónica* but ended up sitting between the horns of the bull, both looking rather surprised. The bull threw his rider but did not attack him and was lured away. García received the *banderillas*. People cheered madly and he waved the *banderillas* towards the box as if dedicating them and walked towards the waiting bull. He put both the *banderillas* in his mouth, raised his arms and stamped his feet to attract the bull. The bull charged and García stepped back a few paces but let him come very close and with a small movement of his head put both *banderillas* into the bull's neck. There was enormous applause, yelling and waving of handkerchiefs.

The bull did not like the trick and pursued García who was running around the ring, proudly showing his jacket which was torn, and did not see the bull behind him. He had to dive over the barrier and the bull followed him, jumping over it, and chased him back again. The bull did not go for the cloth any more but for the man. If he had been a stronger bull he would have killed him very quickly but he only tossed him, knocked him about and chased him all over the ring as if he was playing with him. The crowd roared with laughter but they suddenly became very angry when he could not kill the bull. He tried a dozen times and the bull finally gave way and fell but had to be killed with a knife.

The crowd was in an ugly temper by now and gave applause to the next bull but not to the *matador*. He was a handsome young man in a tight silver-blue suit. His hair was black, glistening with oil, but his face was pale and he seemed to be nervous and frightened. He approached the bull and made him run. He made a number of close passes but there was no applause. When the *picadores* came out all hell broke loose. I did not know what was wrong and asked the man in front of me but he only pointed to the *picador* and called him a mule, a swine and a coward. The *picador* sat on his horse unmoved, square and pale. When the bull was brought to the horse the crowd screamed again. The bull charged. The *picador* sat still without raising his lance. The horse was thrown with the man in the saddle. When the bull was lured away the horse got up trembling but the *picador* did not. The man in front of me screamed, 'Get up you coward, get up you arsehole!' He screamed so loudly that my eardrums felt as if they would split and I slammed his hat down over his face. He turned round to me, red-faced and snarling, but he sat down again and was quiet. The *picador* was carried out and a man made a sign to the crowd to show that he was injured and the uproar died down.

The young *matador* placed the *banderillas* but the bull threw them off so he had to do it again. He did it well this time but the crowd was against him. The bull tore the cloth out of his hand. It was stuck on its horns, covering his head, and the crowd laughed as he ran round blindfolded. Everything went wrong. The booing, yelling and hissing kept on the whole time and the *matador* looked white and ill, his hair hanging over his wet face.

To turn the crowd he performed a desperate trick. He went down on his knees in front of the bull as if he was praying. When the bull charged he made no attempt to get out of the way. Some women screamed in terror but the bull stopped dead in front of the man with his eyes on the cloth. The man stretched out his hand touching the bull's horn. The bull did not move and the man looked round the ring. The people were silent for a moment, before this strange and unexpected scene, then suddenly cheered and applauded which startled the bull and he knocked the man over. He got up but his knees buckled under him. He went slowly to the barrier where he received the sword and went back for the kill.

The bull seemed to know what was coming and did not respond to the cloth, did not charge. The *matador* raised the sword with a trembling hand and lunged at the bull and was tossed. He lay still while the bull buffeted him with his head. He got up and tried again but the sword sprang out as it struck bone and flew into the crowd. The *matador* received a second sword and tried again and fell. He could hardly hold himself upright, fumbling blindly for the sword while the crowd yelled and screamed and started throwing cushions. Another man tried to persuade him to give up and they wrangled with each other. Tears were streaming down his face and he muttered to himself and swore at the bull which was watching him closely. The *matador* raised his sword to the box but the fat men smoking cigars did not respond. He charged at the bull, feebly stumbling and desperate, and finally the sword went in to the hilt. The bull charged and knocked him down, then turned and charged again before stumbling and falling, but he was not dead and had to be finished off with the knife. The *matador* was led out weeping and gesticulating. His friends were holding him up and his arms were flapping up and down as if he were trying to fly. The crowd swore and spat at him and threw bottles and cushions.

Three horses galloped into the ring with jingling bells, their riders waving flags and cracking whips. The bull was fastened to a sort of cross and they dragged him out, galloping and noisy, ploughing a deep furrow through the sand and the eyes of the bull were wide open. The sand was smoothed over behind them, the musicians left their instruments and the crowd got up for the interval.

\* \* \* \* \*

*The narrative breaks off again here. It is not clear whether Jan went on to Málaga with the others or whether he left Cádiz by boat. By mid-September he was in Mallorca, where he met some English people who brought him back with them to London.*

*Once in England he met Kate Mangan (recently separated from her husband, Sherry) at a party and took her back with him to Mallorca. Later they travelled to Portugal. They were in Lisbon when the Spanish civil war began, in July 1936. They made their way back to London, and in October Jan caught a train to Paris, where he enlisted with the International Brigade and was sent down to Marseilles to catch a boat to Spain.[6]*

# PART 2 :   INTERNATIONAL BRIGADE
## 1936-1937

## Chapter 1 — Alicante

As I stood on deck early in the morning the sun was rising in a clear and cloudless sky. Leaning over the railing and looking towards the land, still shrouded in mist lifting quickly as the sun rose, I tried to remember what it was like when I had landed here two years before.

It was the same time of day when I stood on the deck of a small boat trying to get a first glimpse of the town. It was grey and very close and glaring so that only after entering the harbour could I make out the fortress and the first houses and trees. In a short time I should see it again. The faint blue strip of land, in parts still clinging to the sky, of the same colour, would be touched by the sun and a little later the fortress and the town would rise over the water.

I had always known that I should come back. It was the fulfilment of my dream - or was it a realisation of my thoughts on that hill before Totana two years earlier? In less than an hour we should be in Alicante. I say 'we' now, because I was not alone and the ship was much bigger than the one I had come on before. There were six hundred of us, Germans, Poles, French and English and we knew what to do and where we were going.

The deck was crowded with men looking out to the shore. We brought our coffee up from the galley because nobody wanted to stay below. A few small fishing boats passed us on their way out to sea. About two miles from the port four grey cruisers rode at anchor; the first signs of war. We passed a German ship first, then a Dutch, a French and an English ship. They were sent out by their respective governments to safeguard their nationals. They seemed to draw closer together when we passed them, like conspirators, and they started talking to each other with searchlights in a silent, unknown language. Though they were in

Spanish waters they had to do something about us. Maybe they were just bored or perhaps, having so many guns, they wanted to play policeman. We were told to go down out of sight and prepare for trouble. I stayed where I was and looked up at the bridge. The captain did not pay any attention to the men-of-war although I could see the English cruiser signalling to us and, at the same time, getting under way. More silent talk among the four bullies:

'I wonder who she is?'

'I can't see any name.'

'No, it's all painted out.'

'She shows no flag.'

'Lots of people on board – must be a Government ship.'

'Yes, must be reds.'

'Let's force her to run the flag up.'

'She doesn't answer.'

'We'll stop her and look her over.'

'But she's within Spanish waters.'

'Oh yeah? We'll show her.'

The British cruiser was now on her way trying to intercept us. She sailed about a hundred yards before our bows and I could see the officers on the bridge waving towards us. We did not slow down but when it looked as though the cruiser was going to block the entrance to the port, our captain gave orders to hoist the black and red flag of the anarchists. It seemed to baffle them and we passed into the port without any trouble.

The quay looked deserted. It was too early in the morning for anybody to be about. Three Spaniards in overalls and black and red striped caps, carrying short carbines on their shoulders, watched our landing. Because four of us, including myself, had brown overalls and therefore looked more military we were leading the march into town. We were taller than the French and therefore took longer steps, one for every three of the rest, and the French were shouting, 'Eh, les grands là – Hi you big ones, you're out of step.' We tried shorter steps but it did not work and we had to let them pass and march at the back of the column.

A red flag was unfurled and we sang *The Internationale*. At the custom house, just before leaving the port, ten Spanish soldiers with drums and trumpets welcomed us. We halted. They formed two rows in front with the man carrying our flag behind them. The band struck up and we moved on to the quick strain of a Spanish army march. For the first time I felt like a soldier. The trumpets blared a loud and sharp melody twice as quick as our steps and then stopped while the roll of the drums took up the rhythm. Four steps to the trumpet and four steps to the drum. We had to take very short steps to follow but the French did better because they were accustomed to it. The music was similar to that of the French colonial army, its sounds conjuring up vast deserts, heat and lonely outposts.

The streets, deserted a minute before, now were full of people. They cheered and waved. Red, black and red, and yellow, red and purple flags fluttered from the buildings. '¡Viva la República!' they shouted, '¡Viva la democracia!' Someone among us yelled, 'Franco' and everyone answered, 'Abajo.' The people clapped and they ran along with us trying to shake us by the hand, and at every street and square the crowds grew bigger.

I did not look at the people at that moment and, though I felt very happy, I could not shake off that sad and melancholy feeling one has at a homecoming after many years abroad. I would have liked to talk to somebody, to point out the streets and plazas I knew. There was the hotel where I had stayed, the bench I had sat on and a thousand other things, but it was only exciting for me and for nobody else. Everybody was busy singing, waving and shouting to the people around us while, for a time, I saw nothing but that which had been.

It was as I had left it and remembered it and yet it was very different. I would have liked to go for a walk through quiet streets. There was the kiosk where I had my first breakfast, there was the bench I had sat on and watched the sea and saw the tramp walking by, there was the water-cart wetting the dry and dusty streets, as it did every morning, and we had to step aside to let it pass. There was the garden still full of flowers, and the statue of the old man. The trees and bushes had grown in the three years. We halted at the same place where I had stopped to see whether I was on the right road and I hoped we should go on the same way back. A little further on we should come upon the sign which says 'Murcia', and after that the long straight road with small houses on both sides until one comes to the big yellow barracks. But we had to turn and march back through the town again and we took a road which I did not know and, for the first time, I saw the smiling faces, clenched fists and forgot to remember anything.

About a mile out of town we came to a newly built convent school which was our quarters. Our musicians stood on both sides still blowing the trumpets and rolling the drums and we marched smartly into the courtyard. Everything was white: the walls, the gallery which ran round the four sides. The yard was paved with white stones with a fountain in the middle. Though it threw only a thin stream of water, not more than a foot high, one could hear it clearly, the place was so still. It was warm in the centre of the courtyard where the sun was and very cool in the shade of the gallery. Somebody made a speech, but I forget what it was about. I remember it was forbidden to go into town. I had hoped very much to go but now I did not mind.

We had lunch in the early afternoon, consisting of big slices of bread and sardines. We drank the water from the fountain. I went to the gallery and looked into the classrooms. The walls were painted green and the floors were tiled. In each room were two rows of tiny wooden benches. The blackboards still bore the writings of the teachers; on one a little poem, on another the ABC and an arithmetic problem: $71 + 121 - 53$. I'm sure a lot of children had struggled over it.

Through the back of the courtyard was a neglected garden and a small field which was probably the playground. I sat on the wall which separated the school from the road. One could see a little of the town and a strip of sea. A lot of little boys had gathered in the field opposite the wall to stare at us. A bigger boy, about eleven or twelve, came over when I called him. He wore overalls and a little empty pistol holster. He told me his brother was a sentry at our barracks and I walked over with him to the entrance where four young Spaniards were busy unsuccessfully attempting to disperse swarms of children who wanted to look in.

The boy's brother, a handsome young man of not more than sixteen, carried a rifle of which he was very proud. He gave it to me to look at. It was a Mauser of Spanish make and unloaded. 'We don't need cartridges here,' he said, laughing, when I told him he should have some. 'Franco doesn't come here.' He opened his cartridge case which was fastened to a shiny black leather belt. It was filled with tobacco, a little piece of chocolate and cigarette papers. He told me his father was in the army and he was looking after his mother and four brothers. He wanted to go to the front but he was too young. He said his little brother would go and buy things for us if we needed anything. There was a shop about half a mile away. I gave him money and asked him to buy cigarettes, a goatskin bottle and a litre of wine. Soon all the boys were busy running to and fro carrying bottles, chocolate, fruit and cigarettes.

At six o'clock we were told to pack up. Many of us had suitcases which were put on a lorry. An hour later we marched back into town. It was twilight with the many shades of blue which one only sees in Spain. Everything was blue, the streets, the houses, the people, the sky and even the donkeys which passed us coming back from the fields. It got dark quickly. On both sides of the road throngs of people and children followed us. We halted before the French Consulate and we sang the *Marseillaise* and the Consul came out on the balcony to greet us. More people were at the station to see us off. We crowded into the long train and a band struck up the Republican National Anthem while we moved out into the night.

The train was badly lit and very crowded. I got out the only book I had brought with me, De Coster's *Eulenspiegel*, but it was too dark to read. John talked about his experiences on the Aragon front where he had been for a month. It sounded like peaceful and leisurely guerrilla warfare with hardly any organisation. We argued about whether Madrid would be the same. Some of us had seen a newsreel of the bombardment of Irun but John thought there were not enough weapons on either side to make modern warfare possible.[7]

I still remember that when we passed Barcelona two days earlier and heard that we were not going to Aragon but to

Madrid, we were greatly disappointed. I do not know why. Perhaps it was because we heard so much about rising against the rebels. The only fighting seemed to be in Aragon and we would not be in it. The very name, Madrid, had such a final sound. Franco was a long way from Madrid. Some said forty, some even eighty miles away, which must be halfway to the Portuguese frontier, and yet we only spoke about Madrid as if there were nothing beyond it.

We were eight men in the compartment. There were John, Bernard[8] and Chris,[9] fresh from university, Jock, a Scottish miner from Glasgow,[10] another Englishman[11] and two Frenchmen. Jock was a tough little man who always had an odd, bewildered look on his face. He had been in the last war and had stayed in Cologne during the occupation and we talked about the Rhineland. I had great difficulty in understanding his broad Scottish accent. He told me he had liked the Germans very much. 'Ay, and the girls were nice too.' He said he thought the people were very much like the English, especially the miners. He could not understand why they had ever fought each other. Yes, it was strange indeed. Here I sat between the English and the French, an enemy of yesterday. One of my brothers lies buried somewhere in England after being killed on a destroyer after an attack on Dover. Now we were not only comrades but soldiers in the same army, on the way to fight a common enemy.

The two Frenchmen were full of beans. One came from Marseilles, a sailor who had deserted a man-of-war, was very handsome and very dark like an Italian.[12] He was busy making himself smart all the time. He had brought a suitcase which he opened and shut every few minutes. He went out to wash and came back to oil his hair from a frightful-smelling perfume bottle. Then suddenly he had the idea he must change his clothes, started to undress but, as there was no room, he did it outside in the corridor. He appeared in sky-blue silk underwear and then remembered he had forgotten something in the lavatory and walked through the whole train with everybody laughing and shouting at him. When he came back he put on a dark blue silken jersey, a bright red neckerchief and his pants.

Finally, after a last look in the mirror, he seemed satisfied with his appearance.

The Parisian was small and very shabby with no other clothes than the ones he wore.[13] His name was Marcel and he came from Montmartre. He too had been in the army and was later to give us our first training in Albacete. They sang us a song and we tried to learn the words but it was too difficult. They nudged Jock to sing with them which increased the bewildered look on his face, which amused the French very much. 'Ah canne onderstand what u say,' he protested. 'You can't talk French,' and the French copied his accent by making strangled sounds. The song was about a priest who went into a public lavatory followed by many other people. There were lots of verses each worse than the last. Bernard, who was the best at French, did a bit of translating for Jock's benefit. It sounded even more awful in English and Jock's eyes were popping out as he looked helplessly from one to another. The sailor gave us a solo, singing the *Marseillaise* as only the French can sing it, and we replied with *The Old Grey Mare, She Ain't What She Used To Be.*

We all smoked and the compartment soon got very stuffy. The two Johns puffed at their pipes, which amused the French very much. They said it was not elegant, that only old men smoked pipes – old men *avec la barbe.* English tobacco was *bon,* strong but stinking.

I opened the window and leaned out. The train was very slow. There were more than twenty-five coaches, which probably accounted for it, but we were also climbing steadily. It was a very dark night with just a little breeze rustling in the olive trees which grew in the fields below the track.

From the front of the train came faint sounds of music and cheers. We thought at first there was a band on the train but it became louder and nearer. The train hardly moved and in the stillness we could hear the strains of *The Internationale.* It was not played in the way that we knew it but slower, more melodious and tango-like. We all tried to see what it was, squeezing ourselves into the small window. All the windows along the whole train were crowded with men leaning out and looking forward to discover where the sounds came from.

The music grew louder and we could see the lights of a station. The first carriages must have passed it. The lights of the compartment flickered over heads, hands, banners and flags. Cries of '*viva*', deafening now as we drew into the station, drowned out the music except for the boom-boom of some deep brass instrument. Over the din now rose the tune of the Republican anthem. Emerging from the darkness and stillness of a minute ago it suddenly seemed very bright, although there were only a few oil lamps burning, which threw flickering lights and deep shadows. On the bright scarlet flags a few words glittered in golden letters: *Solidaridad Obrero, Proletariado, Libertad, UGT* and *UHP*. Big streamers were carried high on two poles, swaying and sagging: *Arriba la República, una e indivisible.*

There were more flags, more banners being borne down the village street towards the station. There were people running, shouting, waving their hats. We wanted to get down on the platform but it was impossible. There was not room enough to put one's foot down. The comrades behind us nearly pushed us out of the window to gain a glimpse. There were shouts of *'Viva Rusia'; 'Viva la República'; 'Abajo Franco, abajo, abajo',* taken up by everyone, *'À bas, à bas'; 'Down, down'; 'Viva el Proletariado Mundial'.*

Spain had come to greet us. From the villages and small towns, from lonely farms among the hills, from factories and workshops, they had come with their women and children to greet the first brigade of volunteers. The faces were no longer sad, drawn and anxious about the future. Everyone smiled, laughed, shouted and cried. Hands were clasped though one did not know to whom they belonged and it did not matter. They embraced us as if we were long lost brothers. Kisses were planted on cheeks. Women and girls stretched out their hands, a little shy but smiling and putting the other hand modestly over their eyes.

They had brought all their children, the *niños*, the future of Spain, for whom no sacrifice could be great enough. 'Kiss them, our children – kiss the future of Spain.' The children were used to being spoiled, petted and flattered. They were held up to the windows, stretching out mechanically their little arms and were duly kissed on the forehead, on the cheeks, twice over by the French, caressed by the Germans and English with proud mothers and fathers looking on and old grandmothers crying into their petticoats. It was a historic moment for everyone, a moment to be remembered.

The world had sent its best sons to help their threatened brothers in Spain. They looked at us with shiny, wet eyes as if we were a miracle, but more wonderful than any church could offer. No more *mañana* and wait and wait and hope and hope. This was the answer to a million hopes and prayers. The day of delivery was near. Help had come from somewhere, out of the dark, and many more would come. Hopes were running high, courage was restored. Now we cannot lose. *'Viva Rusia! Viva la democracia!'*

'Where are you from?' someone shouted.

'London,' we cried back, 'Paris, Marseilles, Warsaw.'

'But Russia?' they said, 'are you not from Russia?'

They seemed baffled by our 'No'. They had been told the Russians were coming and now help came from everywhere *but* Russia. They must have wondered why we did not wear long shaggy beards and *chacos*. But it did not matter now. The whole world seemed to have rallied. Democracies were standing by to save the Republic of Spain. *¡Viva Francia! ¡Viva Inglaterra! ¡Viva Polonia!*

'Are you thirsty?' they cried. 'Are you hungry?' Baskets of grapes and bottles of wine were pushed into the train. 'Here, take, *con muchas gracias camaradas.* Let's sing a song now, strike up the band!' *The Internationale* and the Republican anthem melted together. Three lines of one, three lines of the other make a great song. But we had to leave. The engine whistled and we drew slowly out of the station. The last hand-shake, the last *'Buena suerte, camarada,'* and the station disappeared, the shouts grew fainter, but the music could be heard for a long time.

As soon as we had sat down, excited and happy, eating grapes and drinking wine, we had to get up again. Another station full of people; a short speech of welcome by the mayor of the village drowned in music and *vivas*. There were many more stations.

From Alicante to Albacete the people had come to greet us. It was a long, triumphant journey, from village to village, but we could not stop everywhere and had to pass on slowly. A flag which was given to us flew from the engine. Everywhere was the same look of hope and gratitude on the faces; well to be remembered and cherished for with every mile we were drawing nearer to the great tomb: Madrid, where the only greeting would be shrapnel, bombs, shells and bullets.

We were very tired when we came to Albacete. Throngs of people were waiting for us and marched with us from the station to the barracks. A white banner was fastened over the entrance: '*Camaradas*, the Fifth Regiment Salutes You.'

# Chapter 2 — Albacete

In the morning we looked over our new quarters. We had slept on mattresses in rooms which were all on the ground floor. Doors with glass panels led to a courtyard. In the yard was a well and two pumps where we could wash. At ten o'clock we were allowed into the town until midday. We had not had any breakfast because things were not yet organised. We had coffee and buns at a café. The town was not very big. It was not old, picturesque or interesting. It lay in a flat, treeless country. There were one or two main streets with shops and cafés and a great number of barbers and pharmacies. There was a *paseo* with a long avenue of plane trees and a few handsome houses where the wealthy had lived. There were a few churches, hospitals and a park with a band stand. A little further off was the bull ring and the great barracks of the Guardia Civil.

The weather was fine; quite warm in the daytime but very cold at night. Some men got colds and infected everybody else and soon most of us were coughing and spitting. We had with us three technicians who had given up good jobs in England to work in aircraft factories. The food did not seem to agree with them and they always had indigestion so I spent a lot of time buying medicines for them. They were quiet, middle-aged men, eager to get to their new jobs, but they did not know Spain, where everything moves slowly, even in war. One of them, a small bald-headed man, I liked very much. He hardly ever grumbled, was always helpful and tried to cheer up his more short-tempered comrades. When he was ill I brought him some aspirins and grapes as his comrades did not bother about him.

I met a young German Jew whom I knew from Berlin. He was helping the doctor, a young Polish Jew with a bald head and drooping shoulders, who was always so vague and absent-minded that he forgot who he was talking to from one minute to the next. Hans, the German, spoke English well and a number of other languages. He always sat with us and was helpful about translating. Every day he tried to get our technicians to

Barcelona where they should have gone in the first place. They were wasted hanging around in Albacete. They were even asked to join the army as soldiers. One of them said he did not mind but the others refused, quite rightly.

In charge of our company was a squat and fat French officer who had brought a uniform. He was always amiable and cheerful and spoke some English. He looked very much like Roehm. He was proud to have us in his company as we were so much taller than the French and we always had to march in front. Marcel was put in charge of the English section. He looked very funny ordering us around. We learned French commands. Every morning we trained in the wood just outside the town with many Spaniards looking on. They mimicked Marcel's '*un, deux, un deux*.' They had every reason to be amused. When Marcel said '*à gauche*' some went to the left, others to the right.

The different battalions trained separately. The Germans were always disciplined, marching smartly and singing. They were led by a tall, thin German called Hans who later commanded a division. There were Poles, Italians and Hungarians. There were twenty young Jews, just arrived from Palestine. We were called the XI Brigade, consisting of four battalions. We still wore civilian clothes; there were no uniforms. Seven of us had brought brown overalls and we looked a bit like soldiers, but everybody thought we were pilots and the first week people always gave us a special cheer when we marched through the town.

Meals were given out in the bull ring, in the gangway under the seats. Food was not very good at first but improved later on. We received no pay. Fortunately some of us had brought a little money. We often had lunch or dinner in a small but good restaurant. It was not very expensive and there was wine and beer and plenty to eat. Every evening we could go out until eleven o'clock.

For a few nights John, Bernard and I together with the French officer and Marcel were acting as police. We each got a rifle, a Spanish beret and a warm coat. The rifles were not loaded. Before we went out everybody was trying to handle the rifles and we could see that most of them had never used one. Someone took mine and slipped the bolt back but could not close it. I showed him how to do it by pressing down on the spring and he nearly cut my thumb off. We walked through the town from ten to eleven but the men were orderly. They all went back in time. There were, of course, one or two trouble-makers. Our Jock was one of them; when he was drunk he started slugging everybody. We wanted to send him back to England but he would not go and he became a great nuisance.

There were a few rowdy French who later landed in a labour camp. We had two Irishmen among us who had joined us in Albacete. We could never find out who they were or who had sent them. One was a fat, middle-aged former sea captain and the other, a young man, was always in a bitter and quarrelsome mood. The younger one went about us trying to create discontent about the food, the quarters and everything else. We wanted to get rid of them but nobody knew anything about them. Everybody disliked them but when we left Albacete they stayed behind and we never heard any more of them.

Chris was ill one morning and stayed in bed. We had been out the whole day marching about and when we came back he had been taken to hospital. That evening we went out to visit him. It was about a mile out of town. There were Spanish sentries on the roads. When we came to the hospital, a big gloomy place, we heard that Chris had been taken somewhere else but they did not know where. On the way back we went through the red light district, consisting of a few bars and dance halls in a dirty street. We had a drink; there were only a few girls who sat around rather bored and lonely. It was not forbidden to go there but there were none of our men around. We talked with some Spanish soldiers. One of them had just returned from Madrid. He said it was very bad and the bombs scared him. He demonstrated them by making a number of extraordinary noises which ended in a loud 'boom-boom'. He was a little man with black curly hair and reminded me of the barber in Elche.

We went into a small wine shop in a side street to buy cigarettes. It was badly lit. There was a bar with a few bottles in it. Two peasants sat in a corner playing cards. A Spanish dandy, smartly dressed, stood at the bar very drunk. He insisted on buying us a drink. The barman was a young man with fair hair.

There were some anarchist posters on the wall. He saw me looking at them and smiled.

'I'm an anarchist,' he said.

'Yes,' said the dandy. 'He's a bloody anarchist but I'm a socialist.'

'Since when?' asked the barman, winking at me.

'I always was,' protested the dandy.

I ordered drinks. 'It doesn't matter now,' I said. 'Anarchists, communists, socialists, it's all the same – *El Frente Popular*.'

'It is and it isn't,' replied the barman.

'Are you going to join the army?'

'We've done our fighting. We've already got a few collective farms. You'd better take him,' he said, pointing at the dandy.

"I'm going anyway," said the dandy.

'What good are your collective farms if Franco takes them?' I said.

'He won't take them,' said the barman. The peasants listened to us but did not say anything.

'While you're busy making collective farms, who is going to fight?'

'We did our fighting,' he repeated.

'If everybody says that who's going to stop Franco?'

'He can't win.'

'You believe that,' I said, 'but you can't know.'

'You can't reason with an anarchist,' said the dandy. 'Have a drink, gentlemen.'

'Have a drink on the house, comrade,' said the barman. One of the peasants came over and insisted on paying for us.

'How young are you?' he said. 'This war is terrible. All the young men are going away. Who's going to tend the fields?'

'It'll soon be over,' I said. 'Then they'll be coming back.'

'*Si Dios quiere* – God willing.'

'There is no God,' said the dandy.

'Listen to him,' said the barman. 'He's been a socialist since August. He used to go to church.'

'Who's going to look after the fields?' the old peasant lamented.

'He is,' I said, pointing to the barman. He smiled.

'I don't think you like us,' I said.

'That's not true,' he said. 'We don't have the same ideas, that's all.'

'What does it matter, for God's sake? We can't win without these others.'

'But there's a difference.'

'So what?'

'One day everybody will be good, helpful and live in peace with his brother.'

'That's a dream.'

'*Podría ser* – it could be a reality.'

'You're talking like a preacher,' I said.

'We've done all we can. Now it's up to the people,' he said.

'You're short-sighted. What good is socialism in Albacete? Franco is advancing on Madrid.'

'He can't win,' said the barman. I gave up. We had another drink and said goodbye. The dandy lay asleep over a table. I shook hands with the barman.

'*Salud, camarada.* I may see you in Madrid,' I said.

'*¿Quién sabe?* – Who knows?' he replied.

Then I said goodbye to the peasant.

'You're so young,' he said. 'What will become of the fields? *Vayan con Dios, niños, vayan con Dios.*'

It was nine o'clock and we went to the restaurant where we sometimes ate. The waiter was a fat man in a white jacket. He was always pleased to see me because I spoke some Spanish and could translate for the others. We had a table near the window. The place was crowded. On the wall hung a poster which said, 'Vigilance! The ears of the enemy are everywhere.' Our French officer was there with other Frenchmen. He came over to shake hands and ask after Chris. He wanted to pay for our meal but we refused and had a drink instead. We ate soup, a plate of small fried fish, meat and potatoes, and grapes.

When we had finished there was a row going on near the kitchen. I saw the waiter arguing with three Frenchmen. The proprietor came from the kitchen and tried to reason with them. One of the three was a trouble-maker with a flushed face and ugly features. The waiter brought us something and I asked him what was the matter. He said the men refused to pay. I got up and spoke to them. The proprietor said it was all right – the *señores* had no money, they didn't need to pay. I insisted that they should. I spoke to the officer but he said that he could not do anything about it. I stopped the Frenchmen at the door and told them to pay up, but the tall one got cocky and said it was not my affair and I should keep out of it – the Government would pay. The two others with him were not quite as drunk and looked uncomfortable. One of them took some money out but the drunk pushed him outside. I wanted to pay for them but the proprietor would not accept my money. The next morning I reported the men. The Commander promised to see to it and the bill was paid.

The next afternoon a few hundred men arrived on the train from Barcelona. Ten English marched in front of the column carrying three rifles and a Lewis gun. We had to leave our quarters and went to the barracks of the *Guardia Civil*, a square, two-storeyed building with a huge courtyard in the middle from which doors led into the rooms. It had not been in use for some time and was filthy so we set about cleaning it up. Mattresses were brought in and two latrines were erected in the patio.

Among the new British arrivals were five trained soldiers. There was Fred,[14] twenty-nine years old from London with his inseparable friend Steve, a small Cockney with a big nose and blond hair.[15] There was Jock, a Scot, who had done a prison term for mutiny.[16] He later rose to the rank of colonel. There was Joe, an ex-fighter from the Red Army in China.[17] There was George, a pale, thin young man with a red beard which made him look like Christ,[18] and Pat, a young Irishman.[19] They were cheerful company and I soon made friends with Fred, Steve and Joe.

At first they high-hatted us a bit because we knew nothing about the army. They scorned the idea of Political Commissars, they were soldiers first, they said. We had a great many arguments about it. They thought that the Political Commissar would meddle with tactical and military matters and said it was impossible to have two commands. They did not understand that the job of a Political Commissar was as important as that of any other officer.

The three friends had a small room opposite ours. When we did not go out marching or doing exercises there was little else to do. We went over to their room and they instructed us in handling rifles. There was no ammunition. Some of us had handled a rifle before but most of the men did not know anything about them. Steve explained, with a voice like a real sergeant-major. They drew charts on the wall to show us how a bullet travelled and how a strong wind would affect its flight and other useful things. These instructions were very welcome because we knew by now how to march and turn *à gauche* and *à droite*. The three comrades paraded before us in military style. They slammed the rifle up and down and they did it as smartly as any Coldstream Guards. We looked on with awe and admiration.

The instructions usually ended in political discussions with different and passionate ideas on everything and from all sides. We talked about prisoners and what to do with them. We wondered whether the rebels took prisoners. What would they do with members of the Brigade? It would be worse, of course, for the German and Italian émigrés. We had heard about the massacres in Sevilla, Burgos, Badajoz and other cities where thousands of men and women were shot by Franco's men. Most of us were for taking prisoners because among the enemy were a great number who were fighting against their will. We did not believe that terror should be met with terror; some of us even talked about the brothers on the other side. I did not like it and said so. I had heard those phrases in Germany, about the Nazis. We were to win them over by discussion and reasoning, but they knocked the hell out of us.

There was a lot of talk about 'red terror'. Even here in Albacete there was a rumour that fascists were being shot by anarchists, yet I never saw or heard it, nor did anybody else I know. I do not think there was one among us able or willing to shoot a man in cold blood. There would come a day when two Moors, who were not killed but taken prisoner, would cost us a hundred men.

'So you're going to take prisoners?' said Fred.

Most of us said yes.

'Even if they shoot you when they take you?'

John said, 'If they're well treated they won't be afraid of being taken and others may come over.'

'If we kill them we wouldn't be better than fascists. I'm against it,' said Pat. 'I'm a Catholic. I came out because Franco is killing women and children.'

'Franco is a Catholic too,' I said.

'No, he's put himself outside the Church. He's a murderer.'

'Listen to them,' said Steve. 'Dead men are no good to us. Prisoners may give us a lot of useful information.'

'You'll be afraid to shoot anyone,' said Fred.

'You're talking rot,' John replied heatedly. 'We'll be as good soldiers as anybody else. We didn't come out to shoot prisoners. It's not the policy of the Spanish Government, neither is it ours.'

'How are you going to win the war?' asked Joe.

'We shall win it – but not by copying fascist methods.'

'What do you say?' Fred asked me. 'You're a German. You know better than we do how fascists fight.'

'I don't know,' I said. 'Friends of mine have been killed in prison yet I don't like the idea of shooting defenceless people. Maybe I'm wrong. In fact I believe I'm wrong. But there's still a faint belief in me that men are misguided and falsely led. There was a friend of mine, in Silesia, and we talked a lot about the same problem. We went to all the Nazi meetings to explain our policy. They replied by beating us up. Every time a number of men were badly injured. They didn't want to go any more except to fight back. The Party was against it. They wanted to show the people that we were not terrorists but Richard, my friend, said they were wrong. He used to say, "We can't win by being better than they are. We are not as brutal as the Nazis and I'm proud of it, but still, I always feel it's no good. If people hate us they believe everything they're told about us; it doesn't make any difference whether we're good or bad. I believe in meeting terror with terror." He believed in discipline, however, and did as he was told even though he was against it. He was killed in 1933.'

'Are you going to shoot prisoners or not?' asked Fred.

'If I'm told to, I shall do it,' I said, 'because I believe it's the only way to stop them doing it.'

'That's one,' said Fred.

'We haven't been in a war yet and we don't know how it is. We are theorising about things we don't know.'

'But it's important,' said Steve. 'We are only five trained soldiers among twenty-one. How is anyone to take responsibility if everyone has his private ideas? You must forget politics and be soldiers.'

'This is a new kind of war,' said John, but Fred and Steve protested.

'I'm not going to see a prisoner shot,' said Pat. 'I'd rather go back.'

'Let's break it off,' I said. 'This doesn't do any good.' I walked away with Steve. 'You frighten the boys with this sort of talk,' I said. 'They'll soon think you're a bad man.'

'I'm worried,' he said. 'I never shot a prisoner yet and I hope I don't have to. It's only the responsibility. They're too soft.'

'They'll make good soldiers all the same.'

'I hope so,' he said, 'but there's no training, no rifles, nothing. And all this talk about warfare worries me.'

'It's not your responsibility.'

'I know, but all the same we feel we have to look after you. That's why we started the bloody talk.'

On our way out of town we often passed the railway station. Over the last few days a great many refugees had arrived. They came from Toledo and villages south of Madrid. They were mostly women and children and old people. We could see them washing and cooking among the tracks. They slept in the freight cars. They never stayed more than a day or two before travelling on down to the coast, but others arrived in an endless stream.

For a few days we had an epidemic in our barracks. The water was bad. I was ill with fever and diarrhoea. The latrines were crowded from morning until night. A few serious cases were sent to hospital. I had a bad headache so I could not read and it was boring lying there in the room during the daytime when everybody was out. The doctor came and looked at me. It was a French one this time, a young man with a beard which framed his face so that he looked like a capuchin monkey. He gave me an injection. The young Irishman we did not like brought me a bottle of brandy. I did not want to take it but he insisted. I had not spoken to him for days and I do not know why he bothered about me. I drank a great part of the brandy and felt better the next morning.

I had breakfast in a coffee house near by, because it was too far to go to the bull ring. Hans went with me.[20] He told me we would leave Albacete in a few days for La Roda, a town near by, where we would be trained properly. I asked him why he did not join us as he always wanted to be with the English. He said he would stay with the doctor because he did not want to fight.

'I'd be a bad soldier,' he said. 'I wouldn't be any good at the front – I feel I shall be more useful looking after the wounded.' He looked at me. 'I hope you don't think I'm a coward.'

'No,' I said. 'There must be nurses. It's just as important. I couldn't do it myself.'

'I'm glad you think so.'

'You have been a good nursemaid to us all,' I said. 'Maybe you'll have to look after us again.'

'I hope not,' he said. 'I hope you all come back.'

In the afternoon we lined up in the barracks square. André Marty spoke and after him another Frenchman. After a general outline of the war, its course and what was expected of us, he said we were not yet in the Spanish Army. In a few days we would leave for another place, to be trained. We had volunteered but there might be a few men who had changed their minds and felt now that they would rather not go up to the front. If there were such men they should step forward now. Nobody left the ranks. 'They can come, later on, to the bureau,' the Frenchman said, 'where they will receive a ticket back to France.' On Sunday there would be a bullfight in our honour. He closed his speech with an appeal to our discipline and we sang *The Internationale* and were dismissed.

Our technicians left that afternoon for Barcelona. Someone came round and took our names, ages and addresses of relatives. Those who still had their passports were asked to give them up to be kept for them.

At two o'clock the next Sunday afternoon we marched to the bull ring. It was a grey, sultry day. Everybody was excited about seeing the fight. It was my first one for some years and I hoped it would be a good one. We had to wait in columns until the Spaniards had taken their seats. At a quarter to four we marched in. The band struck up and the people cheered and waved flags. I felt like a *matador* performing the *paseo*. We saluted the mayor of the town and our officers. A quarter of the seats were reserved for us and we scrambled up to the amphitheatre. I had lost my comrades and sat among Frenchmen.

Then came the *paseo* of the real bullfighters. They looked middle-aged and wore old and faded costumes which did not fit well. They gave the Red Front salute. There were no horses so I knew there would not be any big bulls. The first turn was the clowns. A man in a white dress, with a white painted face, came into the ring. He carried a white wooden box which he placed on the ground. He stepped up on to it, folded his arms and waited. There was a deep silence. A door opened and the bull rushed out. He was brown and of a good size. He stamped and ran around, jumping, until he saw the clown. The clown did not move; he did not seem to breathe and looked like a statue. The bull pawed the sand with his forefeet and charged. He looked as if he would run his horns through the man but a few inches from the box he stopped dead, shook his head angrily and turned away. The clown took his box and went out and everybody cheered and clapped.

When the doors opened again a small procession of white clad men appeared, two carrying a stretcher. The first clown followed it, wringing his hands in despair. The crowd laughed. The stretcher was put down near the barrier and the clown lay down on it. He folded his hands over his chest and they placed a white sheet over him. When the bull came out again he made straight for the stretcher. The crowd yelled and the clown looked up from under the sheet. He jumped up in the nick of time and leaped to safety while the angry bull tore and trampled the stretcher.

The real fight was ghastly. The bulls were young and small and the fighters no better than amateurs. They could not kill cleanly and it was a slaughter. It made a bad impression on our men and I wished we had not come. Even the Spaniards booed the performance. Next to me sat a strong, tough Frenchman. He was very upset and yelled, '*Moi, je sui boucher de métier. Qu'est-ce que c'est?* I'm a butcher by trade. What's all this? This is not the way to kill a bull. *C'est terrible.*' He waved a small knife round his head. His friends were holding him back. 'Let me go down – I know how to do it. I'll show them. They're tormenting the beast. I won't stand for it.'

So spoke a volunteer of the Brigade, a butcher by profession, one of those men who, in reactionary papers, were termed 'reds – brutal scum – underworld.' Steve's words came back to me. 'They're too soft. I'm worried.'

It was a very bad show. Most of our men left in the interval. I walked out with them. I met Jock, who was upset and angry. 'Those bastards,' he said. 'What kind of people are they? What kind of country is this?' I told him about the good fights I had seen and he calmed down, but he got terribly drunk that night. We were all very depressed. The close and grey day seemed to make it worse; it was as if before a thunder storm,.

The next day we had to leave. We packed our things and cleaned the rooms. We received a blanket each and underclothes, but no uniforms. The whole afternoon we sat and waited in the courtyard. We left at four. I said goodbye to Hans. Even the two mysterious Irishmen shook our hands and wished us good luck. We went to the station. We left at five and arrived two hours later at La Roda. From the station to our barracks crowds of people followed us, cheering. It was so dark we could not see them.

# Chapter 3 — La Roda

Our quarters were in a fifth century convent. It was built of yellow sandstone with high white walls round it. Over the main entrance was a coat of arms carved in stone. It had a small garden in front with grass and trees. The windows on the front reached to the ground with iron bars in front of them but the inside of the building was always cool and damp because of the enormously thick walls. On the ground floor was a refectory with a door leading to the courtyard at the back and a number of cellars with tiny windows above ground level. There was a staircase landing to the first floor where there was another big room and rows of cells.

In the early morning I went out to wash myself. The well stood in a courtyard before a little cottage in which two elderly women lived. Behind the cottage was a gate between two crumbling walls and a worn track led through it to a barren hill. On the hill stood a church pointing its square yellow tower into a cold and cloudless sky. It was an ugly church, big, plain and forbidding. I looked up and suddenly saw, high up in the belfry, what appeared to be two people hanging by their necks, their long shirts fluttering in the morning breeze. The sight of the gruesome decoration filled me with horror and fear and for some time I stood there motionless until other men noticed it too, standing round in groups looking up with incredulous eyes and speaking in whispers.

I went through the gate and climbed the track towards the church but when I came near enough I saw that the figures were not human beings but the statues of Jesus and Mary which someone had taken from the church and hanged out of the tower. Many times I had seen these bloodstained and agonising symbols of Christianity in stone, in paint, even in wax, placed behind iron bars to make them look more life-like and real but they never looked more remote, sinister and threatening than on this October morning against a radiant blue sky.

I sat down on the church steps. I saw Pat coming up the steep path from the gate. He sat down next to me. He was looking up at the tower.

'They shouldn't have done that.'

'Why not?' I asked.

'You won't understand. You're not a Catholic.'

'I thought you'd finished with it.'

He looked very unhappy. 'I don't know. You can't get rid of all you learned and believed at once.' He looked up again. 'It frightens me,' he said. 'I wish they hadn't done it.'

'It's very stupid,' I said. 'That's all I feel about it. It doesn't matter; they're only figures.'

'They're symbols.'

'Symbols of what? One doesn't need figures, crosses and other such things to symbolise the suffering in this country.'

'But they're beautiful.'

'Sure they're beautiful. But I think there is no artist born yet who has portrayed the injustice, cruelty and suffering under which these people live. No, there is no need for such waxworks to fire the imagination. Look around; look at the people.'

'You know this country better than I do.'

'You know it just as well. Spain, Ireland, what's the difference?'

Steve came up the path and hailed us. He wore no shirt and was drying his hair with a towel.

'What's all the gloom about?'

'Pat's conscience is bothering him,' I said.

'He picked a fine time.' Steve was trying to open the door behind us.

'It's locked,' said Pat. 'I tried to get in.'

'I bet he wanted to say his morning prayers,' said Steve.

'No,' said Pat. 'I heard there were dead people inside. Fascists who've been shot and left in the church.'

'Go on,' said Steve.

'Who told you?' I asked.

'Everybody says so. They've locked the church so that nobody can see it. The key's with the mayor.'

'There's nothing a bloody Irishman doesn't believe,' said Steve.

'Let him alone,' I said. 'I'm going to get that key from the mayor and show him it isn't true.'

'I didn't believe it,' said Pat, 'but everybody's talking about it.'

'They're talking a lot of rot,' I said. 'I wonder who invents all these stories.'

'We heard it in the village.'

'Yes, and do you believe everything a fascist tells you? Remember the stories in Albacete, about people being shot at night, streets full of corpses? Have you ever seen them?'

'No,' he said.

'Then why the hell do you believe it?'

'He's a Catholic,' said Steve. 'They believe in things they don't see.' He put his towel around his shoulders. 'Well, I'm going back, I'm getting cold.'

'Perhaps I'm very foolish,' said Pat, after Steve had left. 'Those figures have upset me. See how they move in the wind? I thought they were real.' After a silence he said, 'Do you think that Christ ever lived?'

'I don't know,' I said. 'If he did he was killed for what he believed in. Those are only waxworks. There's nothing to be upset about. Christ wasn't hanged at La Roda.'

'I wish I was like you. You never had any religion and it doesn't bother you. I'm always worrying and I want to do the right thing.'

'You can still go back,' I said. He took out a number of newspaper cuttings and gave them to me. They were accounts, from different papers, of the massacres in Badajoz, Sevilla, Burgos.

'This is true, isn't it?'

'Yes.'

'And they're bombing women and children?'

'Yes,' I said. 'When we go up to Madrid you'll see for yourself.'

He put back the cuttings. 'I can't go back,' he said. 'You must think I'm a crazy Irishman who likes fighting but I never did. But now I don't mind.'

'You'll have to shoot people.'

'I don't mind,' he said. 'Franco mustn't win, that's all I know. I'm sure I'm doing the right thing.'

We went back to the courtyard. The men were washing or digging latrines. I did not wait for the coffee but went out into the street behind the convent. There was a *churro* baker living in a small shop. One could get half a dozen for twenty-five cents with a cup of coffee thrown in. Fred and Steve were already there, sitting on a bench which ran round the wall. The *churros* were crisp and brown and dripping with oil. They were better than the dry, hard piece of bread we used to get for breakfast. Only our coffee was better.

'How's the Irish Free State?' asked Steve. Fred asked me what was the matter with Pat.

'He's all right,' I said. 'He didn't like the decoration on the church tower.'

'I don't like it myself,' said Fred. 'It gives me the creeps.'

'They should have hanged a fat priest,' said Steve. 'Nothing gives me the creeps like a fat priest.'

Our training began in earnest. Every day, after breakfast and after lunch, we marched through the village to the nearby fields to receive instruction. We still had no rifles or uniforms. We started by doing gymnastics and after that learned how to advance and obey commands. A fat Frenchman was in charge of our section. He looked like Oliver Hardy but shorter and even fatter, a real humpty-dumpty, and was called *Bou-Boule* by the French. He was quick and astonishingly agile, however, so that we could hardly follow him. He had been in the Great War and knew his stuff. I had great confidence in him and was sorry that we lost him later on, before Madrid, where he became a cook, a job for which he was well suited.

We learned to advance in columns of five and watched *Bou-Boule* giving us signs with his hand and we marched on, halted or lay down as he directed. We did not know our objective and just followed him, running, crouching and crawling over fields and ditches. We rested a while, picking flowers and chewing grass while 'enemy' aeroplanes were overhead. After the all clear signal we stormed over a stubble field towards the big wall, *Bou-Boule* always in front of us. He leapt at the wall like a rubber ball, stuck there in some magical way before disappearing on the other side, and we all went after him.

In front of us were the first houses of the village. The attack was over. We lined up in a circle to listen to the criticism given by Captain Blanche but few understood and those who did, did not translate. Apparently we had done well and driven the army out of the village. Not very difficult, we thought, and looked around, sweating and thirsty, for something to drink. Peasants from the houses near by, who had watched our strange behaviour with open amusement, brought us water in big stone jugs. We tried to drink in the Spanish way, by tilting the jug a few inches above the mouth and letting a thin stream trickle straight into our throats. The peasants laughed and shrieked when the water went into our eyes and noses and over our shirts. While we coughed and spat they showed us how to do it.

We usually sang when we marched back to the barracks, that is to say the French sang and whenever the English tried too it sounded frightfully dreary and the French had to make two steps for our one. Somebody tried *Tipperary* but was hushed down and then they sang *Left, Left* which had no melody at all and another song, with the old German Christmas tune of *Tannenbaum*, which always made me feel as if I were marching to my own funeral, the French sang the *Marseillaise* and, again, we had to make short, quick steps, or *The Internationale* which went well for everybody. Of all the war songs the one I liked best, besides *Bandiera Rossa*, was the juicy French song in the style of *Mademoiselle from Armentières* about 'O, ma belle Cathérine.'

Before meals there was usually time to walk about in the town. There was still enough food and drink; the market was full of fruit and vegetables. I remember when we came home, just before lunch, we all used to rush to a bakery near the market place where horribly sweet cakes could be bought for a few pence. In the evenings and afternoons we had coffee or drinks at a nearby *fonda* where one could get cheap wine, *coñac Domecq* and bottled beer. With Fred and Steve I discovered, by chance, a private house where they sold good sherry and the family offered to make us supper for three pesetas each if we ordered in advance. We promised to come back the next night. Some of us still had a little English money which we exchanged at a bad rate for pesetas. Those who had none were invited to take part in the feast too.

The next afternoon we were out as usual but with three rifles this time. They were heavy Swiss rifles with a cartridge clip holding ten rounds instead of five. Three of us had to come forward at a time and *Bou-Boule* explained how to hold a rifle while standing, kneeling or lying down. Before he was through with us a sergeant from the next section borrowed the rifles. Soon after that we heard a shot. The sergeant had been showing someone how to insert the cartridge and his pupil had pressed the trigger accidentally and the bullet had gone off, nearly hitting some children playing near by. We left the field and marched further away from the village. I carried one of the rifles on my back. It weighed a ton and I hoped we would not really have to use them.

We were split up into small sections to learn observation. Fred, Steve, Joe and myself had a nice place behind a haystack on a hill and waited there for further orders. It was warm and the hay smelled sweet and bees were humming around in the faint breeze. The company runner came up, a tiny but tough looking Frenchman who never seemed to get tired, and explained to Fred what we were supposed to do. Somewhere in front of our hill the enemy would try to advance and if we could see any movement we were to dispatch a runner with a written message down to headquarters about a mile behind us. Nothing happened for a long time. We smoked, chatted and joked and Steve gave a fine imitation of Bing Crosby with a lot of '*bou-bou-bou*'. After a while we saw some men creeping about, but not where we expected them. However, we decided it would be best to report them. Fred wrote a note and I said I would go. He said I was a sucker and I took the message.

I was instructed to keep my head down and move along as if I were under fire. I crept along terraced vineyards down to the road. When I looked back I saw my comrades watching me lazily and I felt very silly. I crossed the road and darted along a ditch which ran parallel with the road towards headquarters. I was sweating and panting and the blasted rifle bumped up and down on my back.

Nothing more happened except that we saw more groups of men walking rather aimlessly about the fields. As they walked upright without trying to conceal themselves we took no notice of the 'enemy'. Or were they ours, who knows?

There was a beautiful sunset with lots of orange and dark purple clouds. An aeroplane flew overhead. The great fields were bare after the harvest. It was not attractive country, with its white plains and hills stretching for miles without trees, but the last glorious days of autumn gave it a sad and melancholy beauty. Very soon the winter would cover everything with rain and snow, transforming it into a desert of mud and clay. The sun lingered about the walls of La Roda and gilded the towers of the convent while the big church and the hill upon which it stood were already in the shadow of the clouds, looking more sinister and threatening than ever.

The short criticism revealed that we had made some mistakes in our manoeuvre but what it was exactly we did not know. We marched back along the road towards the town and the road was white against the brown fields and very dusty. Peasants were coming back from harvesting the saffron. The roads were covered with its purple flowers and bright orange pollen. Together with the white sand it was a beautiful carpet on which we walked, crushing the flowers with our heavy boots, a bright, orange-red, blood-like stream was left behind over which the clouds of dust slowly rolled along before settling down again.

We walked as we liked, in groups of twenty, and only when we came to the town did we straighten up and step briskly to the shouts of command: '*Compagnie, Section, Marches, un deux, un deux, un deux*, left, left. Halt!' We stood before the convent. '*À gauche.*' We turned sharply to the left; some, as usual, turned to the right, facing nothing. '*Saluts.* Dismissed.'

We had a quick wash and brush-up and rejoiced that there would be no soup for us that day. It was still too early for our dinner but we walked to the house to make sure that our meal was being prepared. I went in to see the patron who was preparing stacks of onions, peppers, aubergines and meat. 'Don't forget,' I said. He was holding the pots up for me to see.

'*¿Bueno?*'

'*Magnífico,*' I said. 'We'll be back at eight on the dot.'

I went back and described what I had seen to the hungry, waiting gun section of *Compagnie 2 Française*. They said it sounded swell. We went into a nearby café filled with flies, and Spaniards playing dominoes and billiards. We had lots of *vino blanco*, which was dry and good, and our appetites grew with every bottle.

At eight sharp the seven of us appeared on the scene of the feast. The meal was not yet ready but we could smell it and it smelled good. The cook, a little Spaniard, and his wife who worked in the kitchen, seemed a little afraid when we entered. I cannot blame them because nearly all of us were six foot tall and, before we sat down on the wooden benches round the large table we towered over them like giants.

My Spanish came in handy. I talked to the cook and said the food smelled delicious and though I had had many a good meal in Spain I was sure that this was going to be the best. I put him at ease and he brought us a bottle of his good sherry and a big plate of olives. The stew was ready and it was the finest I have ever tasted, especially after the weeks of bean soup which we had for lunch and dinner.

We made short work of the meal and there was no grumbling, which is very rare indeed among the English. There was nobody who said, 'Ah, what about a nice cup of tea,' or 'Remember the steak and kidney pies, boys?' They all said it was the finest meal they ever ate. Steve said, 'What about some lunch tomorrow,' and we all laughed. They asked me to try to fix a lunch for the next day, which I did.

We had some coffee in a smart-looking café run by anarchists and a few more drinks and got pretty tight, but at ten o'clock we were back at the barracks. I was not sleepy so I sat in the garden in front of the convent. I had bought a new goatskin bottle filled with red wine, though I could not remember where I had got it from, and Fred joined me to finish it. From where we sat we could see the lights from the windows and the coat of arms over the doorway.

'I talked to Blanche today,' Fred said.

'Yes?'

'I told him we had four trained machine gunners and he said we should form a company in the Battalion. I should like you to join my section.'

'Thanks,' I said. 'That will be fine.'

'We had better stick together. I spoke to Steve when you went away with the message this afternoon. "He's taking this war too seriously," I told Steve. "We've got to look after him." '

'You're drunk,' I said.

'Sure I'm drunk, otherwise I wouldn't tell you this. We like you. When I saw you running down the hill this afternoon, I felt that it wasn't part of the training but that the war was on. I said to Steve, "He won't live long. He'll always push himself to the front to do the dirty work; we have to look after him." '

'I didn't do so badly up to now,' I said.

'But you haven't been a soldier. Steve and I have been in the army for years; we'll help you along.'

'What about you? You haven't been in any war yet.'

'I can take care of myself. I'll be alive when this war is over, so will Steve, and so will you if you listen to me. You don't want to get killed, do you?'

'I haven't thought about it,' I said. 'We don't know what this war's like.'

'I know,' he agreed.

'No, you don't,' I replied. 'I heard a lot of rubbish about guerrilla warfare. Maybe it was like that on the Aragon front but I have seen pictures of Irun and it looked like a very modern war to me.'

'Whatever it's like you won't do the dirty work, I'll see to that.'

'All right.'

He was bending his arm and said, 'I'm strong, see?'

I couldn't help laughing. 'This war isn't being fought with fists,' I said.

'I'm going back when this war is over, with Steve and you. We're going to celebrate in the Yorkshire Grey on Camden Street.'

'I know the pub, I've been there often.'

'Funny, I've never seen you,' he said. 'Anyway, we'll all meet there after this war is over.'

'As heroes?'

'No, but alive.'

'I'd rather stay,' I said. 'I like this country. You don't know it yet. This isn't Spain. You haven't seen anything yet. You may like to stay here too.'

'I may come back but I shall have to go to England for a while.'

'I'm going to stay,' I said.

'You'd better see that you stay alive; that's more important. Nothing is worth dying for.'

'Why did you come out?' I asked him.

'All right, don't listen to me.'

'You're drunk,' I said. 'Before I met you somebody said you were no good, but I don't believe it. You're not even tough. And if you tell me you've come out just to look after yourself I know it isn't true. We don't know yet what the war will be like really, or who's going to die and who's going to live.'

'You're a sucker.'

'All right, I'm a sucker, but you remind me of the tough guys in the movies who get soft in the end and turn out to be the good fellows. I don't like the last part of it, and you don't like it either, but that's what we're going to be. It's funny how everybody likes to play tough.'

'I'm not going to be a sucker.'

'All right,' I said. 'But there's something funny I have to tell you. We've decided to give you the command of the English section. There were one or two who protested, saying that you weren't reliable enough, but the others are all for you. Now you aren't responsible for just yourself or for me but for twenty men, perhaps even more later on. You're going to lead us and you'll have to take care of us all, and you'll get the stripes whether you like it or not.'

There was a long silence and then he said, 'Is that true?'

I said, 'Of course, you can refuse.' But I could see that he was pleased. It was getting chilly and, as we had finished the wine, we went inside.

'I would like to join you,' I said, 'if you still want me.'

'I'll help you to carry your things over to our place,' he said a little later. 'Forget what I said. I was drunk. Forget everything, will you?'

Some things are difficult to forget. Sometimes, when I go to the Yorkshire Grey, I cannot help feeling that they have let me down, or perhaps I have let them down too. But if I waited a thousand years they would not come back and there is nobody I care to talk to and the joke is really on Fred, who took such good care of all of us and could not take care of himself. He turned out to be the good fellow one sees in the films, but there were no happy endings. A bullet and a piece of wire saw to that.

The next morning after breakfast, which was earlier than usual, we were told to take our blankets and kits. Those who had suitcases were lucky as usual as they did not have to carry them. We did not know where we were going or whether we would return. A hundred different stories circulated. We would go straight to the front; it was just part of the training; and so on, but nobody knew anything. It was still cool from the night air with that peculiar smell of earth and vegetation. The sun had risen, but it was obscured by a thick mist. I filled my wine bottle at a well.

We went through side roads out of the town. The church was still visible for a long time. Its tower looked like a periscope, watchful and, in spite of the bright morning, as gloomy as ever. We saw no villages or farms on our way. After two and a half hours we rested in a pine wood. It was now very hot and my water bottle was soon empty. We only stayed a short while and then marched back. Burke passed out on the way and he was taken back by a peasant in a cart.[21]

After lunch Captain Blanche made a speech in the dining room. I could not understand all he said. Nobody was allowed to leave our quarters. He wanted twenty volunteers, but only those who knew how to handle a rifle. There were reports of clashes with anarchists. They were on their way to La Roda. I volunteered with six other English, including Steve, Fred and John; the rest were Frenchmen. Blanche took us to a farm which was on the long, wide road leading to the station. The farm lay behind a high, grey wall; the iron gate was closed and we entered through a small side door. The inside was like a fortress with several walled courtyards with stables round them and a few houses. We received rifles and cartridges. When we loaded them we could see that some men had never handled them before and we had to ask them to point them the other way and to take their fingers off the triggers.

Sentries were posted on the road and behind the gate and we sat around waiting. We did not believe the stories about the anarchists. John said it was nonsense. Why should they try to fight us? Fred thought that fascists might be behind the story, trying to create trouble. Nothing happened and it grew dark. Our dinner was brought from the barracks. At nine o'clock, Alfredo, a young French Canadian who was in charge of our company, sent us back to the barracks.[22] We never found out what was behind all this. Perhaps it was just a test to see what we would do in an emergency.

On a hill just above the church we received our first lesson on the machine gun. We had had a lively discussion the night before because Fred and Steve wanted to be in the infantry. They thought we would not get enough training. We did not have any rifles; there was no possibility of enough training and practice. Others of us had set our hearts on being machine gunners and finally persuaded them to stay with us.

Alfredo was popular and liked by everyone. With him was a sergeant, Marcel, a tough young Frenchman with flaming red hair and face. He carried the heavy St. Étienne all the way up the hill. A blanket was spread out and the gun mounted on it. During the whole morning we learned the names of all the different parts. They were translated and we learned them in English. We took turns in taking the gun apart and reassembling it. After a few hours we went further away to try it out. A few peasants working in the fields nearby were told to take shelter. Marcel fired the gun but after the first three or four rounds it jammed. We had brought our own Lewis gun and Joe tried it out. It went well and we hoped we would get more Lewis guns. They were also much easier to carry.

At midnight there was a blackout in the town. Fascist aeroplanes had been sighted. We had another dinner but in a different place this time; it was a real restaurant on the first floor of a house. The windows were tightly closed and we ate by candle light. Nobody was in the streets when we went back. It was dark and threatening. Occasionally dogs barked at us and donkeys brayed in fright. It reminded me of the villages I had tramped through on those nights in the past; the same darkness, the same feeling of intrusion, fear and hostility.

Every day a great number of trucks passed through La Roda on the way to Madrid. They were loaded with munitions. The trucks were new and had come from Russia. Sometimes they stopped for petrol and we talked to the drivers. Yes, they were carrying ammunition. We asked them for news. Franco was advancing rapidly. The war was drawing nearer.

On a wet and grey Sunday morning we were told that our rifles had arrived. They were distributed in a big barn just outside the town. The floor was littered with long coffin-like cases. We lined up in single file and each received a rifle and a bayonet. The rifles were covered in grease. They were of American make, Remington 1916. Someone said they came from Ireland; perhaps he was right. We fixed the bayonets on the rifles and marched back, looking like soldiers for the first time. We spent the day cleaning them. We had no old rags so we used old shirts and under-clothes. Fred managed to get a few leather slings and he gave me one. Most men used string instead.

In the afternoon of the next day we went out for our one and only shooting practice in an old, disused stone quarry. White paper discs were used as targets; the distance was two hundred yards. Each man got five rounds. Four men at a time fired and Marcel called out the score. It was nearly dark when my turn came; flames shot out of the rifle. When everybody had shot their rounds, we lined up on a sunken road below a field from where a French communist deputy, who had just come from Paris, spoke to us.

'Comrades, I'm glad to have an opportunity to speak to you before you go to the front. Most of you have handled a rifle for the first time today. Ammunition is scarce. Five rounds is all we can give you. You are untrained. You are going out to face a ruthless, well-armed and well-trained enemy. You are fighting for a great cause. The eyes of all the freedom-loving people in the world are upon you. It rests with you whether democracy will survive or be destroyed for ever, not only in Spain but in many other countries. I am sure you know this and you will fight well.'

We cheered and waved our rifles. He was deeply moved and continued: 'Many of you may not come back. You have come from all over Europe to lay down your lives for democracy. What you lack in weapons you will make up for in courage. I am sure you will do your best. *Salud* and *bonne chance!*'

We sang the *Marseillaise*. The sky had changed to a light green with red and yellow edges sinking into the soft, dark blue of the night. There was no sound beyond the footsteps in the sand and the wind rustling over the fields.

The next day we were issued with uniforms consisting of dark blue skiing pants and jackets which looked like those worn by the *serenos* or night watchmen. They were of thick blue cloth with black braid. They were made for smaller people and did not fit at all. Most of us did not take them and we were glad that we had brought boots as these were *petit* size also. Only the under-clothing was good. Each man received a beret. I still had the Spanish militia cap which I got when I was on police duty. Our company looked a fantastic sight. The berets and the short jackets made us look like a bunch of artists from Montmartre. In that outfit we paraded before Marty[23] and other officers. Only the Germans had proper, grey uniforms.

The next afternoon we packed our things and left for the station. The train was late and we had to wait for hours. We received 150 rounds of ammunition each and linen bandoliers which we slung crosswise over our coats. Stretchers and first aid kits were unloaded.

# Chapter 4 — Casa de Campo

It took only four hours to Aranjuez. We were all very tired after the long wait in La Roda. The train carried no light and we slept most of the time. I was wondering what Aranjuez would be like. The name reminded me of Andalusia with its old, walled towns, gardens, palm trees and sunshine. It could not be like that though, because I knew it was near Madrid and, therefore, must be high up. I hoped it would be a nice place as it was our last stop before going on to Madrid.

When we arrived in Aranjuez the station was in darkness. We groped for our rifles and rucksacks and lined up along the train. The station consisted only of a platform with a roof such as one sees in any small country place. All the tracks were jammed with freight and passenger trains. It was cold and damp and we wrapped ourselves in our blankets. When we stumbled over the tracks, past the station, a hurricane lamp, hanging from the ceiling, cast a little light over the rifles in front of me and, for a moment, its light fell upon a bright red flag.

Outside the station the yard was full of trucks. Somebody pointed out the Soviet stars on the bonnets. The motors were roaring and sputtering as, one by one, they filled with soldiers and disappeared along the road. Our truck was the last as its engine was cold and we soon lost the others on the way. The Spanish driver and our French sergeant argued most of the way about *la route* while they looked out for somebody to ask, but the roads were deserted. '*La carretera a Madrid*,' the driver said, 'I know it well, but this is not the main road. I have orders to take this road.' It was very cold and everybody was frozen stiff. It was so crowded we all had to lie on top of each other. My legs were stuck under somebody's behind and I felt them going numb and stiff but I could not shift without upsetting everybody.

Towards morning it rained for a while but when the sun rose it stopped. We halted at a crossroads and piled out into the road, stamping up and down and slapping our arms around us to get warm again. The driver and the Frenchman had started the argument again. They had lost their way completely. We should have arrived at Madrid by eight o'clock and it was already seven and we were nowhere near it. An hour later we came to a small town. A few Spanish soldiers, sitting in the market-place, told us we had nearly landed in Franco's army when we told them how we had come. Everybody thought this was very funny but that was mainly because they had cheered up when they discovered a café which had just opened. We had plenty of hot coffee and *churros* and glasses of *anís* from a bottle Fred had bought somewhere. Our driver came to hurry us up. We asked him if he knew the way now and also how much money he got for handing us over to Franco, which made him very angry. We laughed and joked with him all the way. Franco was sixty miles from Madrid; everybody knew that. Those Spaniards certainly made us laugh. After we left the town, the road went over hills into the mountains. The landscape hardly changed until we reached a plateau from where we had our first glimpse of Madrid.

A straight road, many miles long, led through the suburbs with small houses on both sides, a number of petrol stations and big signs advertising the Palace, Florida and Metropole hotels. We passed a few battered-looking aeroplanes, on our right, standing in front of tin sheds. There were very few people about. We thought it strange that they did not take any notice of us but they were too busy looking up into the sky where half a dozen silvery planes were circling about. 'They must be ours,' we all said with one voice, but when we came towards the centre of the town we met a number of motorbikes, with their sirens going full blast, racing through the streets. We still thought they were our planes because the people did not make any attempt to seek shelter, until we heard the explosions of falling bombs about half a mile off.

We did not go through the centre of the town but skirted round it until we stopped in a broad avenue flanked by old trees and gardens. We got down and sat in the garden while our driver went away to enquire about our barracks. He did not come back for hours. It was already past midday and we were getting very hungry. Fred and Steve went off to buy some sandwiches. Two *carabineros* in their green uniforms with rifles slung over their shoulders came up and looked at our truck. They then came over to us and started asking a lot of questions. I was pointed out to them as someone who understood Spanish. I did not like them and I could see plainly that they did not like us. They asked me how many we were, what nationality, and whether we expected more. I pretended not to understand. Members of the Fifth Column was written all over them. They saw I regarded them with suspicion and they tried, unsuccessfully, to appear a bit more friendly. They looked at my rifle.

'It's Russian,' they said.

'No,' I said, 'it's American,' but they did not believe me. I was glad when they went off, though not without trying to get more information from the others, and they might have known everything but for the fact that no one understood them.

In the early afternoon our driver came back. We had resigned ourselves to spending the rest of our lives in the truck. After a while we halted outside a barracks, some way out of town, and got out again. At last, this must be our place, but it was not. We were given a meal. Young soldiers, girls from the Communist Youth, brought us plates of soup and bread and we ate at a long table sitting on benches. We felt better after having eaten. We also had plenty of wine. When we had finished someone took a photograph of us in the courtyard. They asked us to sing so we sang *The Internationale*. It was not a good performance as most of us did not know the words. I sang in German and it turned out to be longer than the English and I lagged behind. However, the Spaniards seemed pleased and after many handshakes and salutes we departed on our unending journey.

We reached a market square and saw a number of German and French soldiers walking about and knew we had arrived. The others had been there since nine o'clock in the morning. Captain Blanche was glad to see us. Our quarters were in the loft of a barn belonging to a farm. It was a big building with a gallery running round the inside and a lot of store rooms. A heap of potatoes had been left behind which we shovelled into sacks. A gun was mounted in the middle of the room. It was soon dark. One of us went out to buy candles and by their light we learned to handle the gun. Blanche came in with a big, stout man in a great-coat and a brass hat. It was General Kleber. We had never heard of him, nor did we know his nationality, but he inspired confidence.[24]

'Hello, boys,' he said. 'How are you doing?' We replied that we were doing fine. Steve whispered to me that he was probably a German. He pushed me forward and told me to ask for Lewis guns. I spoke German but Kleber answered in English, probably thinking it was not my language.

'We have five trained Lewis gunners among us, Comrade,' I said. 'We brought one gun with us but we have no ammunition.'

'I am glad to hear we have some trained soldiers. How many are you?'

'Twenty-one,' I said.

'How many guns do you want?'

Steve said that we needed three.

'You don't like the French gun, do you?' said Kleber.

'It's all right but we don't understand it well.'

We did not like to say it was no good, in case he was French.

'I'll get you some tomorrow; I think we have five.'

We were glad to hear that.

'What about ammunition?' I asked.

'There's plenty. Well, I'll see you tomorrow. I hope you're comfortable.'

We said that we were.

'Good night, General,' said Steve.

Kleber was repressing a smile. 'Good night, Comrade,' he said.

We left the French to learn their gun and lay down.

Next morning we marched into the fields. It was very bare and flat country. It was sunny at first but soon clouded over. We marched until we came to a deep ravine which had cut across three fields. The Edgar André battalion was already there trying out their Maxim. We had to wait until they had finished. Marcel, a young Frenchman with flaming red hair, was in charge of us. He was very strong and could carry the heavy guns for miles. He was trying out the French gun. The ammunition was in short metal belts, twenty-five rounds in each. It did not work well. There were lots of stoppages and the gun had to be taken apart several times. Marcel, his face as red as his hair, was swearing and cursing. We did not pay much attention. We would be getting Lewis guns anyway.

We lay on our backs looking into the sky, chewing grass, making sarcastic comments about French technique.

'I wonder how you won the last war with that contraption,' said Fred. 'It's out of date.'

'It must have been used in the French Revolution,' someone said.

Marcel took it with good humour. 'We won the war, didn't we?'

'No, we did,' said Fred.

'You with your bloody *Louis*, it won't kill a bug.'

'But they make a noise,' said Fred, 'they make a noise, sergeant. What's the matter with you? It'll take you all day to fire twenty-five rounds.'

Marcel was working hard. 'I'll show you,' he said, but still the gun would not work.

'Try to put in one bullet at a time,' said Fred.

'*Merde!*'

'Be gentle with the old machine, otherwise it will fall apart.'

Marcel gave up. We marched back without having fired. Just before we reached the village a number of aeroplanes appeared.

'*Couchez-vous, couchez-vous.*' We fell on our faces thinking it was part of the training. The planes flew on to Madrid. In the afternoon we marched for a few hours in full kit. It was grey and cold. From the direction of Madrid great explosions could be heard. We wondered what it was. We had no dinner but received a tin of something and a piece of bread and went back to the field. Peasants with shovels were coming home. I hailed one: '*Hola, paisano,*' and asked him about his work.

He said he had been digging trenches, pointing into the distance. '*Al frente.*'

I told Fred who said, 'Ask him where it is.'

'*¿Está muy lejos?*'

'*Sí, sí,*' the peasant replied. '*Tres, cuatro kilómetros.*'

'He says it's only two miles, but I know Spaniards can never judge distances.'

We took up positions underneath a hill. Alfredo came and told us we had to stay there all night. It was just part of the training.

'The enemy is a long way off. You're the third line. You must challenge everybody. The word is *Commune de Paris*. You call "*Alto*" and if you get the right answer, say "*Passez*". *Compris? Bon. Bonne nuit.*'

We were organising the watches. I drew from twelve to two. The war was on at last. I was so excited I could not sleep. I talked to Fred and Steve for a while. At twelve o'clock I took over. I walked up and down with my blanket and rifle. It was not very cold. I liked being a soldier. I saw the comrades sleeping under their blankets and felt responsible for them. Was there not something moving? No, nothing. I remembered Fred's words. 'At night every tree looks like an enemy. Don't pay any attention to it. Close your eyes for a second then look again.'

It began to rain. I saw a man coming over the hill. '*¡Alto!*' I yelled. My voice sounded very loud. '*Le signe – le parole.*'

'Shit,' the dark figure said, 'I can't see a damn thing. What's this?'

'Second company, French,' I said. I was very disappointed. I kept on hailing people. They all answered differently, mostly swearing and cursing or begging me not to shoot. Only one answered correctly, '*Commune de Paris.*'

'*Passez*,' I said. It was Fred, doing his round.

'Haven't you been to sleep yet?' I said.

'No, I'm going to lie down.'

We compared our watches. It was one o'clock.

'Is this part of the training?'

'I don't know,' he said. 'Things don't look so good. We may have to go to Madrid tomorrow.'

'What are those explosions?'

'Only bombs,' he said. 'They're a long way off still.' It was beginning to rain. 'You'd better put your blanket over you,' he said. 'I'm going to try to sleep. Wake me if anything happens.'

Steve was the next man. I lent him my watch. We walked up and down for a while and talked. Dawn came very slowly, but the sun was not visible. It was suddenly a grey and wintry November day with a biting wind. The different battalions went back to the village. Alfredo told us that our Lewis guns had arrived. They were still in the trucks but he would give them to us later on.

In the afternoon we were called out to parade in full kit. Nothing was to be left behind. We marched past Kleber and Blanche with bayonets fixed on our rifles. After the parade we stood around under the leafless, dripping trees, wondering where to go next. We were told to go back to our quarters. In the meantime our room had been used as a lavatory by some Frenchmen who seemed unable to help themselves from dirtying every place they happened to be in. Before we could find whoever it was to teach them a lesson we had to leave.

We went to the station where a train was waiting for us. Smoking was not allowed. Blinds were drawn although there were no lights. Rifles were loaded for the first time. The train was creeping slowly along through the darkness. I slept and when I woke up the train was not moving. It was quiet and one could hear the steam escaping from the engine.

At half past four we reached the central station, Madrid. It was still raining outside and we waited in the station hall. There was an open square outside with a railway embankment behind it. Suddenly a huge shadow rolled over it, blacker than the dark sky. I saw the muzzle of a huge gun. A searchlight flashed on and groped among the low clouds and was then extinguished. The armoured train disappeared, reappeared, and was gone quickly and silently.

We went into the square. The rifles were stacked together in pyramids. It was beginning to get light. We were cold and hungry but no breakfast came. We could walk around as we liked. There were hotels and cafés near by but they were still shut. A Scottish ambulance stood near a hotel. We had a few Scots among us and they went running up to the ambulance people but received a sour, unfriendly welcome. They showed clearly that they did not like us. They hardly answered a question. They had come out to give medical aid but they did not seem to sympathise with the People's Army.

We found a *churro* baker in the street. In a short time he was sold out. There was no coffee to be had. A few well-clothed young men stood near by regarding us with hostility.

At half past nine the four battalions of the XI Brigade began their march through Madrid. The shops were open, the streets crowded. We had flags and carried the guns and ammunition on our shoulders for everyone to see. Throngs of people, on both sides of the street, shouted *vivas* and walked with us. The sun came through the clouds and it was hot carrying the heavy equipment. We reached the outskirts, passing a big prison on our left which was said to be full of fascists. We were told they were later evacuated to Valencia for safety.

After we left the last houses behind we came to a great block of new, red brick buildings. We rested there. In the big courtyards between the buildings young Spanish students were learning to march to the signal of trumpets. They came over to us and examined our guns and rifles. They were a cheerful, happy lot. One told me that this was the University City, not yet completed. The buildings next to us were the Clínico and the Casa de Medicina. Further along the road there was a building standing alone before a range of hills which was the Casa de Filosofía y Letras.

After our rest we reached that building. A broad road ran past it and turned at a right angle along the front where it stopped at a slope. The roads were half-finished. There were big fields which would probably be sports grounds and gardens. One half of the building was made into a hospital. A flag with a red cross hung from the roof. Some wounded men and nurses were sitting in the windows and waved greetings to us.

We went into the building by the big portal in front with steps leading up to it. It received light from a glass window more than forty feet high. Everything looked new and smelled of paint. From the main hall corridors ran along both sides of the wings with staircases leading to the upper floors. We took a room on the second floor, next to a bathroom. The floors were covered with dark green linoleum. We had a wash in the bathroom. I was washing my shirt and socks and when I went down I had missed lunch.

A few young trees had been planted on the opposite side of the road. They stood among loose stones, cement blocks and sand heaps. A truck unloaded our five Lewis guns and a great deal of ammunition. Our experts were now busy cleaning them and putting them together. There were parts missing from most of them. Out of the five we completed two and, with the one we had already, that made three in working order. We spent most of the afternoon cleaning drums and bullets. It was a gloriously sunny day.

I was sitting on a sand heap with Muller, a German ex-soldier, the only other German in the battalion, when a group of aeroplanes appeared over us. Everyone was running for shelter. The planes circled around. I wanted to get up to go further away into the field but Muller said, 'Where are you going? This is as safe as anywhere else.'

I said that we had better get out of sight.

'Nonsense,' he said. 'They can't see you unless you start moving.'

He was unscrewing his revolver with a penknife. He was always busy doing something.

'You can run away from shells but not from bombs.'

Someone put his head round the sand pile. Muller was laughing like hell. 'You think they can't hit you there, do you?' he said in French. The man looked scared and did not answer. Muller turned to me, 'Boy, they come so fast you don't know when it hits you. If they do it's a mistake, see? They can't aim at you.'

'What about the building?'

'They can't hit that either,' said the imperturbable Muller. 'They're too high up.'

I saw that the red cross flag had disappeared. I heard later that a telephone message came from Madrid to say that hospitals had been bombarded deliberately. From then on no hospital showed the red cross.

In the evening we dug a number of small gun emplacements on top of the ridge. It was about a mile long and reinforced with cement in places. Large fields stretched in front of and below it, ending in a big road just before the wood, the Casa de Campo.

Just before dark, Blanche's runner came to ask for three men able to handle a machine gun. Steve, MacLaurin[25] and Tommy[26] went with him. I wanted to go too but Fred would not let me.

They went so quickly that I could not say goodbye to Steve. We watched them walking away. There was a railway embankment not far from us and we saw the armoured train rolling along it never to return.

I had the last watch early in the morning from five to seven. I woke up a few times during the night. The wounded were being evacuated. Coffee was being given out at six in the morning in front of the building. I had to stay on watch until seven and when I went over there was none left. The cook gave me a cup of wine. I had left my rucksack in our room and went up to get it. On the way back terrific bangs hammered on the roof. The building trembled. Soldiers were running down to the ground floor. We stood on the steps. The last of the wounded were put into ambulances. Six shells hit the building, two exploded outside on the road.

During a lull I ran over to our gun. Muller was there swearing and cursing. 'They can see us as clear as day from the hills,' he yelled. 'Get down into the fields.'

He was not in charge of our section and we did not know what to do. After the fascist gunner had hit the hospital they concentrated on us. I was very scared. Burke and someone else rolled down the slope into the field. Only Jock and I were left on the gun. He looked bewildered, but he always did. It was an awful, helpless feeling lying there without any shelter. The gun pit was only two feet deep. Shells exploded in the fields and then crept along the ridge. I bolted down the slope. I saw John and Bernard about five hundred yards off but with their gun.

Again the building was under fire and black smoke poured from the windows. Fred came running and swore at us, telling us to get the gun. We went back to fetch it. Nobody was injured in this first bombardment; only one Frenchman was knocked unconscious. We were all dazed, it had come so quickly.

We advanced towards the wood. There were deep channels in the field just before the road, from which earth and stone had been taken for the building. We filed through them and entered the wood. There was a lane through the wood flanked by hills and thickly shaded by trees and bushes. There was a ditch on one side of the lane with water trickling along it. We placed two guns in the lane. We were not afraid any more. At least they could not see us here. Runners went to and fro. We were informed that an attack was likely after the bombardment.

There were Germans fighting in front of us. They would come back if the line should break and we were not to shoot. We were told that Moors were confronting us; they would be wearing green turbans. We strained our eyes towards the green thicket before us. An officer came running down the road from the front. He told us to look out. Hand grenades exploded, machine guns stuttered but the Germans were holding on grimly and the line did not break. Shelling had started again, but from the other direction, from our lines. The small ones just skimmed the tree tops wailing and whistling, the big ones made a queer rustling sound high in the air. The fascists stopped firing. During the whole afternoon our guns fired. Once an aeroplane came down and we feared it would crash on top of us.

It was nice down there in the wood; quite warm in spite of the shade. The trees were very green with hardly a brown leaf, only the grass was yellow and withered. The sun shone through the branches throwing small, yellow lights on the dark ground. I was trying out my rifle to make sure it would not jam. It was lucky I did. The bullet came off the cartridge and stuck in the barrel. I tried out all my ammunition. I crept up to the third gun on the hill and borrowed a ramrod.

There was a movement in front of us. Three Spanish soldiers came out from among the trees. They walked with their hands up and looked scared. I asked them where they were going. They told me they were going to fetch something. They did not have their rifles with them and, probably, had just run away.

After dark we left the wood. There was a newly dug trench in the field, where we rested. It was a bad trench, straight, wide and shallow. Steve had not come back yet. Heavy firing could be heard all around us. I sat next to Fred; I could see he was worried. I was just falling asleep when Muller came to say we had to send a guard down the road. Fred said I should go. I went to the road with Muller; there were two Spaniards as well. We were to stop all cars and examine their papers. If they did not stop, should we shoot? He did not know. I walked up and down the road. Stray bullets came over. Cars came tearing along the road without lights. We hailed them but they did not stop, only an ambulance obeyed our order. After two hours I was relieved and went back to lie down. Everybody was asleep.

The next day was grey and cold. We ate part of our iron rations for breakfast. I went back to the building to look for a rucksack. There were a great number of blankets, sacks, ammunition and two rifles lying about. I found a French hand grenade container which I took. Shelling started again. They shelled the roads on our left where long, grey columns of men moved towards the wood. The XII Brigade had arrived. We watched the shelling.

Fred had gone away to see Alfredo. When he came back he looked very pale. Our battalion had lost about a hundred men on the previous night. There were no details. Two Englishmen were alive but they did not know who. Captain Blanche was dead. Fred sat worrying and brooding the whole day. I tried to comfort him. He was irritable and spoke of Steve as if he were dead. I said that I was sure he was not. After a while he said, 'You drew a picture of Steve the other day – I would like to have it.' I took it out and gave it to him and he put it in his pocket.

# Chapter 5 — Aravaca

We left the trenches in the afternoon and crossed the road towards the wood. The bombardment had ceased. It was getting dark. In half an hour they would fire a few more shells, just to say goodnight. They never bombarded at night in the early stages of the war. Sometimes they would shell Madrid where they were bound to hit something or kill somebody. They never bothered us. Maybe they were short of ammunition, or perhaps they did not like to miss the effect of shelling.

We entered the wood where some trees still had leaves. They were mostly young trees standing close together and they gave me a feeling of shelter and security though many of them were cut and bruised by shells. We waited near a small river until it was quite dark. The gun sections were rearranged. I was put on number two gun. After dark we moved on. We took our position on the slope of a ridge. It was difficult to stay on the top and we tried to hack small steps to get a footing.

The fascists were opposite us behind a long white wall. A field, not more than three hundred yards long separated us. It was very quiet. They must have heard us coming because they opened fire with rifles and machine guns. The trees behind us were higher than the crest so they could not see us. The wall showed white in the darkness and we fired along the top. It was too dark. We waited for the flashes and fired at them. I kept on rolling down the slope because the grass was damp. My rifle got full of sand and I had to clean it.

We had our dinner from our iron rations, unfolded our blankets and arranged the watches for the night. It was too early to sleep and the shooting increased and died down like a wave. Fred came along and asked us to stop firing because a few men were out in front of us trying to dynamite the wall. Fortunately it was not true because to our left and right they continued firing. We fired only when we thought we had fixed the flash of a gun opposite. They sent up Very-lights. They must have expected us to attack. It was a beautiful sight. At first we kept our heads well down but we could not resist watching.

Bullets came over but far too high and they ricocheted off the trees with a moaning sound; tracer bullets looking like fire-flies; and explosive bullets with the nasty double report. It was quite safe to watch because I had a few tree stumps in front of me.

The Very-lights exploded in the air and a pale green light would rise and move slowly, trembling over the field towards us, touching it and the trees with a ghostly light. Then they would sink and slowly fade out. It was like a fairy-tale wood where bright, glittering stars gleamed through the black trees. At every light there was a tremendous burst of gunfire. We did not reply any more; it was a waste of ammunition.

I heard somebody crying on my left, but it was too dark to see who it was. Somebody was taken away and I asked who it was but nobody knew. We heard later that it was one of our gun crew who had shot himself through the hand by holding it before his rifle. They knew he had not been wounded because the powder on his hand gave him away.

It started raining towards morning but I managed to sleep a little. The firing had ceased completely. It was midday when the weather cleared a bit and we spread our jackets and blankets over the bushes to dry. We wanted to make a fire but it would not burn and only smouldered, so we had to put it out because the smoke could be seen from the air.

Fred came along in the evening and told us to be ready to move, but he did not know where we were going. There was talk about a big attack the next morning. We waited, ready to march, until a battalion of Catalans, which was to take over our position, arrived. They were expected to relieve us at nine o'clock but it was two o'clock in the morning when they arrived. We marched towards the road where trucks waited to take over our machine guns and ammunition. Everybody talked about the attack in the morning and we were all excited.

Fred had just talked to our commanding officer and gave us the details. The attack was to be at dawn, but it might be later as the relief had come so late. It was not possible to be in our new position at four o'clock as had been planned. Seventy planes would bomb the enemy lines for an hour and, with thirty tanks in front of us, we would go into the attack. This was good news indeed. We could have cheered we were so happy. Fred said the tanks would go as far as the enemy lines and then turn back. He warned us not to get in a panic and to keep out of their way. We promised to do our best.

The battalion moved on. After an hour we halted again. We waited and it grew very cold. We marched on and halted again. On our left was a new power station which had not been finished on account of the war. We were told to go inside and take a rest. Nobody knew why. We thought it was because of aeroplanes but we did not hear any. We lay down on the floor, tightly packed, and no light was allowed. There was not enough room for everybody so we were treading on and bumping into each other. It was frightfully cold on the stone floor, but no one dared to unfold his blanket in case we should move off in a hurry.

We waited for two hours. Nobody slept. We were talking about the attack and somebody said the attack was off. We marched on. Dawn was breaking when we came to the Puente de los Franceses. It was nearly day; the sky was clear and it was going to be sunny. We heard the rumble of tanks behind us. It sounded like an earthquake. As they overtook us, we counted twenty-five. They looked enormous and threatening against the skyline. There was going to be an attack after all. The sight of the tanks did us good. Somebody said they were Russian tanks but somebody else said they were French. We did not care whether they were Chinese as long as they would go in front of us.

The sun rose. We still marched. It was nearly eight o'clock when we reached a village. We halted and received a cup of coffee, a little brandy and a piece of bread. We waited again. Somebody said the attack was off. Somebody always says something. We told him to get stuffed. A supply lorry rattled past us. Somebody cried, 'It's Joe!' We all ran after him and dragged him from the lorry to shake his hand. While we were having our coffee he told us what had happened. Fred sat a little apart from us.

'Where's Steve?' he asked Joe, but he did not look at him.

'I don't know,' Joe said.

'Is he dead?'

'I don't know,' Joe said. 'He's missing, that's all I know. I saw him firing a gun from his shoulder, after Mac was dead. That's the last time I saw him.'

'What about Tommy?' we asked him.

'He is in hospital with four bullets in his stomach. He was trying to save Mac and the gun when he got it.'

Nobody said anything. Fred walked away.

'Blanche is dead,' Joe said, 'and eighty other men. It was like this,' he went on. 'The village was empty when we entered it. The Moors had left in a hurry, and left only a few men behind. There was no fighting. We made two prisoners. Had we shot them on the spot everything would have been different. They were locked up but one escaped. I think they had left the village because they thought we outnumbered them. The man who escaped told them, probably, that we weren't more than two hundred, and back they came like fucking lightning. We hadn't any hand grenades. It was so dark you couldn't see a thing. Well, you know the rest. I found this Mauser,' Joe added, holding it up for us to see.

'It's no good to you,' we said, 'there isn't any ammunition for Mausers.'

'I'll get it from the Moors,' Joe said, 'I'm going to shoot them with their own fucking rifle.'

We were called away to get our guns and ammunition from the trucks. Two men had to carry the gun in turn, the rest of us carried the drums and small sacks. The battalion lined up ready to march. We had a new commander, a wiry little Frenchman in a smart, long overcoat and leather leggings. He wore a beret with three bars.

We marched. It was a beautiful morning. The roads ran like trenches between the rolling fields. The ground was still misty. We heard a plane overhead. When the mist lifted we saw it was only one small plane. It was not ours. It was an enemy plane observing us from a great height. Machine guns started firing at us from a great distance. We walked bent and, with our sacks, we looked like the Seven Dwarfs in Snow White. The banks of the sunken roads were only five feet high. We crossed a field, running all the way. The drums and rifles clattered on our backs and grew heavier every minute.

It was very warm. We crept along another sunken road. Sometimes the bank would be reduced to road level and we halted and only a few at a time crossed the open space. Our commander and his runner came up from behind. He crouched next to me breathing heavily. He had a lean, sunburnt face with a hooked nose. He looked worried and I wondered, later on, whether he felt that death was upon him. I told him that his coat was too heavy for this sort of exercise. He smiled at me.

We moved on and halted, and moved on again. We wondered whether this was already the attack. We heard no guns and no bombing; there was only the whining and whistling of bullets going over the road. Around midday we were out of the line of fire and could walk upright again. We rested in a valley with trees and a stream. We crossed the stream by a water mill and filled our bottles. During the afternoon we made our way over hills covered with heather and beech trees. It was clear and we could see the country for miles. Looking back we saw the church tower of the village we had left in the morning. It was not far away. We saw three tanks down on the road going back towards the village.

We crossed a few fields. There was another big field in front of us and a white windmill without sails. Further to the left was a line of trees and a farm.

We had nearly reached the mill. I saw our commander and his runner entering it when the shelling started. The shells went over us and exploded a few hundred yards behind. The barrage crept back over us and back again. I was lying flat on my stomach when three shells exploded to my right. I saw smoke coming out of the mill and the top collapsed. I crawled away from the mill towards the line of trees. Under the trees was a trench with a few Spanish soldiers crouching in it. We crept along the trench and over the top towards the farm in front of us. Before we reached it a few shells destroyed it. Only one wall remained standing, with a nice circular hole in it where a shell had gone through without exploding.

After ten minutes the bombardment stopped as suddenly as it had started. We were told to man the trenches. I saw a man running towards us, his face streaming with blood. It looked fiery red in the light of the setting sun. It grew dark. The trench was not very deep and parts of it were covered with boards and bushes. The few Spaniards collected their rifles and blankets and left. They seemed glad to get out. I asked one of them for water. He had none. 'This is better,' he said, giving me a bottle of *anís*. I refused to take it all, but he insisted and poured half into my bottle. We parted with '*Salud*' and '*Buenas noches*' but it was a bad night.

I shared the *anís* among my gun crew. Fred came with a bottle of brandy which somebody had given him and we had another drink. It was frightfully cold. The sky was clear, it was freezing and the rifles were soon covered with rime. The fields in front of us were blotted out by mist which rose and filled our trench. I was not tired enough to sleep and walked about to keep myself warm.

I took over the gun at midnight. After two hours I woke the next man, but he refused to take over and started an infernal row. I was angry as hell but said nothing. At about three o'clock some idiot started firing and in a minute, left and right, everybody blazed away because they thought we were being attacked. I had my finger on the trigger of the gun but could not see anything so did not fire.

It was quiet again. I would have given a lot for a glass of brandy. I smoked, although it was forbidden, by covering the cigarette with my blanket. Pat relieved me at five o'clock and I slept a little. In the morning I left the trench with a few other men to fetch coffee and bread. The food lorries stood in the wood half a mile behind our position. We were told not to go back as our machine gun company was to take up a position further back. I went to fetch my rifle and blanket. When I returned I met a company of Poles going to take over the trench. After breakfast I slept a little in a clearing. The sun was out, my clothes dried, and I felt comfortable and warm. We cleaned our rifles and cleaned the drums of ammunition.

On the road which went through the wood I saw four men carrying something in a blanket. From out of the blanket stuck a yellow, clenched fist. The men called to me but I could not understand what they said and I went over to them. They had put the bundle down. '*Es un inglés,*' one of the men said. I lifted the blanket. Although there was only one eye and the skull had caved in on one side over the mouth, like a helmet, I recognised our commander. Both legs were missing.

'Where did you find him?' I asked.

'In the mill.'

'It's our captain,' I said.

'There was another one,' they said, 'but there wasn't much left of him.'

We covered him up but his fist stuck out as before.

'The Red Front salute,' one of the men said. 'He died saluting.'

It was too silly. 'When you lose your legs,' I said, 'you will raise both fists, whether you want to or not.'

The wood was divided by one road and our part had a brick wall round it. We decided to make an emplacement for the gun between the trees and the wall. While we were working the bombardment started. It lasted six hours. They had the range of our trenches and hit them every time. Long-range batteries shelled the wood and the road to cut off reinforcements, but nobody was hit.

They were having hell in front of us and we were working hard too. Eventually we had nothing more to do but wait and I went to the gate in the wall which led to the road. There were ditches on both sides and a big oak tree stood in the middle of the road. The wood still looked very green in the sunlight; more like late summer than November.

An ambulance came tearing up the road, stopped abruptly and a bearded French doctor, in a heavy sheepskin jacket, jumped out and started cursing a couple of stretcher bearers who waited there. A farm, about half a mile back, had been made into a first-aid station and he wanted to know why the wounded had not appeared yet. The man pointed to the front and the doctor swore and yelled and called for volunteers to carry stretchers. Four stretcher bearers had been killed. Some men stepped forward, put their rifles down and took the stretchers.

The doctor threw his coat on the ground and started unpacking cases and bundles. We helped him, placing things near the ditch where the grass was fairly clean. The doctor and his solemn-looking assistant gabbled at each other in Russian. Their driver came up to say that he was going back.

The shelling came over our part of the wood again so I went back to see whether our gun was all right. A few batteries fired at the same time, making a 'rum-rum' noise and after that silence and then loud explosions. I walked through the wood and came upon the farm. I filled my bottle with water from a well. The doors and windows of the big house were open and I could see the walls covered with pictures and knick-knacks and a large, empty hall. When I came back to the gate the first of the wounded were being carried down the road.

There was a strange noise during the silence between the firing; it sounded like the throbbing of machinery. It came from the stretchers. There was no screaming, only this frightful whistling noise. The wounded were set down and laid on the road by the bearers who went back panting and sweating. Most of the men had been hit by shrapnel and the doctor got busy cutting shoes and clothing and then started to wash and cut and bandage.

One man had his arms sliced in half lengthwise from shoulder to hands and it looked like a picture in an anatomical book. Others were hit all over their bodies and legs; a mass of small and large holes appeared out of which the tendons and white bones stuck. They were calling for water and I opened their tunics to see whether they were wounded in the stomach and then gave them little sips out of my bottle.

They all looked strangely alike, their faces pale, waxen, yellow, their eyes dark and still with the expression of surprise and horror at the terrible moment when the shell had burst upon them. Their hair was full of sand as if they had been buried. I fumbled for a cigarette and lit one. One of the wounded was talking to me in Polish and I could not understand what he said. He looked at my cigarette and I put it in his mouth. He sucked it greedily and then died, the smoke still trickling from his mouth.

The place was soon littered with torn boots, uniforms and underwear, bloody bandages, belts and cartridges. One man was lying on his face, a jagged piece of metal fastening his helmet to his head. They could not get it out and he was taken away in the ambulance with others already bandaged. Stretcher after stretcher came down the road and with them again the pumping noise. The bombardment grew more intense and the stretcher bearers walked more slowly and wearily. They took spades with them to bury the mutilated dead.

We were ordered to man the guns and we expected an attack. Some men hastily tried to dynamite the big tree in the road to make a barricade against tanks but they did not succeed. Muller, the German sergeant, called me to get hand grenades. A Spanish soldier was waiting for me near the farm house and I climbed on the back of his motorcycle. We went along an avenue of trees and open fields until we came upon three small and badly camouflaged batteries with the ammunition wagons standing near by. The crew of Spaniards was sitting round having lunch. I told them what I wanted and rested for a minute smoking a cigarette. They offered me a leather flask of wine and I drank most of it. One pointed towards the front and asked me what was going on and how things were going. I suddenly felt angry, got up and said I had to go. The motorcycle stood in the road and I yelled for the driver. He appeared with twenty-five hand grenades of Spanish make which one had to light with a cigarette. There were small hooks on the tins and we hung them all over me so that I looked like a porcupine and we went back. A few grenades fell on to the road and we turned back to pick them up. I stowed the grenades behind the wall and went back to the gun.

Muller sat peacefully on a tree trunk cleaning his nails with a bayonet. He asked me where I had been and I told him about the batteries and the Spaniards who were busy having lunch.

'Well, I hope they don't start firing as well,' he said. 'They won't hit anything but us. Did you see any tanks?'

'No.'

He put his bayonet away and unpacked a little sack which was full of odds and ends he had picked up, such as screwdrivers, screws, cartridge clips, parts of old guns and so on. He took out a big revolver and started cleaning it and, while I watched him, he said, 'You mustn't get upset about the guns. This sort of thing happens in any war.'

'What's the point of having them?'

'Perhaps no orders, no ammunition, no *nada*.'

'It's been a bad day for the Poles.'

'It's nothing,' he said. 'Why, I remember our last offensive in 1918, round Verdun. We had lined up a thousand guns, big and small, and they were bombarding for six days and six nights. After that we went over the top to clean up the leavings and when we came to the first trench it was empty and no bodies. We came to the second trench and it was the same. My lieutenant went white as a sheet. They had retreated during the bombardment and we had shelled empty positions. Then the French started giving us hell. Oh boy, you should have been there. This is nothing.'

'At least you had guns on both sides.'

'It didn't make any difference, did it?'

'That's true,' I said.

He rolled a few cigarettes with a contraption he had bought in Madrid. We smoked and after a while I went up a tree to look over the wall.

'See anything?'

'No,' I said. 'Nothing but the duds underneath the wall.'

I heard him chuckling to himself.

'I saw them,' he said. 'They're German. Boy, wouldn't it be funny if they had killed us.'

'Listen,' I said.

We listened and could hear the deep drone of approaching aeroplanes. I could not see them at first because of the trees.

'They sound like big ones,' said Muller.

'Yes,' I said. 'They're bombers, I can see them now.'

'How many?'

'About twenty.'

'Don't tell me they're ours.'

'No,' I said, 'they're fascists all right.'

The planes circled round the wood for some time but probably thought we were already well supplied with shells and flew off towards Madrid. I came down from the tree and sat down beside Muller. He had tied his sack up but the revolver was still out.

'How long do you think this war will last?'

'I don't know,' I said. 'Maybe a year, maybe two.'

'You're crazy,' he said. 'The war will be over by February or March at the latest.'

'I don't think so.'

'By March we'll have won this war.'

'We haven't won anything today.'

'Don't let it bother you. Why, I remember the summer of 1917.'

'Yes,' I said, 'I know, but this is different. They seem to get more guns and planes every day.'

'We'll get some more too. I heard the Russians have sent us a lot of stuff. We'll be able to attack soon.'

'I hope so,' I said. 'I hope it won't be an attack like yesterday.'

'What are you going to do after the war?'

'I shall stay here,' I said.

'So shall I. I'm going to stay in the army.'

'Perhaps there won't be any army.'

'You're nuts,' he said. 'There'll always be an army and there'll always be a war.'

'Yes, as long as there are Mullers,' I said.

He laughed. 'What's the matter, don't you like being a soldier?'

'Yes,' I said, 'but not in just any war.'

'This is my third war.'

'Maybe it's your last one,' I said.

'Ah shit. They tried it too often. I'm going to see another war yet.'

'Why didn't you join Franco?'

'That's simple,' he said. 'I don't like fascists, but I like being a soldier. Maybe there'll be socialism everywhere one day. That's all right with me, but somehow I don't like the idea that there won't be any armies and no wars. It doesn't suit me to have a home and a family. It isn't that I don't like to work. I like to work hard, but as a soldier. It's the only life. After the Great War I felt as lonely as hell. When I'd done my five years in the Foreign Legion and they asked me whether I'd like to leave I felt like an orphan who was going to be kicked out into the world. You'll feel the same when this war's over and you have to take the uniform off.'

'You're just a romantic,' I said.

'Maybe I am. You told me you've been in Africa. Didn't you ever feel you wanted to go back?'

'Yes,' I said. 'Very often.'

'Well, that's how I feel about the army. Homesick. You'll understand it all one day. What do you say? Let's both stay in the Spanish army. We'll be officers by then.'

'All right, Muller,' I said. 'I'll think it over.'

It was late in the afternoon. It was getting cool and the shelling had stopped. I took out my woollen balaclava and pulled it over my head.

'That's a nice useful thing,' Muller said. 'I wish I had one like that.' He was holding up a revolver for me to see. 'I'll give you this for the hood.'

I took the revolver and looked at it. It had no cartridge clip and no cartridges.

'What do I do with it, throw it?' I said.

'You may find some cartridges later on.'

'When I do I'll come back for it.'

When I went back to the road the wounded and the doctor had gone. The ditch was nearly filled with bandages and empty boxes. A stretcher with one leg broken was left behind, the canvas showing only in a few places through the bloodstains. A solitary boot stood near by, the toe-cap missing. Some men were resting near the road and others walked about in groups. They talked in whispers. It seemed very quiet after the bombardment. A group of officers had gathered round the big tree. One of them, our new commander, after whom the battalion was named, talked with Fred.

I thought we were going back into the trench when the order came to get the guns down from the wall. The sacks for our drums had disappeared so I went back to the farm with Muller in search of new ones.

When it was dark the food lorries arrived. They were known fondly by the French as 'La Soupe' because that was all they ever served. My name was called out and they gave me a letter. It was the only time I ever got one. It was too dark to read it and I did not want to strike a match. I put it away and forgot about it until I found it again some days later. It was like opening a letter for somebody else. I just read the date and threw it away.

We had our soup under the trees behind the wall and after that were told to stay there. We unrolled our blankets and lay down. A little later we had to get up and go back to the farm. Behind the farm was a big barn full of hay and we were told to sleep there. It was warm and cosy. My feet were hurting me so I took my boots off and fell asleep.

I dreamt I was asleep in a barn and suddenly somebody yelled, 'The fascists are coming!' I woke up and saw black shadows against the door. I groped for my boots and could not find them. I felt I had to have my boots before I could do anything and, while I looked for them, everybody fought and shot and yelled around me. Somebody got hold of me, I woke up and saw the barn door was open. I saw the shadows of men and reached for my boots and found them at once close to my rifle. Somebody was shaking me and saying, 'Get up, everybody up.' We had to be silent, no lights were allowed. Most of our things had got buried in the hay and everyone was fishing hastily for his belongings. We lined up in the courtyard. It was very cold. There was a moon and big, fast-moving clouds. We shivered in the cold night for more than an hour.

We marched back towards the trench in the field with the ruined mill but, before we reached it, we turned sharp left, marching parallel with the trench for a while. We then turned left again. We had to cross many fields and lanes until we came upon a big road. Though it was dark it looked familiar. It was the same road we had passed along twenty-four hours before.

From time to time we came upon groups of Spanish soldiers hovering in their blankets on the steep banks of the sunken road, where they had dug a few holes big enough to lie in. We rested for a few minutes. We marched in single file on both sides of the road in order not to be in the way of trucks which raced past us towards Madrid.

Fred came up from behind and disappeared in front of me. After a time I saw a wire glittering about two hundred yards ahead. It was stretched across the road about a foot above the ground. The headlights of a motor car coming up behind us picked it out. I heard shouts of '¡Alto!' from the soldiers guarding the wire. The lights rested on them for a moment and then the car (I could see it was an ambulance) passed them at a terrific speed and the wire snapped and coiled through the air and it was dark again. Men were running in front of me, shouts came from everywhere. I came upon a group standing around a body on the ground. It was Pat. The wire had caught him round the chest. He was moaning and I could hear him say over and over again, 'they're killing their own comrades.'

Our officers came running up and told us to move on. We waited but were again called to march on. Everybody was upset and angry. 'Why couldn't they stop?' somebody said. 'Why didn't they let the wire down?' Another one said, 'We should have shot at the car.' Someone else said it was an ambulance.

'Where's Fred?' I asked. Nobody knew. Through the whole night we marched and halted and marched again. Nobody had seen Fred but we thought he had stayed behind to look after Pat.

We reached the Puente de los Franceses in the early morning and rested there, but it was too cold to sleep. When it was light we had some coffee, brandy and bread. I saw Alfredo coming towards us looking very white, tired and distressed. He told us to step forward while our French comrades looked on from a distance. He told us that Fred was dead. The wire had caught him around his throat and killed him.

Nobody said anything. We walked away, everybody by himself, up and down the road, without looking at anybody or anything. The fat Belgian who had given out the coffee came with a brandy bottle still half full. He went up to every one of us and raised the tin cups, which we were still holding in our hands, and poured a little brandy into them. His face was red but no tears came, although he was sobbing and the brandy shot into the cups in little jerks.

From the road a number of footpaths went through a thin wood of pines and beeches with thick underbrush. We lay down there and rested. We opened our iron rations, consisting of tins, with bayonets and started to eat. The tins came from Russia.

There were vegetables, fish balls and bully beef. It was very good. We elected Joe our new commander. After our meal we went deeper into the wood, which ended in a ravine. We were told to man the ridge on the right hand side. Marcel and Muller asked for an Englishman to go with them to the university. Burke went with them. We placed our gun on top of the ridge. The grass was very wet with dew but the sun was already very warm.

A Spanish cavalry patrol came through the ravine. The horses looked well fed with shiny coats. The men looked very smart in their blue capes. They had short carbines which hung from the saddles in shiny, yellow leather holsters. Everything was quiet. No shot was fired.

Joe had found a large stable not far away which he said was full of blankets. I went with him. The stables lay in a valley. There was a house on a hill above the stable, with a tennis court. The stable looked very clean and well built. There was hardly a farm around these parts which was as good a building. The walls were whitewashed and tiled halfway up. The floors were cement. Great blankets and rubber sheets hung on the pegs. The blankets were white with a black crown embroidered on one corner. Joe found a light blue cape which he took but threw away later as the colour was too bright. I took a blanket and a rubber sheet.

We went up to the house. It had a great number of small dressing rooms with mirrors fixed over washbasins and a number of showers. Some men from our company were already there. The water was very cold. I washed my hair and started to shave but the soap would not lather. The tennis court looked very neglected with weeds growing all over it We did not dare to go out as it lay exposed to the fascists. We took a few small sacks with us for our ammunition.

In the afternoon we left the ravine and went into open country. We came to a deep lane. I climbed the bank to look over and saw a large flat field freshly ploughed, and the roofs of the university about two miles off. Just as we were leaving the lane we were fired on with shrapnel. The sky was dotted with white clouds but they were high and a little way off. Some men had already reached the field and lay there while we went back and took shelter in the lane. Aeroplanes came and dropped four bombs into the field and four enormous black cascades rose into the air. We retreated back along the lane until we reached the stable. From there we advanced in single file. We were shot at by machine guns but we were too well protected by the hills; it was only on their tops that we had to run.

It was very warm and we left our bags and blankets behind. We would fetch them later on. We advanced about a mile and then had to stop because the aeroplanes were overhead. They fired their machine guns, flying low. We had to lie there until evening. The planes kept on coming back until it was too dark to see. With another comrade I went back to look for our blankets. They had disappeared. I found my rucksack. It was empty. We searched about and collected five blankets but they were not ours. We would have to sleep all together in a heap to keep warm.

The food trucks had arrived but they were on the road near the stables; it was too far to carry the soup down to us. We left two men at the gun and walked to the road and ate our dinner there. It was a very cold night. Bernard suddenly became very ill, feverish and shivering. We told him to go and try to find a hospital. He came back after a time as he had lost his way. We gave him two blankets.

At four in the morning we left. We marched along roads, through woods and fields until we reached the outskirts of Madrid. There were a few houses. We had to go down into the deeply dug foundations of a huge building site where we waited near some wooden hoardings. The black outlines of the university loomed dark against the sky.

From the nearest building we could hear Spaniards talking. They were anarchists from Barcelona who had come up with their leader, Durruti. We waited until morning. We were next to the Clínico building. We had to run along a wide courtyard. There was rifle fire. We crept along behind the paving stones of the unfinished road and reached the entrance. It was barricaded and a machine gun was posted in front of it. The entrance hall was small. Staircases led into deep cellars. There was a door leading to an office. The windows were shattered. I looked out and saw Alfredo standing at the corner with a dozen men, waiting for a lull in the firing to reach the second block.

136

We sat around in the entrance. Coffee was brought in. God knows how they managed to reach us. We had bread and butter as well. Some men sang. There were shouts of 'shut up' and 'be quiet' and the singing stopped. A wounded man was brought in by stretcher bearers. They placed the stretcher on the ground. The man was covered by a blanket. Where his head was, large patches of blood showed through the covering. One of the stretcher bearers lifted the blanket, looked at the man and put it back. He shook his head at his colleague. We ate our bread. After a while the wounded man moved under blanket. His knees rose up and the patch over his head grew bigger. He stretched and then stiffened and was dead.

There was a bustle outside the entrance. Two men brought Alfredo in, his head streaming with blood. They sat him down, leaning against the wall. The stretcher bearers bandaged him. I went over to him and gave him a cup of wine and a cigarette. We were told to go up to the first floor. At the top of the broad staircase was a curved gallery with four big windows facing the square and the Clínico, which the fascists held. On the right was the Casa Velásquez. Every window was broken and the glass lay thick on the floor. We swept it up and threw it into the cellar. The square in front of the building was about eight hundred yards long and wide. It looked like a huge arena after a fight. A donkey lay dead in the middle.

I walked through the building. It was a maze of corridors and rooms. It had been hit by heavy bombs. The lift and part of the roof lay in the lift shaft on the first floor. There was a quantity of surgical instruments neatly arranged in glass cases. I met Alfredo on the stairs. He still looked very pale but he said he was all right.

We stayed two days. There was no water. We found two big barrels of red wine in the cellar. Nobody would drink it at first. The fascists had been driven out of here and some thought it might be poisoned. Finally somebody tried it. We watched him and, when we saw it had no ill effects, we filled our bottles. The wine was sour and it made us more thirsty so we had to go back to get some more of it.

We had two sentries at night; one watched in the gallery and another, a long way off, in a destroyed wing of the building. This was in a room with only two walls left standing. It was easy to reach in the daytime but at night one had to grope through rooms and corridors which did not run straight. I liked watching there. Half a mile away a village was burning. Red flames shot up from time to time. There were other fires towards Madrid.

The next day the Casa de Velásquez was heavily shelled by our batteries. It was a white building like a castle, with two towers. We saw the towers crumbling away and the roof started burning. The fascists replied with shells and bombs and our building rocked and shook. I had the first watch, from nine to eleven, in the far-off room. The village was still smouldering. A dark red glow lay over it. A few Spaniards passed on the road close to me so I challenged them and they answered 'anarchists'. John came at eleven to relieve me. I heard his steps for a long time. I was not tired and stayed with him for an hour. He said he did not like this part.

When I got back I saw the men packing up. I had to go back to John to tell him that we were leaving. When we marched away they found that one man was missing. He joined us the next day. He had overslept and woke up in the dark and empty building.[27] We reached the Puente de los Franceses in the early hours. Trucks took us to Fuencarral for our first rest.

# Chapter 6 — Fuencarral

After midnight we arrived in Fuencarral in a drenching rain-storm. Before reaching the village we left the road and sloshed over ploughed fields full of puddles of water. We halted there and stood around like cattle waiting for the byre to open. The rest of the battalion had found quarters somewhere. We were all tired and some started to prepare to sleep on the wet ground when Alfredo came up and led us to a big, empty tool shed.

It was too small for all of us but we crowded in anyhow until everybody had found a place to sit or lie down. Joe and Mac stayed outside although they could have found room, but Joe always took any inconvenience as something intended to annoy him personally.[28] I slept for a few hours, my head resting on somebody's boots.

In the morning it was still raining and we stayed where we were. It was like a Sunday, when one is allowed to sleep a little longer just waiting for breakfast. I went to have a look at the village. We were a few hundred yards from it. The fields were flat, black and sodden with rain. The earth stuck to one's boots in large heavy lumps and refused to come off. The village was as ugly as the countryside, with grey houses like barns, just one long street with cobblestones and two church towers pointing to the wet sky. Everything looked grey, dirty and hopeless. I turned on to the road to Madrid, which crossed another just before the village, and walked back.

The coffee had arrived. I saw the cans and the sacks of bread being taken from the lorries. Three small tanks stood on the field next to our shed. They were stuck deep in the mud and it looked as if they would never get out again. The green and brown stripes of the camouflage were hardly visible under the crust of dirt and mud.

We had our coffee and also a big piece of butter with our bread. I ate all the butter, although it was too much, as it was impossible to keep it. There were still a few men in the shed while the others went exploring. I sat down, leaning against a pillar, and ate slowly. There was some coffee left in one of the cans and we received a second cup. I watched the other comrades sitting there leaning against the walls on which hung rifles, helmets and hand grenades, most of the last without the rubber safety cap. It struck me how everybody had changed in the course of a few weeks. I had not seen myself since the first day at the University City, but there was probably not much difference between myself and those grey-clad, grey-faced men with week-old beards and unkempt hair. Some were in their hoods, like the one I wore. They had to hold the hood down from the mouth to be able to eat. Others were draped in their blankets and shawls which transformed them into fantastic, scarecrow shapes. Everybody looked very tired. We stared before us as if there were something interesting about the ground or our boots. Each one looked as if he were thinking hard about a difficult problem which was puzzling him, but their faces were blank, their eyes did not see, the brain thought nothing. We might have been part of the wall or the field outside, a brick, a clod of earth, if it were not for something which made us breathe and chew. If somebody who knew us could have seen us now I am sure he would not have recognised us. We had become soldiers; we were taking life and death as it came without side-stepping. Death sat with us for a while until we shook off his paralysing hand and started talking, all at once.

The rain had stopped. There was even a faint gleam of sunlight. I got up and went out. We had been told not to go too far away as we would move on presently. I went as far as the first house of the village. It was a small shop. I opened the door, which rang a noisy bell hanging behind it. The shop was dark and empty; there were a few old cakes in tins and the place smelt of stale groceries and salt fish. I did not see anything I wanted to buy and I heard someone coming from the house to the shop. I asked the woman who came for cigarettes but she had none. Perhaps some chocolate? No, nothing. Her eyes fell on the leather bottle which I carried. 'We've got some wine,' she said, 'if you would like to buy some.' Did I want to buy some? I was sorry I only had one bottle. She filled it and handed it to me and I gave her two pesetas. When I left the shop I tasted it in the street outside. It was very sweet, muscatel.

I walked to the centre of the village. There was a small lane on the left, ploughed up by cars and soggy with water. At the end of the road was a church; the door stood open so I went in. Inside it was dark and gloomy and the only light came from behind the altar through coloured glass windows. Soldiers were resting and sleeping on mattresses on the floor. Near the entrance hung a big kettle over a fire, with clouds of white steam pouring out of it. Men were peeling potatoes and vegetables for dinner. The altar was still just as it had been left, with candlesticks and faded flowers in two small vases upon a dark red silken cloth.

In the centre of the village was a small open square with a town hall, now the temporary headquarters of the Brigade. There were two branches in the square but no trees. I was looking for a first aid station and found it in a big shop with whitened glass windows. The trigger finger of my right hand was swollen and painful. I had injured it some days before and dirt had got into the wound and it was now so inflamed I could hardly bend it.

There were two rooms in the shop and about a dozen beds with a few sick men but no wounded. The male nurse in charge did not want to open my finger and told me to wait for the doctor, who would be back shortly. I waited a long time but the doctor did not come so I went out again.

The main street and the square were crowded with soldiers. There was hardly room to walk, with trucks roaring through the streets to and from Madrid. I wanted a haircut but both barber shops were already crowded with waiting men. I met Joe and we had an *anís* in one of the bars. There was no place to sit down and no other drink but *anís* and very bad brandy. When we came out a truck stopped in front of us and Joe recognised an English comrade who, with eleven others, was serving in the German Thaelmann Battalion. I asked after Chris, who was in the armoury of the XII Brigade, and he told me he was all right, he was probably around somewhere.

While we were talking a truck raced past us and ran over a dog which was crossing the road. Its back was broken and it screamed and howled but managed to crawl away on its forelegs.

141

I followed it and took out my small revolver, which I had bought in Paris, and shot it. The dog was not dead so I shot it again but still did not kill it. A soldier with a rifle finished it off. The bullet, fired at short range, tore a huge hole in the chest of the dog and it lay dead on a rubbish heap, its mouth open in a fearsome grin.

'That gun of yours isn't much good in an emergency,' said the English comrade when I came back.

'No,' I said. 'I'm glad I never had to rely on it. This is the first time I've tried it out.'

A number of Spaniards had collected round the dog and looked at it and then again at me. They probably wondered why I took the trouble to shoot it.

I asked the Englishman how he liked being with the Germans. He said they got on well and he would not like to be with anybody else. They were all well looked after compared to us. He wore a good uniform and boots and was surprised that we were still walking around in our old overalls and thin trench coats. The Germans, being good organisers, had demanded uniforms, coats and proper cartridge belts, while we still wore canvas bandoliers on our shoulders. He told us they even received half a bottle of brandy a day while at the front. In the French battalion nobody bothered much until one made a row. The Germans even had political meetings and discussions at the front and they were thinking of printing their own newspaper. We said that we would try to do the same because we did not know much about what was going on except when we got an old French or English newspaper. We said goodbye and Joe and I sat down on the kerb near our quarters and watched the traffic.

A motorbike with a sidecar rushed by, driven by a soldier. A girl, with very blond hair which blew behind her in the wind, waved to us and we waved back.

Joe yelled, 'Where are you going to, beautiful?' and the girl shouted, 'See you later,' and was gone.

Joe was quite excited. 'Boy,' he said, 'she's a looker. I wonder where she went?'

'She'll be in one of the hospitals round here,' I said, 'she was wearing a Red Cross armlet.'

He looked into a small pocket mirror.

'It's all right, Joe,' I said, 'you look handsome enough.'

'I'll try to find out where she went,' Joe said and got up.

When I got back to our shed everyone was packing and ready to go. I collected my rifle and blanket and we marched to the square. Trucks were waiting and filled quickly. One lorry broke down in front and blocked the street for a time. I left my blanket and sack on a truck and walked about. Behind us was a car with two men standing on top. One wore a leather jacket and he was taking photographs. His blond hair fell over his face on one side and the way he was bending his head and one shoulder while taking the pictures seemed familiar. He turned around and I saw that it was Walter. I could not believe it at first.

'Hello, Walter!' I yelled. 'Hello!'

He looked down at me. I saw he did not recognise me. He jumped from the car and came nearer.

'Hello, Walter,' I said. 'Don't you remember me?'

'No,' he said, and then I realised that I was still wearing my hood. I took it off.

'God,' he said, 'Jan.'

We shook hands and could not speak for a while.

'When did you come back to Spain?' he asked.

'Two months ago. Are you in the army too?' I replied.

'No, I'm a photographer for the Government.'

My comrades were shouting to me to get on the truck.

'Quick,' I said, 'where can I find you? I may get leave in Madrid.'

'*Juventud*,' he said, 'the youth paper. Anyone will tell you.'

He followed me to the truck.

'Where is Putz?' I asked.

'Didn't you know?'

'No,' I said. 'What is it?'

'She's dead,' he said. 'She was killed in Aragón, three months ago.'

Our truck rolled away. I looked at Walter and he waved his hand. Joe was sitting next to me.

'I know where the girl is,' he said. 'She's a nurse in our battalion. Is anything the matter?'

143

*Putz in Aragon, 1936*

'No,' I said. 'I just met an old friend.'

We passed a sign on our right. It said 'Burgos 145 kilometres'. We stopped before a white building and got down. I took my things, when everybody had gone, and walked slowly to the entrance. I felt very tired. I wanted to think of Putz, but I could not. There was a blank every time I thought of her. There was some mistake, surely, it could not be and yet I knew it was true, but something kept on saying, 'there must be a mistake – people are often reported dead and it proves false.' I had to find out, but when and where and how? I knew she was dead. It was no good pretending it was not so. It did not hurt much. It was unreal, like anything else in the war. A bad dream. After one wakes up, it is all over and past. What did it matter? How long is one going to live? A few days, perhaps a few weeks.

Joe was standing at the door talking to the blonde girl. There was another girl with her, smaller and darker, and both wore grey uniforms with trousers. 'There's a German,' Joe said, pointing at us. We shook hands. The smaller one of the two was German. The blonde, tall girl was a Swede who spoke five languages fluently. They were not very young, but quite good-looking. I showed them my hand and asked them to have a look at it. We went through a long hall into a couple of small rooms which had been converted into a hospital. The German nurse opened up my finger with a pair of scissors which she sterilized, and cleaned and bandaged it. It throbbed a bit but did not hurt.

'You need a shave,' the nurse said, 'you look like Christ.' She said there was plenty of hot water and showers on the first floor. 'Come back in the afternoon. I'll make you another bandage because this one will be wet,' she added.

'I'll come back,' I said, and I went to look for a room to put my things down in.

The English were quartered in two small rooms on the ground floor. I found a place in a corner, under a window from which one could see the Guadarrama mountains. We had no beds or straw. My blanket was still wet when I put it on the floor. I took a towel and a fresh shirt out of my bag and went out to wash. There were four showers with hot water and I had to wait for about half an hour. I just managed to wash myself and a pair of socks when the water suddenly stopped. I had a shave with cold water, having borrowed a piece of looking-glass from a Frenchman, and put on the clean shirt. I was shivering as I came out into the cold air.

Clouds were hanging very low. It looked like more rain, and the snow on the mountains looked dirty and grey. The fields were black with bits of ice and snow on the many puddles. A cold wind blew down from the mountains. I went inside again and lay down for an hour but could not sleep. The floor was hard and I put an ammunition case covered with a dirty shirt under my head. Somebody sang *Goodbye Hawaii*. It was not a bad voice but it was a rotten song; if one did not listen to the words it sounded soft and soothing and made one sleepy.

Our French *responsable*, who had a long black beard, brought us our money: a hundred pesetas for the last ten days. I still had my last pay and wondered what to do with it. I hoped to go to Madrid the next day.

In the late afternoon I went back to the hospital to have my hand bandaged. Joe came with me. We sat in a small room which had no window but electric light. Two mattresses lay on the floor where the girls slept. It was nearly dinner time but they invited us to stay and eat with them. We had a two gallon flask of wine from which we drank. A Russian male nurse, whom we christened Ivanovitch, and a Spanish infantry officer joined us. The Russian, a square and silent fellow, bustled around the girls with dog-like devotion. The Spaniard, a small, elegant, good-looking man, spoke beautiful Spanish. We talked in three languages.

The German girl, a trained nurse, had lived in Barcelona for some years and had joined the Red Cross as soon as the war broke out, while Greta, the blonde Swede, a former marathon dancer, had served on the Aragón front at first aid stations.[29] They were both very cheerful and courageous and good comrades. They told us they were temporarily attached to our battalion in spite of our doctor who did not approve of women nurses at the front. Joe had a crush on Greta but was very shy and a little bewildered by her forcefulness and boyish manner. I was getting drunk in a heavy, drowsy sort of way.

The Spaniard came from Andalusia and we talked about the places I knew. I told him how much I liked them and that pleased him.

'Ah, *señor*,' he kept on saying (he never said *camarada*), 'you should have gone (here and there) and visited (this and that) . . . *Es muy bonita, muy linda, muy grande.*' He blew kisses on his hand to invisible, beautiful mountains, cities and rivers. The girls begged him to sing for us. He was an opera singer and had studied for years in Italy. He went out to try to find a guitar but was unsuccessful. He asked me what I would like to hear and I named an aria from Mozart's Figaro. He sang. I have never heard a more beautiful baritone. Maybe I am wrong; I had not heard good music for a long time and I was drunk and full of *weltschmerz*. The girls asked for Spanish songs. He sang old and new folk tunes, gypsy songs and flamenco. It was wonderful to watch the expression on his face, completely unselfconscious; his whole body seemed to move and tremble, filling that small room with glorious, unearthly sounds. For the first time I experienced the power music has over human beings. The girls were just melting away, so was I, so was everyone else including the immoveable Ivanovitch.

I never thought the *Kreuzer Sonata* was a good book, but now I knew what it meant to think, to act, to feel as the musician commanded. It was like drunkenness, just the one glass too many, after which one would lose control and be borne here and there, acting strangely and unexpectedly, saying things which one did not want to say, and everything one feels is exaggerated a thousand fold. I felt god-like and ready to do the impossible.

He kept on singing and I wished he would never stop. We listened to Spain. It was either hot or cold but never warm; icy wind and scorching sun. There was a trembling and a weeping in the air; flowing tears and figures dressed in black; bull rings and whorehouses, dark cathedrals full of prayers and laments; fertile green valleys and wind-swept barren hills. It was either wild and exciting or calm and still; there was nothing in between. The quavering, screaming voices of Africa mingled with the mournful, slow melodies of an Andalusian lullaby.

Then I looked at the singer – I do not even know his name – and I was sorry that he was a soldier. I had never thought that anybody could be too good to fight when so much was at stake, but this man was. If I had had the power I would not have sent him up to the front. Such a voice is like a miracle. It must be the nearest thing to being able to fly without having wings.

We heard *The Internationale* and the Republican anthem a few times every day; like a popular song which is played over and over again it loses its power; it conveys nothing except in certain circumstances. But this voice would never lose its power and, therefore, I wished its owner would not die. When he had finished I thanked him and said I hoped to hear him again the next night.

'*Gracias*,' he said. 'I enjoyed singing for you, but I have to go back to Madrid.'

We broke up and Joe and I went back across the courtyards. It was cold but I did not feel it.

The next morning we received permission to go to Madrid. We waited in small groups outside the gate for trucks to arrive, but for some reason or other none were supplied. It was twelve kilometres to Madrid and nobody wanted to walk all that way. We hailed passing trucks and cars and I got a lift in a petrol truck which took me as far as Tetuán, where there was a metro station. Workmen were busy building a low barricade of cobblestones on each side of the wide street so that only two cars at a time could pass. Sentries were examining the papers of every driver.

I went into the metro and passed the ticket inspector by saying 'Brigada Internacional', as we were not required to pay. On every platform along the whole line were groups of refugees, mostly women and children, who sat on the belongings they had brought with them. As it was early in the morning the trains were not very crowded. People looked at me, smiling and saluting. I talked to a few Spanish militiamen who were full of admiration and compliments for the Brigade. Spaniards are very fond of all kinds of machines, especially those used in war. They saw a little golden machine gun on a cloth disc sewn on the sleeve of my trench coat. '¿*Ametralladora?*' they asked. 'A good machine,' one of them said. 'How rapidly does it fire?'

'Two hundred and fifty rounds a minute,' I said, proudly.

He looked at his friend as if to say, 'Hear that? How can we lose.'

I got out at Gran Vía station. Here, as everywhere else, the station was packed with refugees and they crowded all the tunnels which led to the main stairs. I gave a few silver pesetas to a small child who started playing with them on the floor.

I stopped for a cup of coffee and then walked to the square. The post office, a large building, had been hit by bombs and was partly burned out and was now barricaded with sand bags. I bought a copy of *Juventud* from a newspaper stand to find the address. A policeman told me which tram I should get. I stood outside on the platform. The conductor refused my money when I tried to pay. An elegantly dressed woman with two daughters, next to me, seemed to be afraid and kept as far away from me as possible.

The conductor boomed at me, 'You won't pay, comrade. What kind of people would you think we were if we were to take money from the International Brigade?' He showed me which way to go.

I was in a quarter of Madrid called the *Barrio Salamanca*, not far from the embassies, where the rich people used to live. The streets were quiet with few people about. The houses were five or six storeys high, amply decorated with towers and figures and each one had a huge marble entrance.

After some searching and asking the way I found the *Juventud* office. A soldier, who sat at the door, took me up in a lift to the third floor. One entered what must have been the parlour, a round room with a window overlooking the patio. It was furnished with thick carpets, comfortable settees and armchairs. There seemed to be doors everywhere leading to corridors and other rooms. A young girl asked me what I wanted and I told her I was looking for Walter. He was not in yet and she asked me to sit down and wait. There was a lot of coming and going. Mostly they were young people wearing overalls or leather jackets. The telephone never stopped ringing, doors were banging and the lift creaked up and down.

Presently Walter came in loaded with cameras. He had been up to the University City. I went with him to his dark-room and watched him developing the films. He left the drying and so on to a boy who was helping him and we walked into the *sala*, a long room with big windows.

All the members of the staff ate together. There was soup, bread, oranges and wine. Walter introduced me. Nobody seemed to be more than twenty-five years old. They were an efficient, cool and clear-headed lot of youngsters. One boy of twenty-two was a member of the Junta de Defensa, which Miaja had formed a short time before Caballero and his Cabinet had left Madrid hurriedly, thinking it was about to fall. President Azaña sat securely in Barcelona. A young girl, the editor of the paper, asked me for a story but I could only give her a general account of the fighting.

After lunch Walter and I went back into town. We sat in a café and talked about old times. Fatima was in Paris. The child had been born in Málaga and was now two years old. He showed me a picture. After a time I asked him about Putz. She was in Barcelona at the outbreak of the war and had joined the ill-fated expedition to Mallorca together with a German. He was killed and she came back and joined a battalion in Aragón. She was killed soon after. Accounts of it were published in leading Barcelona papers which Walter had seen. He took out a picture of us which he had taken in Granada and gave it to me and I put it in my pocket. There was a long silence. I wished we could have talked about the time when we were tramping around Spain but, since Putz was dead, it was not possible.

'I can't believe it,' I said.

'Neither can I,' said Walter, 'but I'm afraid it's so. I tried everything to get any details but without success. As long as one doesn't know exactly where and how she died (though I dread to know it), it doesn't seem true.'

We felt a bit like strangers and talked about the war. Walter was very enthusiastic about his work. He made a good deal of money, which he spent on bigger and better cameras. He showed me photos of bombs crashing into the streets. He liked the people of Madrid best of all.

'They're marvellous people,' I agreed. 'It's strange that they should have so much courage, though they've never experienced a war.'

'In the first days of November,' Walter said, 'when everything seemed lost, all the women were buying knives to defend themselves if Franco should enter. Today you can't buy a knife in Madrid.'

'I wish they had built fortifications instead.'

He shrugged his shoulders. 'You know how it was. They didn't want to alarm the people. Only when the first shells fell on the city was it known that Franco was at the gates. The papers and the radio kept on telling them the enemy was a long way off. There was no panic when it started. People always seem to be more courageous than their governments think. Only when Caballero and the whole Cabinet fled to Valencia did we think all was lost. Without the Brigade, Madrid would have been taken. I saw the Germans at the University City today. There was Ludwig Renn dragging a machine gun around. They are all fine comrades.'

I told him something of my experiences and after that we left the café and walked through the town. The streets were very crowded as it was in the afternoon. I saw two enormous holes where two five hundred pound bombs had damaged the metro. I bought cigarettes in a tobacco shop which was only open during limited hours. About twenty men were forming a queue but there were still plenty of cigarettes. I bought English and American cigarettes as we were issued with Spanish ones.

We had drinks at one of the elegant bars in the Gran Vía where one could get cocktails mixed by old-time barmen.[30] We had dinner at an automat where one sat at a long sort of bar and ate shrimps, sausages and beer. Walter managed to borrow a car, which usually took him to the front, and brought me back to Fuencarral. I promised to see him again the next day if I could get leave.

I did not see him because he had gone to Teruel. I went into town with Joe, who wanted to buy a pair of boots. He was still wearing the sandals in which he had come out to Spain. There were no boots to be had, only elegant shoes with fancy trimmings. There were elegant men's shops where one could buy expensive silk shirts and pyjamas but they were no good to us. We met John, Mac and Bernard at a café, reading newspapers. We went into a bar later on. On the way I found a small shop which sold boxes of good chocolate. We bought some for the nurses. While crossing the street a few hand grenades exploded very near, thrown from fascist aeroplanes. We took shelter in a big store. A child in its mother's arms cried and we gave it some chocolate.

Later on we saw about thirty planes flying over the town. Nobody took much notice of them. People looked up only occasionally and did not run for shelter until they heard the sound of bombs. We took the metro back to Tetuán in the evening. It was dark when we came out into the street. Only the cars and trucks carried lights. A great number of men from the Brigade were outside the station trying to get a ride back. We walked along the street and later got a lift in a truck outside the town.

The girls were very pleased with the chocolate. I gave some to Bernard and John who liked sweets and they gave me some good brandy which they had bought. We had dinner with the nurses again but did not stay long because we were tired.

The next morning all leave was stopped. We assembled in the field behind the barracks and Dumont made a speech. Some men had behaved badly and got drunk. We had to stay in. That evening there would be a Russian film shown in one of the halls.

We spent the day cleaning our machine gun and learning to take it apart and reassemble it as quickly as possible. In the afternoon planes were seen near the barracks. They discharged white clouds of smoke which drifted slowly across the sky above us. We thought it was a signal for their artillery.

The two nurses came to our room and told us we would be going to the front that day. We did not believe it as we had just heard about the film but Alfredo came in and told us to pack. We said goodbye to the girls.

'I hope they won't mess you up too much,' the German one said. She was already a hard-boiled war nurse.

'Don't worry,' I said. 'You'll recognise me all right.'

'Take care of yourself.'

'I'll duck in time,' I said, and we laughed.

\* \* \* \* \*

We marched through the dark all the way to Madrid. We halted several times. Once I seemed to recognise the building site not far from the university. We came to the *barrio* of Cuatro Caminos which had been evacuated. Some men wore their mess kits open on their backs. They gleamed and shone in the dark. We tried to march quietly but the sound of a few hundred heavy boots echoed through the empty streets. This was no-man's town; the black, glassless windows in the houses looked like eyes watching us, unfriendly and threatening. A fine drizzly rain started to fall. Not far away, to the right, enormous explosions shook the air and the buildings every few minutes. Maybe they were our guns firing or big shells were coming over from Franco's lines to the university. There was a street with factories to our left. We waited in the shadow of a wall. Nobody spoke. After another five hundred yards we entered through a gate into a large factory courtyard. It was paved with stone. There was no shelter and it rained harder. Bright flashes of light lit up the yard every few minutes. It was like lightning and rolling thunder very near. The stutter of machine guns and the sharp reports of rifle fire sounded friendly and familiar.

After waiting for some time we were told to go into the factory for the night. We entered a huge hall. We could not see a thing. There were shelves everywhere and we groped along in the darkness, knocking things over. Bottles and other glass objects crashed to the floor. I managed to find a place near a window where I slept.

It was still dark in the morning when we had our breakfast but candles were lit near the door where it was given out. At daybreak we had a look round. There were miles of shelves, tables piled with soap of every colour and description, bottles of hair oil, perfume and brilliantine, boxes of lanoline and face cream. At the far end of the hall, separated by heavy pillars, were the fireplaces, kettles and drums; one still contained soap. Shells had damaged that part very badly. The wall had collapsed and the windows were broken. There was an iron staircase leading to a balcony, which had been the packing room, littered with string, labels and paper. We had nothing to do after breakfast so we went round inspecting everything. The cheaper sort of soap had no wrapper. It was in big round or square pieces in hideous colours. We fingered and opened everything to try it out; we were like elephants in a china shop: tough-looking, bearded warriors were opening small perfume bottles and dabbing the stuff on their uniforms. Others smothered their hair with oil. Face cream was rubbed over stubbly, leathery skin without doing much good.

Soon everybody was busy unpacking and trying out the fragrant merchandise. Spanish soldiers came in from time to time, through the hole in the wall, to fetch an armful of soap. We took a few things as well. There was much-needed shaving cream. I took a tin of lanoline and cleaned my boots which were as hard as stone. Another tin was used for cleaning my rifle. A piece of soap and a bottle of hair oil went into my pocket. Everybody was still busy with the beauty treatments. The shaggy, dirty, bearded company was beginning to smell very sweetly; a heavy scent of roses, carnations and violets hung over us. I am glad we did not have to go straight to the front because the fascists would have taken us for a troupe of ballet dancers.

Dumont called us into the courtyard and gave us a dressing down. We were to put back everything we had taken and we did so with much grumbling. I kept my soap. The factory was locked up and we had to stand in the drenching rain as a sort of punishment. I thought he was a bit too hard on us. The place would soon go up in smoke anyway and they should have taken the soap into Madrid and stowed it away properly. We had quite a time out in the yard. The oiled heads and creamy faces looked more comic than ever. The French, especially, were very good at clowning. They addressed each other in effeminate voices.

'*Quel parfum exquis, madame!*'

'*Oui, j'achète toujours chez Gal, vous savez, Gal de Madrid.*'

Some awful looking fellow with a big nose pretended to faint.

'*Ooh la la! Le parfum des roses, ça me tue, je ne pouvais jamais le résister.*'

They slapped each other and danced around and called each other naughty, naughty boys.

We left the factory. It rained on and off, and we took shelter in the ground floor and cellars of a house. The windows looked out on to a back yard but the buildings were so high there was hardly any light. The door leading to the yard was blocked by fallen débris. Most of the windows had no glass. On the first floor of the house opposite there was a kitchen; one could see a table still laid with plates, glasses and food, just as it had been left.

We came to a crossroads in a wood. On the right was a garden with open patches and a driveway. At the end of the drive was a school consisting of three buildings divided by courtyards, and a much bigger building like an aeroplane shed. The courtyards were unpaved and soggy with water. We were glad to get some shelter at last but we were hardly through the door when we had to line up again. We went back to the road and through the wood which was slippery from the wet pine needles. After a while we struck the main road.

It was open country. The road was riddled with shell holes and it looked familiar. The little trees had been planted not long ago. We had to look out not to fall into shell holes which were full of water and looked like large puddles. It was the road to the University City. It was not far away, only an hour or so. It was good to know that one would not have to stay out all night. We had our blankets draped over us; they were heavy with water and there was a streak of yellow light on the horizon reflected by the wet road and the puddles and furrows in the fields.

A despatch rider on a motorbike overtook us. He stopped at the head of the column. After a brief halt he went back the way he came. The rain came down in sheets but we did not care any more. We returned to the quarters we had just left. The rooms were bare. There was a hall full of newly made doors. We laid them on the stone floor and went to sleep. Our clothes and blankets dried during the night.

We had coffee in our room but the meals were served in the big hall. A few broken-down trucks stood around. I helped the cook to peel potatoes and dried my things at the fire. I swept the hall with John and Bernard, just to do something to keep warm. There was a sort of library next to our room with a few books and a lot of old magazines. I found some English ones dealing with the coronation of George V.

Somewhere near, batteries started firing and shook the windows so badly that we thought they would burst. Fascist artillery replied and we heard the explosions, but far away. When I looked out of the window into the courtyard I saw stretcher bearers carrying three Spanish workmen who had been out digging trenches. Two were mortally wounded. The third was crying out and holding his head. Doctors bandaged him in the yard and an ambulance came and took them away.

A few men sneaked out into the town that night. There was a Frenchman, a big-nosed, ratty-looking man, who had been a troublemaker ever since Albacete. He was drunk and did not get up in the morning. Without getting up he pissed on the floor in our room. It was his last bad deed. The French comrades pounced on him and dragged him to his feet. They were slapping him hard and sobering him up. There was a blackboard on the wall and they told him to write a hundred times, '*Je ne dois pas pisser en lit.*' He refused at first but a few more blows made him do what he was told. He was halfway through when Alfredo came in and stopped it. They locked him up and we did not see him any more.

# Chapter 7 — Ciudad Universitaria

It was some time after lunch. Most of us were lying down to rest, while others walked in the garden and wood near by. It was now sunny and quite warm. We were called together and told to pack up and take our guns ready to march. After we had packed, there were still rifles and a Lewis gun lying about. John and two others were missing and could not be found. We went away without them. There was no lorry this time; we had to carry the guns and ammunition and, as we were three men short, everyone was loaded like a mule.

It was a Sunday afternoon. There were only a few people about when we reached the outskirts of the town. Here and there a few old men or women were sitting on chairs in front of their doors. Most of the people would be in the centre of the town taking a *paseo* or sitting in a café. We had to rest every mile or so because of the heavy equipment. It was not very late but the light was already failing in a very clear sky when we came to the evacuated part of Madrid, Moncloa, near the Parque del Oeste. We passed along the avenue where we had stopped on our first arrival. The houses were mostly newly built, four or five storeys high, with broad and well paved streets. The stillness and desolation was strange if one thought that, not more than a mile away, was the Puerta del Sol and the Gran Vía, which would be crowded with people.

Shells and bombs had ruined a great many houses. On our right, looking down the streets which ran at right angles to ours, we saw huge barricades of cobblestones which closed off the town towards the university. We were back at the soap factory and halted. The huge doors to the courtyard were closed and barricaded, the entrance guarded by Spanish soldiers. Two civilians came wandering through the empty streets. One was an Englishman, the other American. Both were reporters in search of a story. The American took some film of us but I doubt if he got anything because it was too dark.

In front of us, at the end of the street, were trenches and barricades which we thought we were to take over, and rumours of a fascist attack on this sector were in the air. We left our rifles and things piled up and walked through the streets looking at the ruins. There was a great house with only the outer walls standing and the interior blown completely out like a piece of scenery for a film. Through the windows one could see into the empty space strewn with débris and blackened by fire. Other houses were cut in half with furniture hanging from the blackened ruins. There was half a ceiling with the lamp still hanging from it. On the upper floor of a house a corner of a room was still intact. One could see the flowered wallpaper, a chair on the floor of which about three feet remained. Two pictures of saints were still hanging undamaged on each side of the corner. On the second floor a bed, pressed between two collapsed ceilings, was ready to fall at any minute, the bedspread of red and white satin hanging from it like a flag. The steel shutters on the shop fronts were torn and bent. From time to time a patrol of Spanish soldiers walked through the streets to see that no one entered the houses.

It was dark now. At nine o'clock the food wagons had not come nor any message from the battalion as to where we were to go. We thought of camping in the soap factory again. The moon was up and an icy wind blew through the streets. Opposite the factory was some wooden fencing with a strip of sand where the pavement did not reach it. A broken wire from a telegraph pole threw little sparks of light. It looked like someone signalling. Then someone shouted for a rifle and pointed to the roof of a house near by. He had seen a light going on and off in one of the windows. Perhaps someone was making a signal to the fascists. We all went to the middle of the road and could see the light. Somebody took a rifle and shot at it. The light went out and did not reappear.

A detachment of soldiers came along the street. The officer in charge spoke Spanish then German and I asked him what he wanted. He was looking for his battalion. I told him to go to Fuencarral where they would be able to help him. He was a German commanding a Catalan company. They all looked very depressed and gloomy. They had come to Madrid about a week before and were already fed up. I asked them how things were in Cataluña. Everything was fine, they said. There was little fighting and better food. They had volunteered for Madrid.

'This is a hell of a place,' the German said. 'I've lost sixty men and this is the rest, look at them.'

He gave me a cigarette and I walked with him down the street.

'They want to go back,' he said. 'Every time I mention the front they start threatening me.'

'Why don't you join the Brigade?' I asked him. 'We have two German battalions.'

'No,' he said, 'it's no good. I'm the only one they listen to. If I leave them they'll go running back to Barcelona. I wish we'd had some experience like this. We came here thinking it would be like Aragón, where you take a pot shot here and there. I haven't seen a damned fascist since we came and I've already lost sixty men out of eight-five through shell fire.'

We stopped and I pointed out the way.

'Perhaps I'll see you again,' I said, and we shook hands.

'Yes,' he said, 'maybe. *Rot front. Salud.*'

I went back and sat down. My blanket did not give me any warmth. The cold seemed to come from everywhere. It rose from the ground, blew from the houses and descended from the sky. We sat there leaning against the fence with only our noses sticking out from the blankets like a flock of miserable birds. We tried to sleep. The moonlight fell into the street but we were in the shadow of the fence when we heard an aeroplane. It flew very low with the engine cut off. It was silent really save for a buzzing noise like a mosquito. It came from the direction of Madrid and we could see the light in the cockpit. It disappeared but came back again, this time still lower. We threw our cigarettes away and wondered whether it had seen us. We pressed nearer to the fence: the shadow was almost gone. The plane came back. We looked up.

'Maybe it's one of ours,' somebody said in the darkness. It was a cue which never failed yet. The actor jumped up on the stage with wailing and whistling. One – two – three bombs about two hundred yards away, the wooden fence bending in the blast.

We got up and waited for the next attack but the plane did not come back. The street was too unsafe in the bright light and we looked for better shelter. We tore away the already damaged shutters from a shop. The falling steel made a hideous noise. We went into a small office with a few chairs and a big writing desk. A door led to a long dark room at the back. The floors were strewn with broken glass which we brushed away as well as we could.

I joined someone else on the desk. There was not much room but it was warmer than lying on the floor. Nobody slept much. The cold was terrible. Men went in and out looking for a better place, or to warm themselves up by moving around. Every time they lifted the shutters the iron slammed back on the stonework and bits of glass crashed down.

I went out to relieve myself and found Joe and Mac lying outside in the street. They were not asleep. In their light blankets they looked like a pair of embalmed corpses. I told them there was room in the shop, but they said they did not like the idea of being buried if the plane should come back. I stamped up and down the street to make myself warm. It was freezing hard and, in the light of the moon, the street looked white as if covered with snow.

I looked at my watch. It was only two o'clock. When I went back inside my place on the table had been taken and I lay down on the floor. It was the coldest night I remember. Perhaps it was because we had not had any food. I was lying there thinking of a big fat bottle of brandy. It made me really warm just to think of it. Every breath I took was hurting me and I still felt the pain long after I was wounded.

At last morning came. We got up and walked about like a lot of cripples. When it was light enough we looked around the shop. The walls were full of pigeon-holes, the floor littered with books and business letters. Somebody must have made a quick departure. Every drawer was open and the contents had fallen out. I tried to read some of the letters. They were full of ornamental drawings which, at first, I could not make out. When I went into the back room I saw it was full of coffins standing on wooden trestles. The coffins were cast of lead, heavily ornamented. Samples of ornament and design were hanging from the ceiling. There were a few men still sleeping peacefully in some of the coffins which had wooden cases inside lined with black cloth. We looked at them with envy. They slept comfortably and even had a sort of cushion to rest their heads on.

A door led from the shop to a glass-covered courtyard and from there to another workshop which was where the carpenter made the wooden coffins. There were a lot of tools and we took a few good screwdrivers which would be useful for our guns, as we had nothing to repair them with.

We went back to the shop and found stairs leading to a cellar which was full of wood and shavings. About twenty Spanish soldiers, including two girls, were sleeping there while somebody made coffee and bread and butter was passed around. The lucky bastards had breakfast in bed. I tried to get a cup of coffee from them but they said they were short themselves. When I told them we had slept upstairs they laughed and said they would not have stayed among the coffins for anything in the world. We had a last look at one of the men sleeping with an arm round a pretty girl; those bastards certainly knew how to make themselves comfortable!

We went back to the street hoping for our coffee and bread to arrive but it did not come and there was no news from the battalion either. For the first time we thought that something must be wrong. Perhaps we had been mistaken and were expected at a different place. Nobody knew. I walked a long way towards the town and found a bakery that was open, where they sold me a few loaves of bread which I took back. I had a glass of *anís* in a wine shop as no café was open yet. It was a bright sunny morning, women and children were already standing in long queues at the various shops. On the way back I met the company runner. We had gone to the wrong place. We should have gone to the University to relieve a Spanish regiment. The runner was out of breath. He had been all over Madrid, he was swearing and cursing, but he seemed glad to have found us at last.

We walked back the way we had come the day before. We rested for a while in front of our old quarters where they tried to get us something to eat, but all the trucks had left. A fascist plane, which had followed us on our way, was still overhead. As it was only one it looked as if we were not going to have trouble. After we had entered a wood, a few guns of ours concealed somewhere behind us started firing. They were very near and at every shot I had the feeling that someone had slapped my face very hard. I was glad when we left them behind.

We came to the end of the wood. There was a steep embankment on which a road ran among a few damaged trees. We rested in the wood. It was no good trying to approach the university in daylight as all the roads and fields were under constant fire. We had hardly settled down when a shell exploded near by, bringing branches and leaves down on us. The plane was still circling overhead and was directing the fire. I do not know whether they wanted to get us or our batteries. Perhaps both. Our batteries did not answer after having fired a dozen shots, in order not to give themselves away.

Shells began to fall in quick succession. They went over us towards the battery positions and we went forward across the open field and rested on the embankment, which gave some protection. There was a small tunnel which led to the field beyond and a few Frenchmen crept in there. The legs and behind of the last man stuck out and we all laughed. The plane could see us now and the observer directed the fire forward. Three shells went into the other side of the embankment and one exploded right on top of the road. We were half lying, half leaning against a sloping wall with our hands around our heads for protection, like the Jews at the Wailing Wall in Jerusalem.

Pieces of shell and stone dug themselves into the earth. The next shells went back into the field and further towards the wood. The plane flew away. I was lying beside an old shell hole next to a few jagged pieces of shell about a foot long. They kept on firing for some hours but mostly into the wood and beyond it. They were also shelling our old quarters; we could hear the crashing of walls and breaking of windows.

I crept up the bank and had a look, crouching behind a tree trunk. The road was badly damaged. When I came down I saw John and Bernard arriving. I told them about the coffin factory and we laughed a lot. I was glad they were back again.

In the afternoon we were told that we should probably have to stay where we were for the night. The firing had stopped and we walked about the fields and through the wood where the sun was still lingering. There was a great number of young pine trees, still very green. The ground was covered with dry brown branches of older trees and we collected them, together with long grass, to make a bed for the night. We put thick layers on the ground and over that our blankets and over them another layer of grass. It was very cosy and warm.

After dark we heard the well-known sound of tins rattling together, coming through the wood. *La Soupe* had arrived. We got an extra big helping with a glass of wine, and iron rations for the next day and a packet of cigarettes. I had my food in bed and, after that, smoked and prepared for a long night's rest. My watch would not be on until five in the morning. I was just going to sleep when we were called to get up and pack. We left for the university.

We walked in single file along the bank and crossed it down to the fields below. There was an old mill and a little stream, the water making the only sound in the night, until we came to a bridge. The moon was out again but clouds blotted it out from time to time. We dispersed all over the fields and halted, waiting for the clouds and the dark.

There was the University Department of Philosophy and Letters, more battered and ruined than ever. The last field was just a mass of shell holes. We reached a small side entrance from which a few newly dug trenches led into the darkness. Soldiers were waiting to be relieved. We passed each other silently. It was very dark and we bumped into bricks and parts of beds, and glass was splintering under our boots.

We knew this place so well that we walked through the maze of corridors, with the sureness of sleep-walkers, until we came to a staircase. On the right was a little light coming from the main entrance which was constructed of glass. We went to the second floor and walked down a long passage with rows of rooms on both sides. The doors were blown out and parts of the rooms were shot away. At the end of the passage we came to a big room with three windows facing the building in which the fascists were still holding out. There were a few iron bedsteads but most of us slept on the floor. From underneath the window came the noise of digging. We were told not to show any light and not to fire as our German comrades were digging trenches underneath.

I took over the last watch at half past four in the morning. Leaning on the window sill, I looked out and after a while my eyes got accustomed to the dark. Under the window, in front of me, was a ravine and to the right of it a railway embankment. I could see the light pillars of the bridge further along. A faint glow of red showed beyond the darkness of the embankment where a village was still smouldering since the first attack on Madrid.

There was no sound on the hill in front of us. From time to time, from far away, came the sound of rifle fire and the bangs of hand grenades. When dawn came everything was blotted out by a mist which rose from the ground, leaving the hills in the distance showing their contours against the sky.

There was the sound of motor cars approaching. They slowed down and stopped somewhere at the back of the building. Then came the noise of cans being unloaded and men talking to each other inside the empty building.

'Alors, salut.'

'Bonne chance, eh?'

'Je te verai encore à six heures.'

Heavy footsteps came up the staircase and along the corridor towards our room.

'Voilà, le café.'

We received a cup of coffee and some bread. The lavatories had no water and we relieved ourselves in an unused room. One of the walls was completely knocked out by a direct hit. The door lay in the middle of the floor. Two big unexploded shells had buried themselves in the concrete floor among bricks, plaster and torn shutters.

Our room was not in a bad condition, although all the windows were shattered and the floor strewn with broken glass. One wall had a big hole where a shell had gone through, which lay unexploded on the floor. On the wall opposite the window, under the ceiling, were a lot of bullet holes. Before one of the windows the shutters had come down and hung suspended by only one thin piece of iron. We tried to knock it down but it would not come off. Before we could place our guns in position we had to dislodge great pieces of glass which still hung dangerously in the window frame.

We walked through the building in search of sand bags to barricade the windows but found only half a dozen and they were only half filled. There was no room which was not damaged. Those parts which had been used as a hospital were full of beds, some whole, others twisted, bent and overturned, and the thin mattresses were blackened by fire. We carried a dozen beds to our room.

On the fourth floor we found the library with the books thrown all over the place. We took down as many as we could carry. They were better than sand bags. We packed them tight against each other in double rows. The Maxim was put on the table in front of the first window with books on both sides to protect the men who were feeding the gun, while the gunner himself was safe behind the gun shield.

The two other windows were blocked half way to the ceiling leaving only a few holes for observation and shooting. The Lewis gun was placed on the floor, after we had knocked a hole under the third window, from where it commanded the field below. We took out all the ammunition belts and drums and cleaned and adjusted them to prevent any stoppages.

From the recreation room on the ground floor we brought up a few comfortable chairs so that the two men on watch could do it sitting in comfort. Stephens[31] brought two posters from the library. They were printed in English. One showed a cathedral, I think it was Segovia, the other a farmer ploughing his field and underneath it in big letters: 'Visit Sunny Spain'. We nailed them on the wall next to the door.

The days were bright and sunny. It was very cold in the evening and at night, but it was much warmer sleeping in there than outside. In the mornings the ground was white with frost but it soon melted in the sun. In the afternoon we often made a small fire, from the wood of drawers and tables, in a back room which had no windows.

*International Brigaders inside the Faculty of Philosophy & Letters,*
*with books from the library supporting the sandbags.*

The fascists were holding the Department of Medicine. One of its buildings was right in front of us but more than nine hundred yards away. We sometimes saw them running down the hill on the right of the building towards positions further back, and fired at them. We could see a few houses of the village to our right, which changed hands every few days. It must have been the fiercest battleground around Madrid. We lost our first eighty men there; many had died there since. The railway track, which was between us and the village, was the same one on which our armoured train disappeared, never to return.

The hills in the distance were covered with woods, the trees yellow and red with autumn. From the rooms on the left of the corridor we could see parts of Madrid with the buildings of the University in front. One of the buildings was burning. In the day one could only see black smoke but in the dark of the night it glowed and flamed inside.

The long, wide street along which we had marched to the University, after our arrival in Madrid, showed the scars of heavy shelling. Three men in dark blue uniforms lay dead and still in the roadway; it looked as if they were asleep, resting there with their faces on the earth and their arms around them for protection.

The room just above us on the third floor was used by the French and Belgian gunners. When I visited them I saw it was the same room which we had occupied the last time. There were still the comfortable settees, only the covers were dirty and faded and they showed signs of hard wear. The windows were closed with books and doors right up to the ceiling, which made the room dark and gloomy.

I went back to the library to find something to read. John and Bernard were there collecting some heavy reading. It must have reminded them of Cambridge. There were works on philosophy in German, French and Latin. I was not in the mood for Schopenhauer or Kant and found some English poets, Shelley and Keats, and John gave me some small volumes on Velázquez and Goya with illustrations which I was very glad to see. I also discovered some sheets of paper for sketching.

When we came back with the books, everyone else went to the library to find some reading matter for themselves, but I am afraid the classics were too difficult for most of us. Although the building had never seen any teaching – it was only just completed before the war broke out – I am glad to say there were many who did appreciate it. I wonder what those people who had planned, built and equipped the university before everything went up in flames would have thought if they could have seen the strange ensemble of students who were now busy reading the new, unused books. It was created for young people, and youth had come from everywhere, all over Europe, as had probably been planned, but they were not the ones the professors would have expected to see. There were no neat suits, shiny shoes and well brushed hair. Most of us had never studied, never heard of philosophy, modern or ancient. This was our first university. I believe the boys would have made good student material. They were hard-working, idealistic, eager to learn and to pass on knowledge to others. Yes, they were pupils that many a teacher or professor would have been glad to enlighten.

However, our task was a different and difficult one, just as our appearance was different. We wore baggy khaki trousers and jackets. We had dirty boots and dirty faces, we were unwashed and unkempt and not too well fed, we had rifles and machine guns at hand instead of pens and notepads. The books would only give us an hour or two of recreation and interest. There were not many we cared to read and the majority were barricading the windows to safeguard life against the dangers of the world. Even the dangers were different from those at other times; not the struggle to the right path of thinking, nor the cry for knowledge and wisdom to get through the dark and dangerous roads of thought.

This time the classics were, as often before, placed between man and man, but were not called upon to settle a dispute through the medium of their thinking. The contents did not matter. They were placed one on top of the other and their silent printed covers – whether friend or foe, modern or classic, whether they agreed or disagreed – had but one purpose. They were there to protect the lives of the men behind them from bullet and shell which were now used to settle the grimmest dispute between two ideas: socialism and fascism.

They protected us well, those wise old men with their long beards and busy pens. I am afraid we were not able to judge justly the different theories they expounded in so many books. Quantity came before quality. The small volumes were found to be too light. A prolific writer was preferred because he filled a large, heavy volume which did not crumple before a bullet.

Yes, it was a strange collection of pupils. There was Joe, sitting on the platform like a schoolmaster, wrestling with a book on old Roman coins. There was Stephens, having found a volume of his favourite poet, Shakespeare, which he read aloud and could recite from memory for hours on end. There were John and

Bernard and Mac, brushing up their knowledge of ancient and modern languages. There was old Jock with his bewildered face, who had got hold of old man Nietzsche which, even if it had been written in English, would have been a puzzle to him. And there was I looking through the art books and Goya's etchings of war, which were grimmer than any reality when one looked at them in a restful and peaceful mood. Then I read a long poem by an English writer whose name I have forgotten. It was about a wood and a burning village which reminded me of the wood at Aravaca and, for a moment, I saw Fred and all the others who died there.

In the evening we went down to the back of the building to see the food trucks arriving and usually got some news from Madrid and other fronts. They came at six in the morning and six at night, but today they were late. The fascists knew by now what time they brought our supplies, and started shooting every night at six, so the trucks came a little before or after that hour.

For the first time since La Roda we saw *Bou-Boule* again. He was now a *responsable* for *La Soupe* and rode in a very small car with the trucks. When the French spied their fat compatriot, whose bulky figure hung over the side of the Ford, they cried, '*Bou-Boule, hai, Bou-Boule, ça va bien?*' They accused him, jokingly, of eating the best of our food himself and measured him to see whether he had got fatter since they had seen him last. He smiled and could hardly speak. He was deeply moved by the enthusiastic welcome, but perhaps he was thinking also of the great number of his friends he did not see among us because they were dead.

We told him to bring drinking water the next morning. There was not a drop in the building and our cup of coffee and the two cups of wine we received were insufficient. We all had our evening meal together on the third floor at the back of the building where it was safe to light candles without being seen. Every night we went there, groping along the dark corridors and staircases. Sometimes stray bullets would come through the windows and the huge gaps in the walls. We left two men to watch while we had our dinner and then brought food back for them. Every night there was the same meal, either lentil or pea soup with a piece of bread and, sometimes, a little sweet such as *membrillo* (quince jelly). The food was not bad and, compared with what the civilians had in Madrid, it was very good indeed.

In the cellar was a large kitchen well equipped with electric stoves and ice-boxes, but it was badly damaged by two enormous bombs which had exploded outside the main entrance, leaving a huge crater more than twenty feet deep and wide. Peter, a fat, blond, red-faced Belgian who was looking after us all like a mother, found a small sack of rice and, as we had a bit of chocolate for our breakfast, he made us a sort of rice pudding which tasted very good, though it was a bit sticky.

I spent most of my time doing drawings of comrades and even made a picture of the landscape through the spy-hole. We were very thirsty but there was still no water so John and Bernard, armed with a dozen water bottles, went out to get some out of the little stream near the mill. It was not more than half a mile away, but in the daytime it was a dangerous undertaking. They came back after an hour, with water, but badly shaken. A plane had attacked them for a time, flying low and dropping hand grenades.

I went down to the kitchen to see whether anything had been left forgotten there. The Russian first aid man from Fuencarral had a nice room next to the kitchen, which was well furnished with a bed and armchairs. The only part which was damaged was the window below the ceiling. He only spoke Russian, a little Spanish and frightful French so our conversation was always fantastic and, I am sure, neither of us understood what the other said. He was talking about the German doctor who I had last seen at the soap factory. What he said about him I do not know but I could see it was not very friendly. When he mentioned the two nurses I asked him where they were.

'*Aquí*,' he said. '*Aquí*,' and he pointed out of the window.

'Are they here?'

'No, no,' he said. "*Le docteur* . . ." and then a burst of Russian curses followed.

I pointed to the window and said, "There?"

'*Sí, sí*,' he said, and we left it at that.

I told him we were hungry, '*Mucha hambre*.' He replied with something unintelligible and showed me his watch, pointed out three o'clock and said, 'You come back – sausage, *wurst*.' He always seemed to have food because he received extra rations in case of any wounded being brought in. In the afternoons he usually gave it away before it went bad, and received fresh supplies in the evening.

On the floor stood a big flask of wine. He gave me a glass but did not drink himself. 'No good,' he said. '*Red wine makes thirsty.*' My water bottle hung still half full on my belt and I offered it to him. He pointed at me saying, 'You *vino*. Me *agua*.'

'It's a bargain,' I said and gave him the water and he filled my bottle with wine instead.

I did not find anything in the kitchen except a plate heaped with coffee grounds. I took it with me much to the disgust of Ivanovitch, or whatever his name was, but he gave me a few pieces of sugar as a present. I took a pot along and went upstairs and collected some water from everyone. The pot was half full and I took it down to the other side of the corridor and made a fire. The wall and the window on that side had blown out. It was a beautiful, cold winter day with no clouds in the sky. There was the windmill shining very white in the brown, sunlit fields. The Guadarrama mountains were white with snow. In the clear atmosphere they seemed very close. Ice lay in the shade of the ruts and shell holes where the sun did not reach. We sat around the fire and warmed ourselves. When the water boiled I threw the coffee grounds in and boiled them well. Alas, it did not taste much of coffee but it was hot and the sugar gave it some flavour.

In the afternoon I got a big plate of beans and sausages from Ivanovitch, which I divided among us.

That night our dinner was cut short by the noise of heavy firing. The candles were extinguished and we ran as fast as we could back to our room. We thought the fascists were storming our building. The din and noise in the room was terrific. Both guns were blazing away and we shot with our rifles as well. It was a very dark night. We could not see anything but the flashes of firing on our right. I fired about ten rounds. After a while we stopped while the French, above and below, were firing for all they were worth. We sent somebody up to tell them to stop. The firing outside, on our right, continued. There was no attack on us and we later found out that the Edgar André battalion had been storming the village. The fascists opposite us had supported their men and somebody mistook their firing for an attack. Fortunately the Germans were well protected by the railway embankment, otherwise we would have fired at them because we had no information that an attack was planned.

When everything was quiet again it was my turn to watch. Very-lights went up around the village. The fascists were still shooting at our building and I found new bullet holes in the window embrasure. Explosive bullets struck the books next to me. From the far hills I saw signals which were taken up and answered from other points miles away. They were probably asking what was going on but I could not see whether the fascists in the back of the building opposite us replied. I wished I could have read those signals. There was a very bright light, like an angry voice, and when it spoke all the others disappeared and listened respectfully, and after it had spoken the small ones came out again and started chattering excitedly in all directions. After an hour everything was dark and quiet and once again one could hear the men, who had been surprised by the shooting, digging below. I woke the next man and went to sleep.

In the morning, after breakfast, we were issued with shovels and picks and went out to dig trenches. There was a short trench leading from the side entrance to the field which was in front of the fascist lines. It was deep enough to walk along upright but it stopped short at a road. Dynamiters were busy digging a tunnel under it. They had only just begun so we had to run across the road, one by one, into the continuation of the trench. It had been begun in the night and was only a few feet deep. The ground was very hard from the frost and it was heavy work. We soon had to take off our jackets. One could only dig by bending very low. We had never done this work before and often threw the sand too high which brought a hail of machine gun bullets over the spot and into the parapet. As we dug deeper the earth became very soft and very dry and would often collapse. Then we had to start all over again.

We paused around midday. Going back to the building was made more difficult by a watchful fascist gunner who had trained his gun on the road. Every time one of us crossed a burst of bullets swept along the road and, every time, just a few seconds too late. When my turn came I sprinted over the road and dropped into the trench but, in the meantime, the miners had deepened it to more than eight feet and I fell headlong with my spade and helmet clattering after me. An anxious stretcher bearer who was watching me came running up because he thought I was hit. We did not go back in the afternoon because it was decided to leave the trench until the tunnel beneath the road was completed.

At about three o'clock we heard a great number of planes in the air but could not see them. Heavy bombs were dropped somewhere between us and Madrid, and at every explosion our building rocked and swayed as if in an earthquake. There was artillery and anti-aircraft fire as well, and I went down to see what was going on. I saw the planes coming back followed by our chasers. I went into the kitchen and had a glass of wine with the Russian and he gave me a plate of beans which I took away with me.

Halfway up the stairs I heard a terrific noise approaching. It sounded like an enormous object travelling through the air at great speed making a sharp and swishing noise. I did not hear the explosion. It was quiet for a moment and then someone yelled, '*Brancardier, brancardier!*' The Russian came up the stairs followed by stretcher bearers and I heard men running along the corridor above.

When I reached the floor I could not see our room for heavy clouds of dust and smoke which drifted towards me. Then I saw John, Joe and Stephens being led along. They had an odd look of surprise on their faces; Joe was holding his nose and John's head was bleeding badly on the right side. Stephens had a deep wound just above the elbow. I made my way to the room through a crowd of Frenchmen who had collected there; some of the very young ones were crying. We told them to go away, got some brooms and swept the bricks, plaster and glass from the floor.

When the dust had settled I saw that a shell had gone through the left wall tearing a big hole right above a bed where somebody had slept. It had fallen onto the middle of the floor under Mac's chair and exploded. Mac was unhurt. The shrapnel balls had pitted the walls with holes. Most of them were on the blackboard behind where Joe had sat and he was very lucky to have escaped with a broken nose. I found pieces of the shell on the beds and also the cap which I put in my pocket.

When we had finished cleaning up the débris the room looked neat and tidy once again. A German artillery officer, with two observers, came rushing in. The officer, a man of about forty-five with a dark beard looking very much like El Campesino, seemed very distressed and upset. I went up to him and said I was German.

'I hope no one's been killed,' he said. I told him we had three wounded and he seemed relieved. He gave me a packet of American cigarettes, which I handed round, and told me he had seen the shell strike the building. It was one of our shrapnel bombs, fired against aeroplanes. He kept on saying he was sorry and it was not the fault of the gunners.

'We have a lot of old ammunition and the timing is very bad. The one which hit you came down, exploded outside your room and struck the wall.'

I translated what he said. We had all wondered why the shell came from a direction where there were no fascists. The officer looked at our beds and asked whether we slept here.

'You're very foolish,' he said. 'You should sleep somewhere else, in a back room, and leave a few men on the gun to watch. If they shell again you'll be through.'

I said I would talk it over with my comrades. The observers had placed their periscope on the table by the first window after taking down the Maxim. Another German came in with a telephone to which a wire was attached.

'What are you going to do?' I asked.

'We're going to give them hell now,' the officer said. 'You watch. Place a few men on the Lewis gun and shoot them when they come out.'

Mac took the gun and we watched. The officer reached for the phone and spoke in German.

'Can you hear me? This is Otto speaking. Fire a few rounds but stay at the phone.'

We heard the report of guns. Three shells went into the hill opposite but did not reach the building.

'Another twenty to fifty metres. Try one round only.'

A cloud of smoke rose from the second floor opposite.

'That's fine,' the officer said. 'Keep on shooting.'

For more than half an hour shell after shell struck the building. They let me look through the periscope and I saw the walls crumbling but our guns were not big enough to damage the structure. The walls of all the university buildings were very thin but the structure was made of steel and the floors were strengthened with steel mesh, which accounted for the extreme resistance to severe damage. After months and even years of bombardment the structure still remained, though nothing else was left, and men were still living and fighting in the ground floors and cellars of the skeletons.

The officer now directed the shelling towards the village on our right. I told him we thought it was in our hands.

'We stormed it last night,' he said, 'but we had to give it up this morning. I'm looking forward to the day when the Brigade has its own artillery. We have quite a number of German and French gunners but we're not getting any guns. This morning they should have been in position at seven o'clock to support the men in the village, but they rolled up at three o'clock in the afternoon and the position was lost.'

'Why don't you get the guns?'

'Hell knows. They're holding them back in Cataluña. That's what we're told, but I don't believe it. Everything is made difficult and I don't know who's responsible. I think it's Miaja but you can't say it aloud. They're afraid the Brigade is getting too influential. They don't like the Fifth Regiment because it's communist. As if it mattered, as long as we beat the fascists. We're doing all the dirty work with frightful losses. We're entitled to get all the guns we need. Those generals make me sick. Kleber was sent away because he was an able commander and didn't like to be pushed around. One day you'll hear that Miaja has won or lost the war – and you have to blame the people who made him great with their propaganda. Well, we have to do our duty.'

He spoke into the telephone again. 'Fire another dozen rounds, and then stop. It's getting too dark. Yes, I'm coming back now.'

I walked with him down to the entrance.

'How many men have you lost?' he asked.

'There are nine of us in our section,' I said, 'We had twenty-one English, but I think the three men who were wounded today will come back soon. Our battalion has lost about one hundred and fifty.'

He shook his head angrily. 'I was in the Great War for four years. The losses were about twenty-five per cent, which we thought was a lot, but this is slaughter in comparison. There's no battalion which hasn't lost at least fifty to eighty men out of a hundred. Not only the Brigade but the Spaniards as well. There's something very wrong here. I don't know what it is, but maybe we'll find out.'

We left the entrance. It was dark now, and I walked behind him along the trench.

'There was Verdun,' he continued, 'but I never had this feeling of being doomed. I'm afraid I'm getting very sentimental, but you shake hands with comrades in the morning and they're dead before the evening, just because a few bloody Spaniards can't get up in the morning. There's no war without sacrifice, but it should not become a waste.'

We came to the tunnel and I said goodbye to him. He gave me his last packet of cigarettes.

'I hope I'll see you again,' I said.

We shook hands.

'I hate saying goodbye now,' he said. 'Give my greetings to the three wounded comrades when they get back, and tell them it wasn't our fault. Keep well yourself and remember what I told you about the room. *Salud.*'

I watched him disappearing into the tunnel and turned back.

The wounded had been taken to Madrid in the returning food truck. That night we got an extra ration of food or sweet, I forget which. It was the French way of showing their sympathy for us in our misfortunes. They liked us and the English section in the French battalion had a very good name.

The next morning we went digging trenches again; this time at a different place, in front of the fascists, and on the same field where we had our first experience of warfare. Only a few hundred yards was exposed to enemy fire, from the building down to the field, and we had to run along that stretch. In the field itself, which was screened by steep embankments against the fascists, we were safe. We could work standing upright.

It was another beautiful day. A great number of planes flew over us, but very high and when they came we lay quiet at the bottom of the trench. Towards midday we watched a fight high up in the air. A great number of bombers, who had just returned from Madrid, were intercepted by half a dozen small silvery-white fighting planes which we had never seen before. Though this time nobody said, 'Those are ours,' they really were ours. When they came lower we could see their wing tips were painted a bright red. We heard the machine guns firing. They were cheering the bombers in all directions. The arrival of Government planes, faster and better than any the fascists had, cheered us enormously. We had grown a bit sceptical of all the stories about Russian planes which were supposed to have arrived, but at last here they were. When we went back we told everybody about it as the planes could not be observed from inside the building.

In the evening John and Joe returned. Stephens had been detained in hospital as his wound was more serious. We were glad to see them back. Joe had a plaster across his nose which looked comic and not half as romantic as John, who wore a thin bandage around his forehead. Joe kept on fiddling with his nose, often looking into a small mirror, but we told him it would be all right and, even if it came out a bit crooked, it would only improve his looks. They wanted to take part in the watch that night but we did not allow it. All the French shook hands with them when we went up to dinner.

We stayed another three days. We slept that night in the back room but went back to our old quarters because, one morning, three shells of ours fell short and exploded just underneath the new room. We left the university the next night. We marched for four hours but without our guns, which went by lorry.

We slept for a few hours in a country house somewhere in the Casa de Campo. It probably belonged to a university professor. Every room had been made into a laboratory full of a thousand glasses, tins, test tubes and retorts.

# Chapter 8 — Madrid

Trucks were waiting the next morning, somewhere near the Puente de los Franceses, and took us to Fuencarral, but this time to another new quarter. It was nearer to the Guadarrama mountains; they did not look so high and impressive. We drove through an iron gateway which led to a cluster of large buildings, very much like a small town, with well paved streets, large halls, a chapel and gardens. It had been an orphanage and home for old people, belonging to the municipality of Madrid. Our company camped in a large, empty hall. There were no beds so we asked for straw, which came in the afternoon. It was not enough and most of us had to sleep on the bare floor.

I rested most of the day as my back was hurting me. Leave was only to be had by special permission but in the afternoon everybody was allowed out. This time the Brigade provided trucks to take us into town and back. Madrid had changed since we saw it last. The approaching streets were closed with tall barricades of stone and heavily guarded. More houses had been destroyed. Nearly all the windows in the shops were filled with sand bags. Tetuán, the working-class quarter, had suffered most. Though a great number of people had been evacuated, a constant stream of refugees from outside the town brought new people. One saw them here and there, walking through the streets with their belongings, sometimes with wagons drawn by a tired, faithful donkey. The metro stations were crowded more than ever because of the constant air raids.

It was a very cold and chilly December afternoon. A damp fog hung over the tormented city as if to hide it from the world. It was better than a clear day, though. Aeroplanes would not come over on such a day as this. The people looked miserable and cold. They were hurrying along the streets or sitting in cafés where some thin tea could be had. There was no coal, no fuel, no bread, no soap. As in Paris, in February 1793, women were searching for *du pain et du savon* but searching only and not screaming as they had done back then. In long, black, silent queues they

179

waited in the wind-swept streets for a few beans or a little milk. They had no warm coats but only shawls to wrap themselves in. It was only five months since the outbreak of the war and they would go on standing there for another twenty-seven months, hungrier and colder, uncomplaining, unafraid, with unshakeable faith. Madrid, a heroic and invincible city. Resist, resist. Let this town be the tomb of fascists! It did not need those words on the posters. They knew why they suffered and for what cause. It made me glad to see all this, and very miserable at the same time. I hoped it would not be in vain. It was not possible to think that after all this we should not win.

*Approach to the Plaza Mayor, Madrid, with banner (anon.)*

There were more soldiers to be seen. Most of the men wore uniforms. Also, for the first time, I saw a lot of stripes and brass hats. I did not know we had so many captains. On a corner of the Gran Vía an old man sold caps, badges and stripes. I stood for a while in an old, quiet square not far from the main streets. There were some trees left and a few benches that had not been taken away for firewood, but it was too cold to sit down. I bought a paper and went to a café. I had a coffee which was made of roasted grain. There were about a dozen elegant-looking girls sitting with officers.

A few shells landed somewhere, shaking the great window but nobody took any notice. I wanted to go into a cinema but I had seen the film so I went back to Fuencarral in time for dinner.

The next day was a Sunday. In the afternoon I went back to Madrid. The streets were strangely empty. I found an elegant bar and settled down to drink. It was early yet and hardly anybody was there and I read newspapers. By the time I had read them all it was getting late, every chair was taken and the bar was crowded. A few airmen at the bar were having a good time. I thought of talking to them but they looked too elegant in their high boots and fur coats. I still wore my old trench-coat and the blue skiing pants with a great hole in the knee. I was sure they would think I wanted to sponge on them. They were very boisterous and loud. A few whores had collected round them. They were giving acounts, very favourable to themselves, of air battles they had fought. They did not say exactly 'I brought one down' but they had riddled the enemy with bullets and he was sure to have crashed later on. They were snobbish and sentimental like all airmen, who think that without them nothing would go right. They were always in danger.

'Tomorrow I have to go up,' one said. 'Perhaps it's my last day. Have another drink chaps.'

If an infantryman should drink to every time he was likely to die he would never be sober. Those loud mouths were no good, I could see that. They received a huge salary. I do not think money makes a good soldier. They were badly needed, but only with great discipline would they do any good. As it was, they were flattered, spoiled and could practically do what they liked. The Russian airmen were good but, of course, they did not fight their battles in bars.[32]

'It was like this, boys. I came up just under the tail and rat-a-tat-tat went the gun.'

'Yes, bullshit,' I thought. 'Let's get out of here.'

I walked to the station to go back to the barracks. The trucks would be waiting at nine-thirty but I did not want to wait so long.

Just before reaching the station I could hear aeroplanes and from all sides people ran down the stairs for shelter. I was caught halfway down and could not move. I stood next to a girl. She was smiling up at the sky and said, '*Aviones.*'

'They've gone,' I said. 'I can't hear them any more.' It was impossible to get down to the platform and I asked the girl where she wanted to go. She was not going anywhere and had come down only for shelter. I invited her for a drink and we went into a café. She was a nice-looking girl. Since I joined the army I had never thought of girls. Later we went back to Cuatro Caminos where the trucks were waiting. It was after nine-thirty. The truck was full and the driver shouted at me, '*Vous venez avec nous?*' I said, '*Non*' and turned away.

I took the girl to a hotel. The concierge was a bit sour when he saw we had no luggage. I had to fill up a large form. I had hoped to have a hot bath but there was only cold water and no heating. The bed was comfortable. I did not enjoy the girl and later I could not sleep. I felt I had done something wrong. I do not mean sleeping with the girl but I had not turned up at the barracks. Never before had I broken discipline and I kept on thinking that I would not find my battalion the next morning. Towards the morning the rifle fire, which could be heard all night, seemed to increase. There were explosions of hand grenades and trench mortars. I kept on imagining my battalion was in action; I would be reported as missing. I was glad when morning came.

It was very cold with fog and rain when we left the hotel. We had some tea at a nearby café and I wondered how I was to get back to Fuencarral when a few Frenchmen came in who I recognised as belonging to XI Brigade. They had a truck outside and they said they would give me a lift. I sat on the back of the truck, holding on to a chain. I had said goodbye to the girl. She stood on the pavement until we left. I was very depressed. Maybe it was the awful cold or the miserable looking people who had waited all through the night for the shops to open.

I felt better when we reached the barracks. The sentries did not challenge us. It was like coming home. John saw me coming in. He told me he had answered for me at roll call. They had changed the gun crews again and I was on his gun. He said he hoped I had had a good time.

That morning we were taken out for a march along the road to Guadalajara, without rifles or packs. For a while we practised advancing over a stretch of hilly fields. It was very clear over the mountains but towards Madrid a thick mist was lying over the countryside. It was so cold that our breath froze in the air. We marched back at about midday. Young Spanish militiamen were drilling in the fields to left and right. Peasants and workmen with picks and shovels were working on fortifications. The finished trenches were full of water. They stretched for miles through the fields, parallel with the mountain range.

In the afternoon there was leave again. I did not feel well. I had pains in my back every time I drew breath so I went to the hospital. It was in a building which consisted of just one hall. Part of it was the dispensary and the rest was filled with camp beds. A number of soldiers were examined by the German doctor, vague and befuddled as ever. A bearded French doctor was there too and the Russian Ivanovitch.

'What's the matter with you?' asked the German doctor. I explained and he told me to take my coat and shirt off. He listened to my chest, went away and forgot about me as he was having an argument with Ivanovitch. The French doctor attended to me and, after listening and tapping my chest, he said I had a slight congestion of the left lung. He told me to go to bed; I would get some medicine later on. Most beds were occupied; there was only a sort of barred, child's cot. I lay down on it. I had to draw my legs up otherwise they would have hung over the end. I had brought a few Spanish papers which I read.

I slept and woke up later in the afternoon. The doctor had gone and all the patients had left, having got suddenly well by some miracle, and Ivanovitch was playing cards with two stretcher bearers. I asked him about my medicine but he said I had to wait until the evening. When the doctor came back the stretcher bearers brought in a woman followed by a lot of relatives. She had been injured about the legs in a car crash. She was bandaged up and taken to Madrid. At nine o'clock I was given two aspirins. I changed to a more comfortable bed but I could not sleep.

The next morning, after breakfast, I got up and put my clothes on. On the way out I met John coming in. His head was hurting him and he looked very ill. He was bandaged again and went to bed. I left him my newspapers. The doctor said I should stay but I told him to go chase himself. I went back to our room and took half a dozen aspirins, swallowed them with some hot water which I borrowed from the kitchen. I slept for more than twelve hours and when I woke up I felt better.

# Chapter 9 — Boadilla

It was a cold, grey afternoon and it was beginning to rain when we lined up. Everybody was grumpy and bad-tempered because we were supposed to go to Madrid on leave for the afternoon. We were already climbing on the trucks when the alarm came through. One truck had already left and they had to chase it halfway to Madrid with a motorbike, and caught up with it just as the boys were sighting the first pub. We had to wait a long time. The ground was too wet to sit down so we huddled together or stamped about. I had picked up an English newspaper earlier and we were all trying to read it before it melted away and the light failed. Finally the trucks arrived and we deposited our Maxim in the ammunition wagon and crowded into an empty lorry. It had no cover. It was raining hard now and we could not sit or stand or lie down; the rifles were in everyone's way and it was just too bad.

It must have been nine or ten at night before we arrived. We had to skirt around the whole of Madrid. The roads were in an awful condition and there were tanks and broken down cars in our way. From time to time we had to put on our headlights to see where we were going and also to show the enemy we were coming. When the lights were on we could see fantastic shapes moving about the fields. They were Spanish soldiers draped in their blankets. One could only see their eyes; with their rifles sticking out at strange angles under their cloaks and their half-covered helmets, they looked like monstrous scarecrows. In the darkness only a searchlight or a Very-light showed the skyline.

During the whole morning we were waiting about in the village. Nobody knew where we were to go and it was still raining. Finally our machine gun section came to rest behind a brick wall while a French sergeant tried to find a place where we could settle down. On our left, just where the wall ended and gave no more protection from the bullets, was a hill, and on that hill was an old farm. Every time the little Frenchman went up and down the hill a spray of machine gun bullets followed hard on his heels. We watched him crawling up and sliding down with cold curiosity, and nobody said, 'Why the hell doesn't he go around that damn place?' Eventually we all did just that, and after staying a few minutes in a small shed where we found a lonely Spanish soldier who was not very friendly when I addressed him, we settled down in the stable of the old farm, which commanded a good view of the hill opposite. The view was, of course, only good from a gunner's point of view, otherwise it looked brown and dismal like Hampstead Heath in December. The stable was open on one side but it had a courtyard with four walls around it. Against one of the walls was a big straw pile nearly reaching the top, on which, with the help of some bricks, we placed our Maxim. As we had a bit of roof and wall facing the enemy we could build a fire behind it, with wood which was lying around, without giving ourselves away. We dried our blankets and ourselves and collected a pile of straw for each man to lie on. We had nothing more to do except our two hour watch each.

From time to time a loud bang and a swish showed that our armoured cars were doing a bit of work, but the enemy only replied with rifle and machine gun fire. I had a *New York Times* which I read twice over, including the advertisements, and with the warm fire, all things considered, it was a beautiful day.

When it grew dark we had to keep the fire very low. At about seven o'clock the food appeared and was given out in our place because it was safe to have a light over the soup pot. *La Soupe* was distributed with a piece of bread and the iron rations for the next day. After that it was my turn to take the gun. I always liked to take the first or second watch because then one was not disturbed during the night. As I had just eaten I felt warm and snug. I peered out into the dark and could not see a thing. I would not have been surprised if a Moor had suddenly put his finger on my nose, it was so black. After two hours of straining my eyes and listening to the snoring of my comrades I woke the next man and went to sleep.

* * * * *

The next day the barrage started in earnest; it was intense. There was hardly any time between the dull report and the explosions. The shells came over, whistling and shrieking, and the barrage crept past us towards the village. A few hundred yards before the first house we made a last stand in a shallow lane but machine gun fire, now well directed from the top of the hill opposite, showed the enemy had a good target. A bullet passed very near me and Joe, next to me, fell back into the ditch holding his head but, luckily, the bullet had only grazed his cheek. We had to retreat further towards the village and, with our guns and heavy ammunition cases, it was slow and difficult as one had to keep one's head down all the way. We saw our last armoured car disappear after firing a couple of low, badly placed shells, and we saw two French comrades running like the devil to get under cover when about three big shells exploded near them, but when the smoke lifted both got up again and disappeared. As we had to go the same way we had to be quick about it because the barrage was now moving to the church and the houses which we had to pass.

We had just left that part of the village behind when half a dozen shells went tearing up the street, sending a shower of dirt and stones over us. The rest of the battalion stood behind a newly built and solid-looking schoolhouse in which the wounded were being cared for. The road here was a dead end and two lorries partly filled with ammunition, spare rifles and stretchers blocked it and could not get out. We crossed the road, labouring up a steep crest towards the wood and creeping along, one by one, in the shelter of a brick wall. We were still under fire but rested nevertheless as nobody knew exactly where to turn, and we were wating for some command. There was a great deal of confusion and, to make things worse, about twenty-five aeroplanes appeared in the sky and hurried us on towards the shelter of the wood. They flew in great leisurely circles above us without bombing, as the wood was already under heavy shrapnel fire.

Bernard, who was in front of me, suddenly uttered a fearful shriek and fell, clutching his throat. His face became a frightful white colour and we thought he was dying as the bullet had struck just underneath his throat and had come out of his back but, after he was bandaged, he could stand up and someone helped him along.

Captain Dumont appeared, unruffled and fearless as usual, with his blue cap, his neat uniform and his little stick. A Polish officer came running up in great excitement brandishing a revolver and trying to get some help from our battalion as the Spaniards on his left flank were in full flight. However, Dumont ordered us further back and we staggered around the wood, weary and utterly worn out, while fragments of shrapnel cut the leaves and branches.

It was in a small, open clearing that I was struck. I felt a fearful blow on my right leg and I must have roared with pain as my leg shot into the air and I thought it had been torn off, though I was clutching it with my hands and it was shaking as if jerked by strings. I was lying on my back though I did not remember having fallen, and I was conscious. John and someone else were bending over me and the other man was cutting my trouser leg open and tying a string round my leg to stop the bleeding and bandaging the wound. They were trying to help me but I could not move. They were urging me on but I did not care and I asked them to leave me behind. I remember their kind and tired faces, the branches of trees, a bit of sky with a shrapnel cloud in it, soldiers passing us and that ratty little Frenchman whom John burdened with his Lewis gun (he threw it away later) so as to be free to help me along.

It was peaceful and quiet all of a sudden, and I smiled. I had just had a long sleep and the earth was cool. I could see a green, dark jungle with enormous grasses and leaves like trees. I wanted to wake very slowly and rest a bit and then it would be light enough to walk on. But I could not, at the moment, remember where I was or where I was going. I opened my eyes and still the dark green was close around me and I heard a voice very far away saying, 'Come on, wake up, pull yourself together, we must be going,' and another voice saying, 'We can't leave him here.' My head was gently moved around and the wood shrank to little patches of grass in which I had lain my face on the earth. I woke up and the pain came back.

I drank nearly all of Mac's wine as my bottle was empty but I could not quench my thirst. It was strange how every wounded man asked at once for a drink. It must have been caused by the loss of blood. My leg was bent but, strangely, my foot was hurting more than the actual wound, which was well above the knee. John and Mac were helping me up and, with my arms round their necks, I hopped along, but the pain was unbearable when I stood up. I was too weak to hold on to them and I could not use my leg at all so it trailed behind me, paralysed. They had to put me down again and were dragging me along the ground. I helped as best I could with my hands and left leg.

The wood was full of banks and deep ditches which gave us good protection from bullets but it was exhausting crawling over them and I had to rest a lot. John and Mac were panting and sweating heavily. I remember a lot of soldiers passing us and, although they saw us, nobody offered any help. They did not seem to be in any hurry. Their faces looked pale under the dark trees; they looked blank and expressionless and strangely pre-occupied.

When we came to a clearing from which one could see the road our political commissar, a stockily built, fine-looking Frenchman who everybody liked, carried me on his shoulder for some time until Jock Clark and someone else carried me on their rifles down to the road. I was still bleeding a lot and I again asked them to put me down because the rifles, on which I sat, were rubbing on my wound.

Suddenly I saw a tank looming over me and the gunner, looking out of his turret, shouted to my comrades to put me on the front between the caterpillar wheels. A blanket was pushed under my head and Jock was sitting in front of me to prevent me slipping down. We rolled along the road with the gun still blazing away above me. I could see a few shrapnel clouds over the wood on my right but they seemed far away. We came upon a lorry which had just brought food and drink for the battalion. They were going back, taking the wounded with them; I could not help thinking of those unfortunate men left in the schoolhouse; nobody could save them now.

Stretcher bearers were helping me off the tank after having opened my coat and trousers to see whether I had a stomach wound and taking my ammunition from me and my revolver, which I did not want to let go. I asked for more drink and filled myself from a huge flask of wine which tasted sour and metallic. I was placed on the open truck with two other wounded men. I saw Burke running along and he smiled, with his ever-dirty face and his blond hair blowing in the wind. He waved to me and shouted, 'Bonne chance' and 'I'll see you soon.'

I shall never see him again. I always knew he would not live through this. There were some men who seemed doomed right from the beginning, one could see it in their faces, I do not know why or how, one just felt it. They did not go around with gloomy faces, on the contrary, they were the most cheerful and brave men, laughing and joking most of the time and with no thought of death. Poor Burke, with his dirty face and his dirty uniform, his big head and his blond hair sticking out in all directions under his *petit*-sized helmet. He was always in the way with his rifle slung carelessly over his shoulder hitting everybody when he turned or treading on one's foot when he marched behind and dropping things about. He was twenty-one years old. He wanted to be an actor and now he was playing the part of a hero on a stage greater than any he could ever have wished for and he played it well. He was a success and he died nobly for a noble cause, but the curtain will not rise for there is none, and he will not get up any more to take his bow and he will hear no applause, for he is really dead.

The truck went bumping and swaying on its way but we had to stop again after a while and two stretchers with badly wounded Poles were placed over the side, so that they hung free, resting only on the stretcher handles. Blood was dripping on to me but I could not move away. Next to me crouched a man with his head over the side of the truck. He had been shot in the face. Congealed blood hung from his mouth like a cloth swaying with the movement of the truck and he was spitting all the time to keep himself from choking, but this frightful red flag waving from his mouth never grew smaller. He looked at me and I knew he wanted to say something and I shall never forget the look in those eyes.

I did not want to look at the stretchers above me so I tried to sit up and look over the side of the truck. The wood had disappeared and we went through flat country with brown and grey fields. I saw Spanish soldiers, singly and in groups, going back, although the front was already miles away. Officers with revolvers in their hands were trying to turn them back but only succeeded in taking their rifles away because once an anarchist runs there is no stopping him. Some even tried to get on our truck but when they saw us they jumped off again. They probably had to walk all the way to Madrid where they could still buy enough drink to get their courage up again.

We came to Las Rozas and peasants were loading their possessions on carts and donkeys. The look of horror was still on every face as the village had just been heavily bombed and we could see the huge black craters in the fields round about.

The first aid station was housed in a large barn and when I was brought in I saw Bernard sitting at the door smiling at me. His neck was now heavily bandaged. We said hello and then a Spanish doctor was busy with my leg. I gave him an American cigarette which pleased him very much and he said that my leg was fine ('*Nada, hombre, nada*') and he said I would be walking around again in no time. He left for a while to attend to other men who were lying about on the floor on dirty, bloodstained mattresses. Presently he came back to tell me that a car was going to Madrid with an officer of the Brigade and, if I thought I could sit up for a while, I could leave in that. I agreed, because I did not want to take up a berth in an ambulance, and I was helped in next to the driver. Behind me sat Bernard with the man who was shot through the face still bleeding, as he could not be bandaged, and after every bump in the road they grunted and groaned. My leg was not bad but I felt ice cold and my hands could hardly hold a cigarette.

Near Fuencarral we were brought into another first aid station and we all got anti-tetanus injections and then went on to Madrid. It was getting dark rapidly and the driver could not find the way and the passers-by we hailed all pointed in different directions, of course. We went through the black, uninhabited suburbs of Madrid where most of the houses were half-destroyed and we saw clouds of smoke over Tetuán, where a street had just been razed to the ground by bombing planes. There was no light anywhere as we tried to find our way along the black and silent streets. We had to turn back several times when we came upon barricades. Twice we reached a hospital. When we presented our papers we found we were at the wrong place and I was carried in and out again. Finally a militiaman came with us, standing on the running board, to show us the way.

I was dead tired by now, my leg was stiff, and I was taken out of the car with difficulty. I was put on a stretcher and we entered the Palace Hotel through a side door.[33] The huge ballroom on the ground floor had been turned into an operating theatre. It was well lit and men and women stood silently at the door, anxiously watching the surgeons operating on and bandaging several people who had been hit in the last raid. My bandage was removed and my wound was cleaned with little pieces of gauze.

*The Palace Hotel, Madrid*

We both smoked a cigarette and I saw for the first time the two holes in my leg where the bullet had passed through. My foot was still hurting so I asked the man to take off my boot, which he did, but he could not find anything wrong. I gave my name, age, Brigade and Battalion numbers, all of which was noted down on a card and then I was taken up in a lift to the third floor. I was brought into room 360. It was a typical hotel room with two beds with white linen and yellow covers. There were two electric lamps on bedside tables and a big polished wardrobe and heavy window curtains reaching almost from the ceiling to the floor. The stretcher bearers undressed me, leaving only my shirt, while a nurse took the covers off the bed and I was put to bed as I was, unwashed and bloody.

It felt good to be in a real bed after all this long time of sleeping in the open. It took me ages to get warm and my hands remained stiff and frozen, but I did not want to put them under the sheet because they were dirty and blood stained. My bedside lamp had a small yellow shade. I could see myself reflected in the large mirror on the wardrobe door. I asked the nurse for some water to wash my hands. When they were clean I put them under the bedclothes, feeling for the bandage. My leg felt thin compared with the other. My foot was hurting me but I could not move it. I tried to stretch my leg but it only hurt more.

The nurse came back with another girl carrying plates, a bowl of soup and some wine. I only drank the wine. It was very cold and I warmed the glass with my hands. 'You must try to eat something,' the nurse said, but I was not hungry. I finished the wine and asked for more. They laughed and said they would try to get some more but, as a rule, only one glass was allowed. I had another glass. It made me tired. 'I'll try to go to sleep now,' I said. They showed me the bell in case I wanted anything and turned the light out. The door was left open. The soldiers and nurses were still talking and laughing outside in the corridor. I had to listen to them and could not sleep. I put the light on again and managed to reach my jacket, which hung on the bedpost. I found two crumpled Chesterfields which I smoked.

I heard somebody say, '*Aquí.*' Another voice said, 'No, further on, 360.' They stopped outside my room. The ceiling light was on; the nurse uncovered the bed next to me. A stretcher was carried in and the wounded man was laid on the bed. He was wrapped in blankets and when they took them off I saw he was naked, with a big bandage round his stomach. They covered him up. He was breathing heavily and his hands tried to tear off the bandage. One of the stretcher bearers came over and talked to me. He pointed to the wounded man and to his stomach and shook his head.

'*Muy malo*,' he said.

'*¿Un español?*' I asked.

'Yes,' he said, 'a Spaniard.'

'He's so young,' one of the nurses said. 'I hope he isn't going to die.'

The wounded man tried to say something but made only terrible gulping noises. His knees rose under the blanket and he had to be held down. I could see his profile; he had a dark skin and black, curly hair. His head fell to the side towards me. His eyes were open but he was unconscious. He was unshaven and looked very tired. A piece of paper was stuck on his forehead, with the number 74. It looked ridiculous, like a human parcel.

'What's the number for?' I asked.

'He had no papers on him,' the stretcher bearer explained, 'so we had to give him a number.'

'Why do you have to stick it on his head?'

The wounded man was kicking his legs. '*Ay, mi madre*,' he said quietly, '*ay, mi madre*.' They were pressing his legs down again and he started screaming, '*¡Ay, mi madre, ay, mi madre!*' dragging out the last syllable so that it sounded like the bleating of a lamb.

'*¡Chis!*' said the nurse, '*chis, chico*.'

Somebody outside called for a doctor. The young man had stopped crying out. His eyes, which were still open, were filled with tears which glittered in the light of the lamp. He had stopped breathing. The nurse shut his eyes with her open hand so that the number on his forehead was covered, and his tears rolled along his nose and dripped down on his pillow. The doctor came and listened to his heart. The stretcher bearers lifted him, in his sheet, on to the stretcher and carried him out. The nurse

194

sat by my bed for a while holding my hand. She cried a bit and then got up to put the light out.

I slept well. When the nurse came in the morning to draw the curtains I saw blue sky but the sun was not on my side of the building. When I leaned on my elbow I could see parts of a garden, a broad road and a house like a palace, covered with turrets. There was a radiator under the window but it was cold. I could see my breath in the cold air. The nurse brought me coffee and milk. When she left, an elderly man in a black and white striped jacket and a white tie came in carrying an elegant feather duster. He wished me good morning and started dusting the furniture. He was a sad man with a sad face, sad eyes and a sad, quiet voice. He was carefully tying back the curtains, brushing away an invisible speck of dust here and there, but there was something futile and forlorn about his movements.

He had been a waiter at the hotel. The old staff was kept on after it was transformed into a hospital. He took my jacket from the bed and asked me if he could put it away. He emptied the pockets and put the contents on the table beside my bed. Two fifty peseta notes, which were my last pay, a few copper coins, two cartridges (which he very carefully laid down), an empty clip, my watch, a lighter and an empty Chesterfield packet.

'I can get you American cigarettes, if you like,' he said, 'but they are very dear.' I gave him a note and asked him to get me some.

'Can you get anything to drink?' I asked. Yes, it was possible, but he could only buy it in the early afternoon, when he was free. He was not sure what he could get, perhaps there was only vermouth left, and I said that would be all right.

When he left, the surgeon and two assistants came in with the nurse. One assistant took down my details again while the nurse removed the bandage. The surgeon was an elderly man, tall with white hair, very distinguished, very reserved.

'Ah,' he said, 'I see you are German. I have studied in Freiburg. *Wie gehts?*' But when I answered in German I could see that he did not understand much. The bandage came off; the leg was dirty and bloodstained and the nurse washed around the wound with alcohol. I could see the two holes where the bullet had gone through, a big hole on the inside and a small one on the outside.

'The bone is all right,' the doctor said. 'Raise your knee. Does it hurt?'

'Not much.'

'Not bad, not bad.' He squeezed my foot and I groaned.

'This looks very strange,' he said, and pressed it again. 'Ah, it hurts you? Well, that is very strange. I must come back tomorrow and examine it more closely.'

They put a new bandage on. After they had left, another man appeared. He was young and pale with spectacles. He wore a tight, black suit, white shirt and a black tie. He was holding a piece of paper and a pen and looking for something on the wall over the next bed.

'There is nobody else,' I said. 'The comrade died last night.'

'Yes, I know,' and he was looking up and down the list and said that he could not find the name.

'He had no name,' I said, 'he wore a number 74.'

'*Gracias.* I will tell the nurse to remake the bed because I have to put someone else in it. We are very short of beds,' he explained. He came over to me and looked at the chart.

'I hope you don't have to sign me off,' I said.

'*No comprendo.*'

'Never mind,' I said. 'It was only a joke.'

He looked at me disapprovingly. Bernard bumped against him when he went out.

'Who's that?' asked Bernard.

'It's the undertaker!'

'That's what I thought,' he said. He wore a thick bandage round his neck.

'How are you, Bernard?'

'I'm all right. My shoulder is hurting a bit, that's all. You're not looking very well,' he said. 'What did the doctor say?'

'He doesn't know yet. He says it will be all right soon.'

Bernard said he was going into the town in the afternoon though he was not allowed to leave the hospital. He had heard that the English had been taken out of the French battalion and were going back to Albacete for a rest.

'I hope to see John,' he said. 'I'll bring him along if I can find him.'

Bernard got up from the bed and looked out of the window and said there were planes about. I could not see them but I could hear them.

'*Nuestros*,' we both said with one voice, and laughed.

# Chapter 10 — Hospitals

I was told that I was going to be sent to Valencia in an ambulance the next morning. At first I had thought I would be going to Murcia because the International Brigade had taken over the hospitals there. Still, Murcia or Valencia, it did not matter to me. I just wanted my operation. Every day my leg seemed to shrink and bend more and the pain grew steadily worse.

The nurse brought me my coffee early next morning and helped me to put on some clothes. It was difficult to get my leg into the trousers and it hurt me; I was so feeble and weak afterwards that I had to rest lying on the bed.

The stretcher bearers carried me downstairs because the lift was too small, and I was left lying near the entrance in the big hall. I waited for hours but the ambulance never showed up. I was taken back up to my room and the *responsable* came to tell me there was no petrol left in Madrid to take the wounded out but he would see to it that I went with the next transport.

For two days I waited and hoped; when they finally came to fetch me again I was convinced there would be a hitch at the last moment. I was right. For some reason or other there was no ambulance to spare and they had requisitioned two old buses to take away the less seriously wounded, at least, to make room in the hospital for others. There was not enough room for my stretcher and I was brought back again. I never wanted to say goodbye again, and I felt very silly turning up in my room again and again like a bad penny.

My current room mate, of course, was glad to see me back because he was alone, but I hardly talked to him, I was so fed up. In the afternoon the French doctor came along and he nearly threw a fit when he saw I was still there. He shouted at me that I must have my operation at once and asked me why I had not gone with the transport provided. I lost my temper and bawled back that it was not my fault that I was still here, and he rushed out to raise hell down at the office.

He was more friendly when he came back and apologised for being rude. He said he had been upset on seeing that I had not gone because he was worried about my leg. 'But tomorrow,' he said, 'you must go for sure. Unfortunately we haven't an ambulance but I told them to put you in the bus on your stretcher.' I said it did not matter to me as long as I could go somehow, the bus ride could not hurt my leg more than it did already. He said there would be a doctor with the transport who would look after me.

That night the telephone rang in my room and somebody asked for me. It was a call from Valencia. I could not reach the phone and I asked my Alsatian room mate to take it, but he could not understand what was said and he was so nervous and flustered that he slammed the receiver back. When I finally managed to reach the phone by crawling over his bed the line was dead.

The next morning I waited, fully dressed. My room mate was going with me. As he could walk I sent him out to make sure that the transport was not leaving without me. Earlier the doctor had given me a big dose of morphine and I was completely free of pain. I felt drowsy and it was not important any more whether I went away or not.

For the third time I said goodbye to the nurses and we all laughed and joked about me being back very soon. One of the nurses went down with me to see that I was comfortable. The bus was not yet full and they put me on the floor. I was glad the door was left open and I could see a little of the street, very grey, very cold, with soldiers standing at the door of the hospital. Further on I saw a lot of hollow-eyed, miserable-looking women huddled in their shawls waiting for food. I had not seen anything but my room and the bit of sky out of the window for two months. Everything was interesting and I was sorry that the door would be closed shortly when we started, and I envied the men who could sit upright and could look out of the windows.

The bus was nearly full when two more stretchers were brought out, but there was only room for one. On the second stretcher I saw a very young Frenchman with both legs missing. I was not as badly wounded, though he appeared to be completely without pain, and I told the doctor who was in charge, a Hungarian woman, that they should put me in a seat to make room for him. She protested, but I insisted, not entirely from unselfishness, because I wanted to look out of the window. They finally put me on a seat next to my room mate and, though it was not very comfortable, I was all right as long as I was still under the influence of the morphine.

It was a cold, depressing day with a sky of lead hanging low over the town. The streets we passed were dirty and many houses lay in ruins looking desolate, save for the silent columns of starving women and children. A huge poster was stuck on a wall: '*Madrid, una ciudad heroica e inexpugnable*'.

Yes, heroic and impregnable. There are many cities all over Spain. Compared with them you are only a huge, ugly village, in spite of your Gran Vía and your Puerta del Sol, in spite of your solitary skyscraper, the Telefónica. But I love you and will remember you always because there is something more valuable than beauty; it is your courage and heroism. 'Madrid' was our watchword; 'a wall' was the anwer. Lorca's *Oh you white wall of Spain – Oh you black bulls of sorrow* will always remind me of it. Was this a farewell to Madrid? Perhaps not. I hoped I would be able to get back soon. But if I should not come back, I say goodbye to you Madrid, and to you Steve Yates, Fred Jones, Burke, Maclaurin, Stephens and all the others, to the known and unknown, to the Germans, French, Poles, Italians and English who died before the walls of Madrid.

As the main road was under constant fire we took a minor one which was very bad; worn out by the thousands of trucks which travelled over it day and night. It was a monotonous and melancholy landscape through which we travelled; windswept, bare hills, sometimes a house or village here and there. I was holding my wounded leg with my hands to stop it bumping on the floor because our bus had hardly any springs, but I still felt all right and I was glad I was not lying on the stretcher and could look out of the window.

About midday we stopped at a hospital in a large village and everybody who was able to walk got out to have lunch. The men on the stretchers and I had ours in the bus. Nurses came with bed pans and bottles. After lunch we started again and my room mate, next to me, had got himself drunk and was very unpleasant. He made advances to the woman doctor who sat opposite us, and he kept on bumping my leg. He accused me of being in love with her myself and he thought it was all very funny. I tried to shut him up. The doctor was a very plain woman and we all felt very awkward and I would have liked to hit him. I was glad when he got tired and fell asleep.

We had left Madrid at about half past ten in the morning. Ever since lunch time my leg had been hurting me and in the afternoon it was giving me hell. Every jolt seemed to hit me right in the stomach and I felt very ill. I asked them to stop the bus. I wanted to lie on the floor but there was not enough room. A comrade who was sitting at the back of the bus, where the seat went all the way across, offered to change with me. I was carried to the back where I sat next to a man who had both arms in plaster. He told me to put my leg on his knee so that I was half stretched out and it was more comfortable. The doctor wanted to give me an injection but she found that she had left the syringe behind.

At about eight o'clock we passed through La Roda; though it was very dark I recognised it immediately. Two Frenchmen, who sat in front of us, started a row; one had remarked that we were already in Albacete, but the other insisted it was La Roda and all hell broke loose. It needs a Frenchman, or a drunk, to start fighting over such a silly and unimportant question as this.

'I tell you I'm right,' yelled one.

'*Non!*' shouted the other.

'*Oui!*'

'*Non!*'

'*Oui!*'

'*Merde alors!*'

'*Je m'en fou.*'

Though both were wounded they started knocking each other about and they fell over my leg and on to the man with the broken arms. The bus stopped and everybody was yelling and the doctor tried to calm them down with '*camaradas*' and '*disciplina*', but only when they realised that I was nearly unconscious did they stop. They still went on haggling with each other, like old fishwives, with each trying to have the last word. I was sorry I was not well. They would not have had to worry any more about Albacete or any other place. I smoked a cigarette and lit one for the man beside me and put it in his mouth.

We reached Albacete an hour later and I was carried through a garden into a hospital. There were three men in the room with me but none of them wounded. A male nurse took my clothes off and put me to bed. He brought me dinner but I was too ill to eat and he went to fetch the doctor, a big German with a kind and gentle face who dressed my wound and gave me an injection. He was a dental surgeon and was trying to organise a dental hospital. He advised me to travel on to Murcia as quickly as possible. He said he knew two very good surgeons there. There was a train leaving that very night and he asked me whether I could stand the journey. I said I would go, because I could not face waiting for yet another journey. They dressed me again and I was carried to the ambulance which took me to the station.

The train was late and we waited for hours in the house of the station master. The hospital train turned out to be just an ordinary train stripped of seats and partitions. The beds were stretchers fastened with leather straps to the ceiling. It was very slow and it carried no lights apart from a few candles. Although it was slow it shook and rattled terribly and we were tossed up and down. I had to hold on to my leg all the time except when we stopped at a station.

Dawn came and it grew pleasantly warm. The sun rose magnificently in a clear sky and, when it was light enough to see, I saw the fertile hills and valleys of the province of Murcia. I forgot the journey, my leg, everything. I had left Madrid only yesterday morning in mid-winter and now it was spring. What a glorious sky! The almond trees were in full blossom and the deep green orange and lemon trees bore the first fruit. The air smelled fresh and very sweet, of flowers, earth and fruit.

We arrived at Murcia. A few peasants waited for a train and everything looked peaceful without a sign of war. An ambulance took us to the hospital and it was the worst ambulance and the worst road I ever experienced. We moaned and groaned at every bump and the driver put his head through a window and said, *'¿Qué pasa?'*

'Be careful,' I said. *'Lentamente.'*

'Just one minute more,' he said, 'just one more road.'

He was worried and drove very slowly but it got worse and worse. Up and down we went and I was holding on to the stretcher above me and was glad I had not got a stomach wound. We swore in English, Polish and French and the driver mumbled in despair, *'Paciencia, camaradas, nada más que un momento, solamente un camino más.'*

The ambulance stopped. The door opened and somebody took us out. I did not see anything. I came to my senses lying in a large, cool hall with a floor of coloured tiles and a big wooden staircase.

# Chapter 11 — Murcia

It was like being borne aloft out of a deep, dark hole. Slowly at first but then faster and faster, I was dragged towards the light. My eyes were still closed. The light was glaring and white and it hurt me. I did not want to wake up but consciousness overtook me, dragging me with it. I heard voices. They seemed to talk to me. Somebody said, 'What time is it?' I opened my eyes a little. I turned away from the light and saw a pair of shoes and two legs and, near to them, a shiny, yellow piece of metal. It stabbed at me. I put my hand out to cover it; it felt cool when my hand closed around it and my fingers were twisting it harder and harder, bending it like a piece of rubber. Somebody was trying to loosen my grip but I was holding on.

I was awake. The shoes shuffled on the floor. There was a table by my bedside with a glass of red wine on top of it. Underneath was the towel rail, which my hand was twisting and bending. The towel lay on the floor. I looked up. I saw khaki cloth and above it, but far away, a face which looked familiar though I could not see any features. It bobbed up and down. When it came nearer it opened in the middle and spoke to me.

'It's all over,' it said. 'You'll be all right, it's all over.'

'It's over,' I repeated.

'Yes,' said the voice. 'You'll be all right.'

Somebody on the other side turned my head but it fell back. There was only one thing to do – hang on to the piece of metal. I wished they would leave me alone but they kept on turning my head and pulling my hand. The rod became unhinged and clattered to the floor. An arm was put round my head to lift it towards the light and a bowl knocked against my teeth, but I was not sick. A cloth wiped sweat off my face and pieces of cotton wool soaked in water were pressed against my mouth. Shadows in front of my bed kept moving up and down. I opened my eyes again. There were two men with red crosses on their arms and one in a white shirt and a white cap. They were talking to me.

'*Alors, ça va? Ça va bien, eh? Courage.*'

There was a noise like a pump. I heard it every time I opened my mouth. A band of iron was fastened round my leg, high up near the hip, and pressed until it came to the bone, and relaxed and came back at me, and it was hurting me all over.

'Get it off,' I said. 'It's too tight.'

The man in white was bending over me and got hold of my arm. He rubbed something over it and pricked it with a needle. It felt good. All the pain went.

'*Voilà, couchez-vous maintenant.*'

I was getting sleepy; I shut my eyes and it was dark again.

\* \* \* \* \*

When I woke up I packed my things and went out. It was early in the year, but it was already hot during the day. I was thirsty. Something cool and flabby was pressed against my lips. Everything was a different shade of blue; the streets, the sky, the people, everything except the church – yellow against a dark sky. A man was hanging from the tower, his long shirt fluttering in the wind. 'I'm thirsty,' he said. 'I'm thirsty, I'm thirsty.'

'They shouldn't have done it,' I said to Pat. We found thin pieces of wood in the garden and fastened them to each other with string until they became a long swaying pole. We fastened some cotton wool on the end of it and, after dipping it in water, we tried to lift it to the tower but it was bending like a blade of grass and broke in two. 'Never mind,' I said. 'He's only a puppet.'

We left the town. The roads were sprinkled with the purple and crimson saffron flower. 'What time is it?' somebody asked. I looked at my watch. It was twelve o'clock. It had started raining and I walked up and down. A man came over the hill and I called, '*¡Alto!* Who goes there?'

'I'm a friend,' the man said, 'don't shoot.'

I let him come near. It was Fred. 'I'm turning in now,' he said. When I looked at my watch it was still twelve o'clock.

I came upon a coffin. It was made of metal but had a wooden lining. I looked up to the road in the wood and stretcher after stretcher was brought down. The stretchers were empty and bloodstained. The stretcher bearers rested for a while until the

205

doctor came and chased them back to the front. 'Where are the wounded?' he was yelling after them. 'What do you expect me to do, get them down myself?'

He took a length of wire from his pocket and gave one end to me to hold and we stretched it across the road. 'That will stop them,' he said, '¿no pasarán, eh?' He was laughing loudly and I said, 'Be quiet, I can hear a plane.' The plane was right above us. We saw the light in the cockpit and the bomb rushed down to the road like a comet. It exploded and the wire coiled through the air. The doctor was jumping up and down on the road laughing and screaming, 'They're killing their own comrades,' he yelled, 'they're killing their own comrades.'

We waited for hours in the sunken road. 'It's too early to go to town,' Hermann said, 'everybody will be in church.' When the people came out they were all in black. They came down the steps towards the market place. The first man carried the coffin of a child. We followed the procession and, after the burial, the mayor gave us five pesetas. He told us to clear off and never come back again. A policeman followed us to the end of the town. When we looked back they had levelled their rifles at us. We fell to the ground and they started shooting. The bullets exploded, tearing big lumps of stone and earth from the ground.

'This is what I call good shooting,' said the observer in front of me, 'here, take a look.' I looked through the periscope and saw the courtyard with a dead donkey and, further on, the white Casa de Velázquez. Shell after shell went in and both towers were in flames. I watched it until it had burnt out and then I went down to the courtyard. I covered the donkey with my blanket and sat down on it.

A lorry drove up and took us away. We arrived at Fuencarral in a drenching rainstorm. The street was crowded with soldiers. They sang:

> Heute sind wir noch zu Mause
> Morgen gehte zum Tore hinaus
> Und wir müsssen wandern
> Von einem Ort zum Andern

Somebody was playing the guitar. When I came nearer I saw it was Walter.

'Don't you remember me?' I asked. He shook his head. I took my balaclava helmet off.

'No,' he said. 'I don't remember you.'

A truck passed between us and knocked down a dog. The dog screamed and crawled away on its forelegs. I tried to catch it; somebody else shot it with a rifle. The bullet made a big hole.

'They're only locals,' our guide said. 'The trick with the *banderillas* isn't bad but they couldn't kill a bull with a rifle. You watch the clowns, they're really funny.'

A stretcher was brought into the bull ring. A clown in a white dress and white face followed it waving and wringing his hands in despair. The crowd laughed. The stretcher was put down in the middle of the ring and the clown lay down on it. He folded his hands over his chest and they placed a white sheet over him. The bull was strong and fast. He made straight for the stretcher and the crowd yelled, which made the clown look up from under the sheet. One horn caught the clown in his right leg above the knee. It hurt me to see it; the bull tried to shake him off by tossing his head. I felt sick and left the ring. I was limping badly when I walked down the stairs so that I had to hold on to the bannister.

Outside the ring stood six coffins, one for each bull. They were filled with grease and a man was busy dragging rifles out of them. It took us a day to clean them. We marched to the rifle range, escorted by *guardias civiles*. The range was two hundred yards. It was dark; each time we fired a flame shot out of the rifle. We had five rounds each. A *guardia civil* noted our scores in a book and called them out. A man in civilian clothes started talking to us and we lined up in a ring around him. After each sentence we heard a cannon shot in the distance.

'You will face a ruthless enemy, without training and ill-equipped. But what you lack in weapons you will make up for in courage. You have come from all over Europe to lay down your lives for democracy. The eyes of all the freedom-loving peoples in the world are watching you. I am sure you will do your best. *Salud* – and *bonne chance!*'

He took out a long piece of paper and read the roll call, but everybody had gone away and there was no answer. I stepped forward when my name was called and answered, 'Present.' He looked up for a moment and I saw tears in his eyes. He began to reel off the names all over again. 'Blanche . . .' and after each name he said, 'killed in action.'

\* \* \* \* \*

The doctor asked me in German how I was.

'Not bad,' I said, 'but I can't sleep.'

He shook his head and said we must do something about it.

'I will give you an injection in the spine. It will put you to sleep.'

'Make it a strong one,' I said, 'I don't want to wake up any more.'

When I woke up it was night. Everybody was asleep. A nurse sat by my bed.

'How are you?' she asked. The pains had started again. I put my hand under the sheet. I was wearing a long boot, very hard and narrow, so that the flesh bulged over the top. At every breath I took it seemed to shrink slowly, squeezing the leg from my body. It was very heavy. I could not move and I tried to lift myself on to my elbows. A terrible feeling of helplessness came over me. I wanted to kick it off.

'Try to breathe deeply,' the nurse said. She was holding my head and wiped my face from time to time. 'You must fight against it,' she said. She put the corner of the blanket into my mouth and I chewed it.

'It's no good,' I said. 'I can't stand it.'

'Be quiet,' she said. 'You mustn't wake your comrades. I can't give you anything, the dispensary is closed. You'll have to wait until tomorrow morning.'

'What time is it?

'Eleven o'clock.'

'Oh God.'

'Sh, be quiet. Breathe in deeply, but don't make any noise when you let it out.'

'What did they do with my leg?' I asked. 'It's too tight.'

'It's in a plaster cast. It always hurts at first. They did a fine operation.'

'It's too tight,' I repeated.

'You don't want to have a short leg, do you?'

Somebody else called for water and she went away. Every time she opened or shut the door I saw a ray of light. When she came back I asked her again for the time.

'Never mind, try to go to sleep.' The bed on my left was empty. 'I'm going to rest for a while,' the nurse said. 'Call me if you want anything.'

I could see a little light through the shutters opposite my bed, but it was of a dark blue colour and not grey. Morning was a long way off. I lay there chewing the blanket. Every few seconds a spasm of pain went through my leg. It started at the foot and rose up into my stomach. I counted up to eight but the next time it came at seven.

The nurse went away to look for a doctor in the morning just as I started yelling.

Opposite my bed was a door leading to a balcony with iron railings. I could see the tops of some trees and the mountains in the distance. There was a road just under the crest and I wished I could walk along it.

At night the doors and all the windows were tightly closed so as to afford no target to aeroplanes. It was hot then and it stank. The nurses went in and out and a dreary, dim light came from a solitary bulb. I never slept and I listened to the murmurs of the sleepers and the cries of those in pain. I could not sleep and could not think when the pain came over me. I gripped the iron railing at the head of the bed above me and clenched my teeth so as not to wake the others. The nights were endless. I counted every second, every minute, and after an eternity a pale light would show through the shutters. Then I began to breathe more freely and the pain seemed to ease. I could already hear the clattering from the kitchen and very soon the doors and windows would be opened and lovely, cool, sweet-smelling air would stream in. I would see the sky with small clouds already touched with pink by the rising sun, the mountains now looking blue and cool. Along with the air would come the beautiful scent of lemon and orange blossom and the smell of earth. This was indeed the best time of the day. Very shortly the sun would come through the iron railings of the balcony, throwing its patterned shadows on to the wall.

Everybody was awake now and, after coffee and a piece of dry bread had been given out, we were washed and our bed pans were removed. Some who were not badly wounded went out into the town.

Girls came in from the town and, with much banging and raising clouds of dust, they would scrub the floors crouching on their knees. Now and then they would squeak when they were clapped on the behind during childish joking between the boys and girls. We got sick and tired of this '*tú malo!*' routine (you're bad; no *you* are) and it went on for a long time for lack of any other language.

A Pole was brought in one day and put into the bed on the far side opposite me. He came from the *Sala de Amputación* and was still unconscious. He was not a big man as Poles often are – big-boned, strong and ungainly like cattle with the sad, innocent look of those animals. He was small, about forty years of age, with a round, shaved head and unshaven beard. He never made a sound, he never cried and later hardly ever spoke except to another Polish comrade who had been kicked in the head by a horse and stayed with us for only a few days.

This young Pole was tall and handsome, washing, cleaning and brushing himself the whole day. He frequently looked into a mirror and looked into it with great satisfaction. He was kind and soft-hearted and he often talked to me in his bad, guttural German. He talked mostly of girls he had seen or met or slept with and, brushing his Douglas Fairbanks moustache with his large hand, he would roar with laughter when he came to a specially spicy story. He was like a great big child. He spoke a little French, a little Spanish, a little German and a little of everything and was everybody's friend.

He often used to sit with his countryman, talking to him or helping him on to the stretcher when he was fetched to be bandaged. He would take him up like a child, placing him on the stretcher, arranging a blanket around him, and no mother could have done it more tenderly or carefully. Every time he did this, his face was twitching with emotion and, when he came to me afterwards, he shook his head with his bottom lip pressed under his teeth and, with his large hand flapping up and down, his expression spoke more convincingly than words how he felt. 'Ah, he is very ill,' he would say, rolling his r's. 'This poor man is badly hurt and he will say nothing. It hurts him very much but he will say nothing.'

We could all see that this man would not live and we all hoped he would die. Every time he was lifted up I saw the bloody bandage right on his hip, his whole leg missing, with not even a stump left. I watched his pained, distorted face and sometimes he would shake his head which revealed his pain louder than any scream. Sometimes he would try to explain his plight to a nurse or to a doctor. He could hardly speak. He would close both his fists pointing to his missing leg to show how big the piece of shell that struck him had been. Or he would place his hand to show how much it had hurt when it hit him and I had to look away. He was suffering hell; his only thoughts were his leg, his pain and his wound.

He did not eat much but drank his glass of wine and when somebody brought me a whole bottle one day, he asked me for a bit and I gave him all of it, although he was not allowed to have so much. For the first time something like a smile appeared on his lined and haggard face.

He never slept. Neither did I. Throughout those long, dreadful nights I saw the glow of his cigarettes which he smoked one after the other. Like two people left alone in this world we listened to the sleepers with open eyes.

It was on a Sunday afternoon when death finally came to him. He was restless the whole morning. The young Polish comrade talked to him at about midday but soon afterwards he started bleeding and was taken out for the second time to be bandaged. In the afternoon I heard a sound like dripping water and saw blood under his bed running over the floor. He had pushed away his bedclothes and his face and shirt were bloody; so was his bed and parts of the wall behind him. The nurse in charge came but they could not move him. Our surgeon had gone to another hospital but his assistants and the nurse fought desperately to keep him alive. They made a tourniquet with chains around his arms and his one leg to stop the flow of blood, they bandaged him and gave him black coffee and he was still conscious. After some time the surgeon returned and they came to fetch him into the operating room. He was back in a short while and they tried to keep him alive with injections but he died shortly afterwards and we were glad for him that it was over.

For the last time he was borne away on a stretcher looking very small and a bit ridiculous, hanging limp in the sheets. His head rolled to the side and they closed the sheets over him. When he was carried out we saluted him and his Polish comrade was crying, sitting on his bed with his head in his hands.

\* \* \* \* \*

Two soldiers came into the ward one evening. They stood with their backs to me and looked round as if searching for someone. One carried a paper parcel. 'Dumont,' one of them said in a loud voice. 'Is there a comrade of the Battalion Dumont here?'

'Yes,' I said. When they turned round I recognised one of them. It was the fat Belgian from our machine gun company. He came to my bed and sat down.

'*Camarade anglais*, how are you? When were you wounded? Ah yes, I remember Boadilla. We had a bad time there, but the Germans got it worse two days later.'

'Yes, I know. You're all right?'

'I've been lucky so far. We're here for a short rest and to fill up the battalion. There are very few of us left.'

He was still holding the paper parcel and he put it down on my bed. 'It's for you,' he said. I opened it and it was full of small cakes. 'I hope you like them.'

I did not say I could not eat them.

'Try one,' he said, and I ate one. He looked round while I ate.

'How's everybody?' I asked.

'There are only a few you know. We were all sorry when you left. We always liked you English.'

'How's Alfredo?'

212

'He's dead. Nearly everybody's dead or wounded. What about the rest of you?' he said. 'Is John still alive? You know, *le Grand*, who was wounded in the head?'

'He's dead too.'

'I cooked you a chocolate pudding on the morning he was wounded, remember?'

'Yes, it was very good.'

'Alfredo was always talking about Fred and the English.'

'When did he die?'

'Not long ago,' he said. 'It came quick. It was over in a moment.'

I wanted to talk about something else.

'Are you forming a new battalion? Is Dumont back?'

'No,' he said. 'We're getting French and Spanish to fill up. We're staying a few days. I'll come again.'

'If there's anybody I know, give them my greetings.'

'I will,' he said. 'I'm glad I saw you.'

'I'm glad you're well,' I said. Then I remembered Muller and asked after him. He was all right. I could not help laughing. They could not kill Muller after all.

'Tell him to visit me. Say I'm the other German from the Dumont.'

'You're German? I didn't know. We always thought you were English. I'll send him round. He'll be glad to see you. Well, I'll be going now.'

'Thanks for the cakes,' I said.

'That's all right. If you need anything, let me know.'

'I will.' We shook hands.

'*Bonne chance, camarade.*'

'*Salud,*' I said. 'And good luck.'

Muller came the same night. It was after nine o'clock and no visitors were allowed but he came in with the grumbling *responsable*. He saw me at once. He was grinning. Nothing could wipe that smile off his face.

'Hello, Muller,' I said.

'I didn't know you were here,' he said. 'I thought you were well, or dead or something.' He sat down. 'I'm leaving tomorrow.

That's why I came tonight. I've often asked about you and somebody said they'd taken your leg off. How are you feeling?'

'I'm all right,' I said. 'I can't sleep, that's the worst.'

'How long will it take?'

'A very long time.'

'Come back to us,' he said, 'and don't join any other outfit.'

'Yes, sure. How's the war?'

'Everything's fine. We're doing well.' He did not say anything about the losses and I did not ask him.

'I'm glad you're as cheerful as ever.'

'No good getting depressed,' he said. 'When you're out of hospital you'll feel better. What an awful place this is.' He shuddered. 'I don't want to be wounded, like you. Let me see, how long have you been in bed?'

'Four months.'

'Oh my God,' he said, 'I'd rather be dead.'

'You'll never die,' I said.

He asked to see my leg and I showed it to him.

'It doesn't look very good. Did you ever try to get up? When you can stand upright it will soon be all right. Let's try it,' he said.

'It's no good,' I said, 'it doesn't work.'

'Let's try it.'

'All right,' I said. 'But put it back if it doesn't work.'

He was bending the leg over the side of the bed and let it down a little. It hurt terribly and sweat broke out all over me.

'Put it back,' I said.

'Never mind,' he said. 'Try it every day. These doctors don't know anything.'

He smoked a cigarette. I was sorry that he was going the next day.

'I'll come back,' he said. 'I'll see you some other time.' The *responsable* was urging him to go.

'What lousy *responsables* you have,' said Muller. 'I'm only cheering him up,' he said to the man. 'That's what you need in these lousy hospitals. Well, *auf Wiedersehen*, I'll see you at the front.'

The door slammed and he was gone.

# Chapter 12 — Valencia

Of course, they had forgotten me at the bureau. Now I was hustled on to the stretcher with one blanket thrown over me and I just remembered in time my whisky bottle and also my Spanish militia cap which I wanted to take home as a souvenir. I was carried out through the ward, all the men smiled and shouted at me and saluted me with the raised fist, and I felt very sad.

'*Salud*,' they cried after me. '*Bonne chance! Machs Gut!* Good luck!' and the door closed behind me. I could see the wounded lying on stretchers along the corridor and we went down the three flights of stairs. We hurried down but it was narrow and steep and John, one of the bearers, had a bad hand and could not support the stretcher properly, so I had to hold on in order not to fall out. The ambulance was waiting outside in the dark with a feeble light burning inside. They shoved me in and I nearly lost my head because a metal flap was not raised in time. Everybody else jumped in, the door closed and we rattled off over awful cobblestones. We were holding on to straps and iron bars and my foot started to pain me again.

The station was ill-lit and dark. An enormous number of people surged about. The train was still there and, although I could see it was already full, there must have been a few hundred more people trying to get on.

The platform was crowded with refugees, soldiers with and without rifles and a few *oficiales* tried in vain to bring some sort of order into the chaos. I had a first-class ticket but it was difficult to come near the train at all, though everybody made way at once when they saw the stretcher. A few Spaniards took me away from my comrades and hoisted me on their shoulders to save my foot from being knocked with parcels and rifles and, on high above the crowd, I swayed along like a Nabob on an elephant.

We found a first-class compartment but it was jammed with people. However, my bearers were determined to put me in it. It is quite easy for a person to get into a train, one just goes up the steps leading to a small platform, then one turns sharp left through the door and there one is. It is a very different matter on a stretcher. I knew it would not work and I watched the proceedings with great interest. First somebody got up on to the platform and my head was hanging down with my legs high above me. While the men behind my head were pushing me up, the man with my legs was nearly pushed out of the other side of the train. So they pulled me back and tried all over again. Up I went, and this time they turned the stretcher sideways so that it would point towards the door, but the space between the two carriages was too small and, even if they had succeeded, they would have had to bend the stretcher at a right angle to get it round the lavatory.

My bearers were getting frantic now and tried it again the first way, while I was giving them sound advice from above about taking off part of the train. They even tried to push me in through an open window, although there was no room, and I stood on my head while this was going on and began to lose my sense of humour. A great crowd had collected round us. It must have been a long time since they saw such a Laurel and Hardy act but, apparently, it was not funny to them and they shouted and screamed and women were wailing, '*Ay, el pobre,*' covering their eyes every time parts of me disappeared. Advice was given to my sweating and, by now, completely crazed bearers and everybody tried to get hold of the stretcher and I was borne hither and thither. Above the din rose the sound of the bell swung by the station master, who cried in despair, 'All aboard, all aboard.'

I was put down while everybody scrambled on to the train and I had a sip of whisky. From far away I saw the stretcher bearer, John, coming towards me with the station master running behind him. Once more I was taken up and we were running towards the last carriage where they finally got rid of me by pushing me into a luggage van. It was full of small wooden cases but there was enough room for me. I said goodbye to John, and the station master reminded me that I had to change at Chinchón.

We were off, but before the train gathered speed two soldiers jumped into my car, and I was glad that I would not be alone. My companions were both German, just back from the front to have a rest. They were nice boys, not over twenty, and they talked a lot about their home in Carinthia. They came from the same village and most of their conversation was, 'You remember this, Karl?' and 'You remember that, Franz?' They were cheerful fellows but they soon went to sleep and I was lying awake sipping my whisky, smoking and thinking about this and that.

From time to time a light stabbed through the iron grille of a window above me, then it was dark again and I heard the endless 'tam-tam' of the rail under me, and at every 'tam' a piercing pain shot up my leg. It was cold and I wished I had got a second blanket. I was sore and I tried to move to my side but, as my legs did not turn with me, it was impossible. I knew that once I could get on to my side I would be able to sleep but I had tried it for weeks past without succeeding and I gave up. I was cursing the doctor who had forgotten to give me a shot of morphine as he had promised. It was icy cold and I had more whisky, but it did not intoxicate me, although it was the first time for many months that I had tasted liquor.

We stopped at many stations. I heard voices, people trampling about, the guard's whistle, and we were on our way again. The train seemed to move more and more slowly after every halt as if it were climbing all the time. Once the door was opened and the wooden cases were taken out and I saw 'Take care – ammunition' written on them. Through the open door, in the grey half-light, I saw a few big guns on the other side of the track covered with tarpaulins and white with ice and snow. The station I saw was partly damaged by bombs. It was here I blessed the donor of my whisky; without it I am sure I would never have reached Valencia alive.

We arrived at Chinchón and the Germans got out but promised to come back for me. An icy wind blew through the open door. I had been waiting a long time when I heard an engine and banging and I saw that I was moving. I was glad because I thought that the train would go right through to Valencia, but it stopped again. I saw nothing but snow-covered tracks and a field and it was very still. After more than an hour it dawned on me that my carriage had been detached from the

217

train and shunted a long way from the station. I shouted out but nobody heard me. After a time I heard voices and suddenly a few Spaniards passed the open door not far away and I was shouting, *'Oiga, camarada!'* and waving my arms.

'*Salud,*' they cried. '*Salud, camarada!*' raising their fists, and they disappeared. It was at this point that I cursed the war, my fate, Hitler, Franco and everybody in and out of Spain, and if the Spaniards had seen me then they would have thought I was a homicidal maniac.

I was sucking on my bottle, trying to figure out a way to get to the door of the train, but it was no good. I was wondering how long it would take them to find me, and I saw myself buried as a skeleton clutching a whisky bottle and perhaps they would put on my grave, 'Here lies Johnny Walker', and I was very sad.

Then to my relief I heard German voices. My comrades had come back and they carried me down the track towards the station, running all the way because we could see another train already under steam. It was not our train. The wind was fierce and snow and rain fell on us. The station master took me into his house, in which a fire was burning. My friends went out again to enquire about the train. I felt a sudden need to pee and I wished I was somewhere else. When I could not hold it any longer I called the station master and asked him for a bottle. He pointed to my whisky but I explained what I wanted it for and he groped about, embarrassed, with ink pots and water glasses. He went in and out with lots of '*hombres!*' and exclamations of despair until he found a metal measure for oil which was sold from the station house. I refused at first but I could not wait any longer and took it. I asked him about the time the train to Valencia would arrive and he shouted at me that it was here already and leaving any minute now. As he finished speaking the German boys returned and they carried me to another luggage van. We said goodbye and they left me to go and look for seats in a compartment.

*The narrative breaks off here. Jan arrived safely in Valencia and was admitted to the Hospital Pasionaria, on the outskirts of the city, near to the port. He spent several weeks convalescing there, until he was strong enough to move on to Barcelona.*

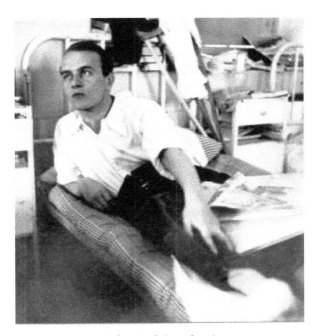

Jan in hospital, in Valencia

# Chapter 13 — Escape from Barcelona

During the long wait in the station the compartment was horribly hot and stuffy because the shutters were down to prevent any light showing. As soon as the train started I switched the light off and opened the window but the train moved slowly, stopping a number of times among fields, and it was still close and hot. The sky was overcast and lightning flickered along the horizon.

I woke early in the morning. Dawn came with a feeble grey light which changed to a dirty yellowish brown over the Mediterranean. There was continuous lightning over the sea but the noise of the thunder was drowned by the wheels of the train. Straight across the water, but invisible, lay Mallorca, from where death took off every day to descend upon the mainland coast.

I had bought some bread and an egg which I had for breakfast but there was nothing to drink. I went to sleep again and, when I awoke, we were nearing Barcelona. I remembered it always bright and sunny, though it could be very dark and cold in winter, but coming through the suburbs on this dreary day it looked like any industrial town in England.

The station was deserted. Most of the people had left the train before Barcelona. An old porter fetched a taxi while I waited on the bench in the big hall. I went to a *pensión* on the Rambla. We drove along the port and turned into the Rambla at the statue of Columbus.

I had heard about air raids in Barcelona and expected to find a great part of the town in ruins but I saw only two damaged houses. Everything looked strange, cold and hostile. It was like arriving for the first time in a place where one knows nobody. Perhaps it was the rain, or coming back alive from a war. It was so early the streets were deserted. The big barracks on the corner of the Barrio Chino had been pulled down revealing an ugly black square.

The *pensión* was on the first floor of a large house near the Plaza Catalunya. Fortunately the lift was still working. The woman who ran the *pensión* knew me. 'What happened to you?' were her first words when she saw me on crutches. I was asked the same question many times as if it were something extraordinary to see a wounded man.

I had some coffee and rested a bit until lunch time. Lunch was served in the dining room, typical with tiled floor and small tables. Nothing had changed. There were the same sort of people: young men who should have been in the army; elderly, fat, swarthy Catalans; and a few young women with dark professions and dark circles under their eyes. One of them asked me if I had met with an accident; the others did not speak to me at all.

After lunch I rested. From my window I could see the space where an old and beautiful church had been pulled down. It had taken them nearly a year to do it; they had just reached the foundations. I wondered why they had done it; perhaps they did not know themselves, perhaps the comrades of the CNT had nothing better to do – such as building fortifications or doing a bit of fighting. I suppose an anarchist brain works differently to mine.

The rain cleared and the sun came out in the afternoon. I went to get my final discharge papers and a visa to leave Spain. There did not seem to be any shortage of petrol as taxis and buses were running as before. I could not help thinking of the times when I was in Madrid and the wounded could not be sent out on account of the petrol shortage, which nearly cost me my leg.

The taxis had CNT-FAI painted prominently on the windscreens to prove that the workers had taken over, but the drivers were the same old tough and unfriendly lot. As I could not walk I had to take taxis and the fact that I was obviously wounded made no difference. Perhaps they too thought I had broken my leg skiing. When I stepped out in front of the barracks where I had to report I asked the driver to wait but he would not unless I gave him five pesetas. He said it was a new law. Such was the gratitude of the fatherland.

The French *responsable* (two bars, an officer) was very vague and non-committal. He said it was difficult to get a visa and even more difficult to get into France. However, he gave me the address of the passport office and refunded my fare from Valencia. When I asked him about money for the *pensión* he told me I should sleep in the barracks. When I pointed out that I was not fit he just shrugged his shoulders.

While I sat there, there was a continuous coming and going of soldiers. One man asked for money for a glass eye saying he would not go home looking as he did. He looked awful. The *responsable* shrugged his shoulders, '*Rien à faire*'. There were some American boys, the survivors of a ship load of volunteers which was torpedoed and sunk off the coast with the loss of several hundred men. They helped me down the stairs and we talked a little outside the barracks.

In the evening the Rambla looked its old familiar self. It was so crowded that the people could only move slowly. There was no blackout, which was asking for trouble. True, the town had only been bombed a few times. The working class quarter, the Barrio Chino, near the port, was fairly dark as it would suffer most, but higher up towards the Plaza Catalunya and beyond the middle class did not like any interference, despite the war. Was there a war on?

I managed to find a chair outside a café opposite the *pensión*. There was still beer to be had and every other sort of drink, though expensive. Even appetisers such as shrimps and little pieces of ham were available, as in the good old days. While I was sitting there watching the crowd I heard strains of music coming nearer.

A huge procession of young men and women, five abreast, came up the Rambla. They carried flags and banners with slogans: 'Against the Criminal Bombardment of Barcelona by the Fascists'. It took more than an hour for the demonstration to pass. There must have been more than four thousand people. From time to time groups were shouting, '*Abajo los criminales fascistas* – we protest against the criminal bombardment.'

It was too silly. If they had demonstrated in Mallorca it would have made some sense, but here Franco would neither hear nor see them. Was there no better cause for a demonstration? 'Food for Madrid', for instance, or 'Defend the Republic' or 'To the Front, Comrades!' I heard no '*¡Viva la República Española!*', only '*¡Viva Catalunya!*' As if Catalunya could survive without Spain. The war had not changed their separatism, it had returned stronger than ever. Did they hope to make a separate peace? I remembered the anarchist in Albacete who said, 'We have taken Albacete, the war is over.' If the people thought the same here there would be a frightful awakening one day. Franco would never compromise. One day Catalunya would be put to the test, but would they fight? Four thousand people. Ten battalions were idly walking down the Rambla. Not a big army, but when three thousand men saved Madrid, four thousand might have saved Málaga.

The great hero of Catalunya, Durruti, was dead but though his picture was on every wall and his name on everyone's lips his spirit was nowhere. They must have left it in Madrid when they brought his body home and it did not return because it was too dangerous and reckless a spirit.

I felt like a stranger in a hostile country. I was glad that I had fought for Spain and in Spain and not for this worthless rabble which sat loud and boisterous in cafés, well lit and well supplied with liquor, while Spain was fighting its desperate battle.

There was no difference between the people who sat here a year ago and these fat, mean, stupid ones with gold rings and watch-chains, reminding me of the profiteers of the last war. The only difference was the party emblems which they displayed prominently. Perhaps that was all that had changed; after all an emblem was easily removed if things should go wrong.

I had a three-course dinner and some good wine for which I was charged twenty pesetas. I felt depressed. I thought of friends now dead, and I drank a lot because even a Catalan cannot spoil good wine. I wished there had been another way out of Spain, by sea or air, so that I did not have to come out with this bad taste and, worse, with the feeling, for the first time, that we might not win the war. Defeat was written all over this town. Defeat before it was defeated; ruin before it was finally ruined. I had a sleepless night, my leg was hurting me, and I felt like crying.

\* \* \* \* \*

The café was one of the best in the Paseo, called the American Bar. There were the usual businessmen and young *señoritos,* the typical customers of a Spanish café. Hardly anyone wore a uniform. There was one difference though. More women were to be seen, young and good looking and dressed in the latest fashion.

An old woman tried to sell me flowers and then a group of youths in blue shirts and red ties were collecting money for the Basque country. On a wall was a poster saying, 'Give for Euskadi – Remember the martyred towns: Durango, Guernica, Eibar'. Hardly anyone gave anything. Wherever one looked there were posters with bombastic slogans, showing soldiers with steel helmets and fixed bayonets storming over a trench towards an indifferent population. 'More tanks, more munitions, more planes'. 'Strong men to the front'. These were the only sign of war.

The passport office was in the Calle Córsica where I had lived in the winter of 1933-1934. I had been warned by the French *responsable* that everything was in a chaotic state since the May rising. Many officials had been sacked and new ones had not been appointed. I was not surprised, therefore, to see a great number of wounded International Brigaders standing in a queue in front of a large building. There were quite a few police, young men of the *Guardia de Asalto* with rifles slung over their shoulders, in the street and in front of the door of the office.

The wounded were grumbling and protesting, trying to get in, but the police drove them back every time they made a move. I asked one of them what it was all about and he said that most of them had waited for days, some even for weeks, to get their exit visas. *'Mañana'* was the usual answer. *'Mañana por la mañana'* he said, spitting, 'Tomorrow and never. They treat us worse than thieves.'

Each of them had his story to tell and they were not nice stories. It looked pretty hopeless for me because I couldn't stand up for more than ten minutes at a time. I moved towards the door where an ill-looking Frenchman was having a violent dispute with one of the guards.

'I have waited here for days,' he shouted, 'and I'm fed up.' The guard pushed him back.

'Take your hands off me,' he said, 'I've been wounded six times.'

Then the guard said something that made my blood boil. 'A pity it wasn't seven times,' he said.

The Frenchman was at him in a flash and his comrades helped him as well as they could with their wounded limbs, but the guards drove them back and arrested the Frenchman, who was beside himself with rage, and took him away.

There was nothing for me to do but to get inside the office or leave, so I decided to go in. I had not been afraid of Franco and I was not afraid of the *Asaltos* either, who were not so hot when it came to fighting, anyway. I opened the door with one hand, keeping an eye on the policeman standing there, trying to think quickly what I should do if he were to stop me. I could lean on the door and swing one crutch, or sit down and use both, but he did not move. If he had pushed me I should have fallen down. Already people had gathered round to see what was going on.

I opened the door and walked in with some of the men following me. There was a marble hall with a richly carved staircase and a few dusty palms in pots. More soldiers were waiting upstairs on the landing in front of closed doors guarded by a dithery old man with white hair. I told him I wanted a visa.

'No, not today; tomorrow perhaps – the officials haven't arrived yet.'

'When will they come?' He didn't know.

'Tomorrow, perhaps the day after tomorrow.'

I walked to one of the doors and the old man rushed after me, but I had already pushed it open with one of my crutches. Three men sitting idle at desks laden with papers looked up angrily. What did I want? They could do nothing for me. I sat down on a chair, took out my papers, put them on the desk and demanded a visa. By now I was ready to raise hell and fight it out with everybody. The man must have felt this, so, very reluctantly and with much disdain, he unfolded the papers and looked at them. After he had read them he took out a big passport form and started writing: Name, Age, Nationality, Distinguishing marks. He looked at my leg and wrote, 'Bullet hole in right leg.' After he had filled it all out he asked me whether I had passport photos. I had none. That seemed to cheer him up. He pushed the papers away and sat back.

'Well, you must get some photos and come back tomorrow.'

'Where can I get a photo?'

'That's your business, not mine.'

I looked at the time. It was already four o'clock.

'How long will you be here?'

'Until five.'

I remembered then that I had seen a man on the Plaza Catalunya who took photos of people feeding pigeons.

'I'll be back before five,' I said, 'and I expect you to be here and my papers ready, signed and all. If it isn't ready I'm going to bring a hand grenade and blow this place up. *¡Sí señor, con una bomba!'*

I went out and left them gasping. With help from some comrades I left the building and found a taxi to take me into town. The man was still on the plaza just photographing a soldier and his sweetheart. I had to sit on a chair.

'Smile please.' But I could only raise a bitter grin. He developed the picture and made a few prints. I returned to the passport office. All the comrades had now gone inside and were waiting at the big door. The old man knew me now and opened it for me. My papers were ready. The official glued my picture on to the form and another on to a card which he filed away. I paid for the stamp and left.

Outside the men were eager to know if I'd had any luck. They congratulated me and showed not the slightest resentment at my success. By now I was so tired that I could hardly hold myself upright. I couldn't find a taxi and had to hobble down the long Paseo de Gracia until I reached a café.

\* \* \* \* \*

Only three people besides myself left the train at Port Bou. All the glass in the station was shattered and one wall was badly scarred by bomb fragments, but the station itself had not been hit. A soldier and a civil guard examined the passes and luggage. An official, a small man with black, oily hair and glasses, asked me if I had any Spanish money. No. Foreign currency? Yes, three pounds. He wanted me to give it up. I protested and said that I had brought it in with me. Had I any receipt or a note in my passport? I said that I had no passport and furthermore I had come in by boat at a time when there were no officials asking questions. The man became very angry and ordered the soldier to search me and I had to go with him into a small room. The soldier looked embarrassed when I stood before him on my crutches.

'I'm not going to search you,' he said. 'Let's just wait a minute.'

After a little while we went out and the soldier told the official he had found nothing. My three pounds were returned and I boarded the train. As it entered a tunnel I saw mattresses and blankets beside the tracks. The people of Port Bou were using it as an air raid shelter at night.

The station at Cerbère was undamaged. There were porters and stalls with chocolate and fruit. The passport officer looked at me sympathetically.

'Your passport?' I gave him my documents.

'This isn't much good,' he said to me. I knew it was not.

'Wounded?'

'Yes.'

'All right. I'll give you a transit visa, but you cannot stay in France.'

That was all. I walked along the narrow corridor which led to the restaurant but I was not through yet. On arrival at the station I had noticed a strange looking individual in a sort of Alpine costume, ginger plus-fours and jacket, panama hat, hob-nailed boots and a climbing stick. Suddenly he stood in front of me with several officers in uniform.

'You are German?'

'No.'

'But it says here you are.'

'I have no nationality.'

'How did you get that leg?'

'I was wounded.'

'Which side did you fight on?'

'For the Government.'

He then spoke rapidly in French with the Belgian and French

# ESPAÑA

### DELEGACION GENERAL DE ORDEN PUBLICO EN CATALUÑA

Barcelona 2 de Junio de 193 7

CERTIFICADO DE IDENTIDAD numero _____ expedido a los
extranjeros actualmente sin nacionalidad, para que les sirva de pasaporte
Orden de 7 diciembre de 1925

Valedero hasta el 1ª de Septiembre de 1937.

Para ir a Francia e Inglaterra.

y volver a España

Nombre Jean

Apellido paterno KIRAZE          Fecha del nacimiento 9-5-1906, en Hambur

„    materno                      gº (Alemania).

Nacionalidad de origen Alemana

Profesión Pintor

Domicilio actual en España Eventual

### DATOS PERSONALES:

Edad

Color del pelo Rubio

„   de los ojos Azules

Nariz Recta

Rostro Ovalado

Señas particulares Está herido en el pie derecho.

Observaciones Expatriado, se refugió en Francia,

de donde vino nuevamente a España, regresando

herido.

El que suscribe certifica la legitimidad de la
firma con la del portador de este do-
cumento.

Firma del naciente

El Delegado General
de
Orden Público en Cataluña

Esta Certificación es valedera más que para volver al país indicado en el y en los países indicados en todas las demás autoridades españolas que figuran a continuación. Se expide únicamente para procurar a los extranjeros sin nacionalidad la identidad que suele servirles de pasaporte y no significa en manera alguna que el portador es protegido del Gobierno Español. Está prohibido prorrogarlo añadir días o este certificado perdiendo en ambos casos su valor. Esta Certificación al dueño que el portador aquí.

*Jan's Nansen Passport, issued in Barcelona*

officers, saying my papers were not legal and that I was a German. They looked at the papers and then at me. I could hardly stand any longer. My armpits were sore from the crutches, it was hot and sweat was pouring down my face. I no longer cared a damn what they did to me.

'Are you going back to Germany?' asked the Alpine type.

'No.'

'Why not?'

'I am going to England.'

'Why did you fight in Spain?'

'That's my business.'

His German was very good and I asked him if he was German, but he protested that he was Danish; I did not believe it.

The French passport officer, who had been standing in the background watching us, came up and said that I was all right, that they should let me go, my document was a Nansen Pass saying that I had no nationality, and I could travel through France.34 The other officers agreed but the 'Dane' seemed disappointed. I had a drink at the buffet but felt very uneasy. Not even the batteries of bottles and food on the counter could cheer me up. The Alpine Dane was still watching me and, after a time, he came over to my table.

'This war is awful,' he began.

'Yes, a great pity.'

'I've seen a lot of wounded coming through,' he said. He continued, 'You fought in the International Brigade?'

'Yes.'

'When you go back to Germany where will you go?'

'I'm not going to Germany.'

'But you're a German.' I did not answer any more. I left the table and the waiter showed me to my room. I asked him to call me in time for the train and to bring me some coffee. I took the elastic bandage off my leg but did not undress. I fell asleep. It was getting dark when I woke up and the waiter came in with the coffee. He stood by the bed watching me while I drank. He had a face which did not show whether he was young or old. When I put the bandage on again he asked me whether I had been wounded.

'Yes.'

'Where?'

'Madrid.'

'Why?'

'Why what?'

'Why did you fight? You're not a Spaniard.'

'For the Republic,' I said. 'For the People.'

'I'm for nobody but myself,' the waiter said. 'Let the people look after themselves. What did you get out of it?'

I pointed at my leg.

He laughed, 'Yes, but what else?'

'Nothing else.'

'Then why fight?'

'Sometimes it's worthwhile.'

'It isn't,' he said. 'I once fought for democracy; it's a lot of bunk. I'm for nobody but myself. Trade is bad since this lousy war,' he went on. 'Nothing but lousy Spaniards coming over.'

'You don't like them?'

'They're lousy. You should see them coming over. They run like rabbits; all of military age. They don't fight, why should you? It's not your war anyway.'

'It's mine and yours,' I said.

'It's a lot of bunk. Would you like some more coffee?'

When I was ready the waiter asked, 'Are you going to Paris?'

I told him I was going to stay in Perpignan for one night.

'I wouldn't if I were you,' he said.

'Why not?'

'It's full of police waiting for boys like you.'

'Thanks for the tip. Then I'd better go straight through.'

'Think nothing of it.'

'I thought you were only out for yourself,' I said.

'I wasn't warning you, I was just telling you.'

'Well, thanks again,' and we said goodbye.

When I went down, the train was ready to leave and the attendant helped me into the sleeper car. He made the bed and told me dinner was in half an hour. Should he reserve me a seat? I explained that I was not well enough to go down the train and asked him for some whisky and a sandwich. The bread was white and crisp and the ham thickly sliced and fresh. One just ordered food and there it was, like a miracle. I drank my whisky sitting on the bed near the window. Dusk was falling with that peculiar darkened but transparent blue of the south.

The train followed the coast line for a while and then slowed down at Perpignan. I drew the curtain and peered round it. There they were, as large as life, detectives in bowler hats and heavy boots watching everyone who left the train, and there I was hiding behind the curtains, having done nothing but fight for democracy, hiding so that I should not be arrested in the country of Liberty, Equality and Fraternity. The world had gone crazy.

After the train started again I undressed and lay down. The sheets were white and cool. Everything was clean and polished. The little reading lamp over my head was reflected in the window against the night sky. The train gathered speed. It made this noise: 'Rum-tum-tum, rum-tum-tum'. 'No return,' it said, 'no return. Nevermore, nevermore.' There was something final about this last journey. I had left Spain for ever. Separated only by a narrow line were a country at peace and a country at war. Peace for how long? What price peace? The outcome of the struggle in Spain would decide it. The democracies looked on unmoved and gave no help. The writing on the wall would not be read, not even if it were written in flaming letters. Two thousand years had finally killed the conscience of the world.

I.B. 113.

No. K.2911.

Date. 27th March, 1939.

Authority issuing certificate —HOME OFFICE.
l'édiction de l'autorité qui délivre le certificat

Place of issue of certificate —LONDON.
Lieu ou l'on délivre le certificat

## CERTIFICATE OF IDENTITY.
## CERTIFICAT D'IDENTITE.

*Signature of Holder*
*Signature du titulaire*

*Hans Kuczke*

DESCRIPTION.
SIGNALEMENT.

The present certificate is issued for the sole purpose of providing the holder with identity papers in lieu of a national passport. It is without prejudice to and in no way affects the national status of the holder obtains a national passport it ceases to be valid and must be surrendered to the issuing authority.

Le présent certificat est délivré à seule fin de fournir au titulaire une pièce d'identité pouvant tenir lieu de passeport national. Il ne préjuge pas la nationalité du titulaire et est sans effet sur icelle.

| | |
|---|---|
| Surname.............. | KURZKE |
| Nom de famille | |
| Forenames.......... | Hans Robert |
| Prénoms | |
| Date of birth........ | 6th May, 1916. |
| Date de naissance | |
| Place of birth....... | HAMBURG. |
| Lieu de naissance | |
| Nationality of origin | |
| Nationalité d'origine | |
| Surname and forenames of Father | |
| Nom de famille et prénoms du père | |
| Surname and forenames of Mother | |
| Nom de famille et prénoms de la mère | |
| Name of wife (maiden) | |
| Nom de la femme (mari) | |
| Names of children | |
| Noms des enfants | |
| Occupation | |
| Profession | |
| Former residence abroad | |
| Ancien domicile à l'étranger | |
| Present residence in the United Kingdom | |
| Résidence actuelle dans le Royaume Uni | |

London, N.W.3.

Police Registration Certificate
Certificat d'enregistrement délivré par la Police.

The undersigned certifies that the photograph and signature hereon are those of the bearer of the present document.

Le soussigné certifie que la photographie et la signature apposées ci-contre sont bien celles du porteur du présent document.

Signature of the issuing authority
Signature de l'autorité.

H.M. CHIEF INSPECTOR,
IMMIGRATION BRANCH,
HOME OFFICE.

| | |
|---|---|
| Age | |
| Âge | |
| Height | |
| Taille | |
| Hair | |
| Cheveux | |
| Eyes | |
| Yeux | |
| Face | |
| Visage | |
| Nose | Straight. |
| Nez | |
| Special peculiarities | |
| Signes particuliers | |
| Remarks | |
| Observations | |

This Certificate is available during its validity for the holder's return to the United Kingdom without visa.

Durant la période de sa validité ce présent certificat sera valable pour la rentrée du titulaire dans le Royaume

*UK Certificate of Identity issued 27 March 1939*

# Afterword by Charlotte Kurzke

*Biographical Notes - Jan Kurzke*

Jan was born Hans Robert Kurzke in Hamburg in 1905. His mother was Danish and his father was from Silesia, a Wehrmacht officer who was a very harsh and brutal parent. There were five children. The two oldest boys were drowned during the First World War and one, at least, is buried at Dover. The family was very poor and Jan left school at fourteen to work in the docks where he used to steal coffee, among other things. At sixteen, he won a scholarship to art school in Hamburg and set about educating himself. In 1927 he moved to Berlin. He became a Marxist and took part in street fights with the Nazis. He was obliged to leave Germany precipitately, aided by Gustaf Grundgens, in February 1931, sailing from Hamburg bound for Cape Town on the SS Ussukuma. He travelled part of the way along the coast of Africa before working his way back northwards to Europe.

He spent six months in Barcelona before he set out on his trek around southern Spain. By the autumn of 1934, he was in Mallorca where he met the English people who brought him to London, where he met my mother Kate. He did not like England and had no intention of staying there.

He and Kate spent the winter of 1935-36 in Spain and went to Portugal during the summer of 1936.

Once they were both back in England after their time in the Spanish war, they remained together and began work on their manuscripts. One great drawback to living in England was that Jan was prohibited from taking paid employment and this stricture remained until the middle of 1941. Jan had his exhibition of drawings and paintings at the Delius Giese Gallery. On the whole, his work was not particularly well received although his drawings and water-colours were admired.

During the Spanish war, he drew constantly: comrades in arms, comrades in hospital and any scenes visible from windows.

It is tragic that all this work seems to have been lost.

When the Second World War broke out, Jan and Kate were on Guernsey. They returned to England where Jan immediately tried to join up. He was rejected, not because of his leg but because of faults in his hearing and eyesight which had not prevented him from being an artist and a crack-shot. He was interned on the Isle of Man from June 1940 to July 1941. This really marked the beginning of the end of his relationship with Kate.

After he returned from the Isle of Man, Jan worked during the day in a horrible factory where skins were processed and tried to paint at night by the light of double summer time.

In 1942, he got a job painting scenery at the Arts Theatre where he met a young actress, Gillian Adams, whom he married in 1945.

After the war, he did a variety of work including painting portraits of children, cleaning and restoring private collections of pictures and also cleaning and restoring church art and decorations for the Church Commission, but somehow he contrived to fall out with everyone who could help him.

He was a man who changed greatly over the years. He was always reserved and disliked emotional scenes. He liked cleanliness and order. He was self-sufficient; there was no household task he could not perform. As a young man, he was talented, courageous, amusing, charming, irresistible to women and very susceptible to them. They all remained devoted to him and he remained very fond of them until he married.

He never naturalised so he could not have travelled even if he had wished to. He did keep up with a few very old friends. In his latter years he was very isolated. He did not paint any more. At the end, he refused to go out socially at all. He tried to close the doors on every past experience and suffered greatly as a result.

It must be said that it was his wife Gillian who kept him in touch with his children and who tried to welcome relatives and friends who wished to make contact with him.

He committed suicide on 15 December 1981.

Cat [?] l'the [?] and [?] 19.10.4.41 [?]

**MALE ENEMY ALIEN—EXEMPTION FROM INTERNMENT—REFUGEE**

(1) Surname (block capitals) _____ KURZKE

    Forename _____

    Alias _____

(2) Date and place of birth _____ 6 - 5 - 05 _____ Hamburg

(3) Nationality _____ German _____

(4) Police Regn. Cert. No. _____ 560740 _____

    Home Office reference, if known _____

    Special Proceeding Card Number, if known ____

(5) Address _____ 73 King Henry's Road N.W.

(6) Normal occupation _____ Artist Portrait Painter

(7) Present Occupation _____ a _____

(8) Name and address of employer _____

(9) Decision of Tribunal _____ Exempt from internment _____ Date 15 [?]

(10) Whether exempted from Articles 6 (a) and 9 (a) (Yes or No) _____ Yes

(11) Whether desires to be repatriated (Yes or No) _____ No

[over]

# Appendix 1: Letters from Bernard Knox to Bill McGuire and Charlotte Kurzke

INDEX

Transcribed from photocopies of the originals held by Charlotte Kurzke; published here courtesy of MacGregor Knox

Bernard Knox
13013 Scarlet Oak Drive
Darnestown
Maryland 20878

June 7, 1990

Dear Bill

Thanks for your advice about tracing my Bollingen Fellowship. I will get down to LgC one of these days and look it up. Meanwhile, I have proudly added it to my curriculum vitae.

We had, in our first English group of eleven or so, a German refugee, a painter, called Jan Kurz  (but it may well have been Kurzke – I never saw it written down). He was wounded at Boadilla as I was, but later in the day and was carried to an aid station by John [Cornford].  I never heard of him again. It may be the same man – he may have got a journalistic assignment after recovering from his wound (which was a bad one – bullet high up in the leg). If you ever come across that battered typescript I'd be glad if you'd check to see if it is the same man. This Jan was the son of a Prussian Reichswehr colonel of artillery and was deaf in one ear because his father had taken him, when a baby to a battalion firing practice. He was a very quiet, cultured chap, and made sketches of some of us when we were out of the line. Unfortunately the first two fellows he sketched got killed right away and nobody wanted to sit for his portraits after that. John did, though. But I imagine all his drawings were lost when he was evacuated from Boadilla – we were very nearly surrounded, and nobody was bothering about baggage.

All the best

Bernard

Bernard Knox
13013 Scarlet Oak Drive
Darnestown
Maryland 20878

January 17, 1991

Dear Charlotte Kurzke,

I enclose a xerox of an account of the Boadilla engagement I wrote a few months later: it mentions meeting your father in the dressing station at Majadahonda. We went into Madrid in the same ambulance, which, however, was not an ambulance but an old taxi with a red cross painted on the roof. There were three of us, Jan painfully wounded in the upper leg, I in the neck and the man in front next to the driver had been shot through both cheeks so that he had difficulty in speaking. This was unfortunate since he knew the way to the hospital (the city was blacked out) and the driver didn't. He would try to give him directions but what he said was unintelligible. Meanwhile the driver kept driving fast and slamming on the brakes when he came near an obstacle (there were plenty around, including wrecked cars and barricades): when that happened all three of us would yell in pain as the sudden stop jarred our wounds. It was a nightmare ride. But eventually we got to the Brigade hospital, which was none other than the (once) luxurious Hotel Palace. After that I did not see Jan again: I think he was moved to Valencia soon and I was kept in Madrid.

I left England with John Cornford and another Cambridge fellow-graduate McLaurin in late August 1936 for Paris, where we were sent to a hotel in the XX'eme arrondissement: it was full of French, Polish, Italian and refugee German volunteers. Exactly when Jan joined us I don't remember: I don't think he left England with us; he must have been in another small English group that joined us in Albacete, the base of the Brigades. At any rate, in Albacete we English numbered about 21, and we were assigned to the machine gun company (*compagnie mitrailleuse*) of the French battalion that was being formed. Jan could have

239

gone to the German battalion, named after the executed communist leader Edgar André, but preferred to stay with the English. There was also a Polish battalion named after Dombrowski (I'm ashamed to say I don't know who he was). The French was called Commune de Paris but everyone called it Battalion Dumont, the name of its popular commander. On November 5th or 6th, these three battalions, constituting the XIth International Brigade (the first, but that's how the military mind works – we joked that it was intended to confuse the enemy) were sent up to Madrid, which was in danger of falling to the Franco troops, who were already in the Western and N.W. suburbs. We were sent to the Ciudad Universitaria, the complex of American-style glass and concrete buildings of the new university, and defended (appropriately enough) a building called Filosofía y Letras. We were then moved to positions along the Manzanares river, afterwards to a failed attack west of Madrid at a place called Aravaca and then back to Filosofía y Letras again. It was by now mid-December and we had lost a good half of our band of 21. At Boadilla, where Franco troops launched an offensive designed to cut Madrid off from the North West road, we lost quite a few more.

I liked Jan very much and saw a lot of him in those six weeks or so at the front. He was a very handsome young man, with aristocratic looks and manners, and a talented artist. He made some sketches of the buildings and of some of us. I don't suppose they survived. He told me the story of his father taking him, when he was a small boy, to the regimental parade at which there was an artillery salute that deafened him in one ear. I have often wondered what happened to him and was glad to hear that he got out of Spain alive. I am sorry I don't remember any more about him – it was a very long time ago.

Best wishes

Bernard Knox

Bernard Knox
13013 Scarlet Oak Drive
Darnestown
Maryland 20878

23 April 1992

Dear Charlotte Kurzke,

I should have written to you before this but I have been madly busy (mostly on things that I won't even be able to remember three months from now) and have been reading Jan's fascinating memoir in the intervals. I do thank you for getting it into readable shape and sending it to me. It brought back a flood of memories, of places, times, and people that I had forgotten.

I wonder about its genesis – what impelled Jan to write it in such detail, above all, when he started to do so. It must have been soon after the events described (or based on notes taken at the time) for the wealth of detail (almost all of it sounded absolutely authentic) would surely be beyond recall at a long distance in time. And the conversations that he reports at such length – they sound in character and true to life and the situation – but how could he remember them so vividly?

The only detail that clashes with my memory is the account of my getting wounded at Boadilla. He has me walking away from the wound after recovering from the initial shock, helped by some of the squad. What I remember (and how could I forget?) is being left behind, after hearing David MacKenzie, who had been a medical student, say, about the fountain of blood pulsing out of my neck "I can't do anything about that" and hearing John Cornford say goodbye to me. They had to go on with the gun and as they left I started to lose consciousness, convinced of course that this was the end and I was on my way out. Unlike many people over here who claim to have "died" in similar circumstances, I didn't hear any angels singing or feel a heavenly peace; like the heroes of the Iliad I was furiously angry. I did pass out and walked back to the village where I found the squad setting up a gun position, and then proceeded to walk through woods for several kilometers to the dressing station at Majadahonda, where I found Jan, with the wound in his leg. He was probably struggling with getting the gun back when John and David came to look after me and when I turned up in the village didn't realize that I had lost consciousness for a while.

But that's a minor matter; everywhere else he catches the reality, the tone, the feel of those terrifying and exhilarating few weeks.

There are places where clearly he and I were with different sections in different places. On the journey to Madrid, for example, I went, with John and David, by train all the way to Alcalá de Henares and from there by truck to Vallecas, an eastern suburb of Madrid. We then went, by rail, round Madrid's northern edge to detrain at the Estación del Norte and then start on the march out to University City.

I didn't find anything to correct in your manuscript; you did a fine job of transcribing what I imagine was a very difficult text.

As for your queries :

The date of the Aravaca flanking movement must be very close to November 8, the day we took position on the Manzanares river. The mill Jan describes was at Aravaca. I would guess we were there from Nov. 10 to 13.

The evacuated suburb was certainly not Cuatro Caminos; it may have been Moncloa, as you surmised. The dates of the Boadilla offensive are confusing since the battle went on for a long time with stops and starts. I am pretty sure we moved up to Boadilla on the 15th of December and that means Jan and I must have been wounded on the 16th.

The names. Tommy? must have been Tom Patton. He was killed at Boadilla. Marcel was a French character who was a particular friend of mine; I sat next to him on the train from Paris to Marseille when we all started out. Alfredo, a Quebecqois, was CO of the machine gun company. There was somebody called Stevens (not, I think, Stephens) but I don't remember anything about him. There was indeed a Christopher Cauldwell in Spain but that was later (he was killed at Jarama); the Christopher who came with us from England was Christopher Thornycroft, who had got fed up with the French and attached himself to the German battalion. There was also a Ron? Symes, who I think was killed at Boadilla. I never heard of Raymond and never met Jan's friend Muller. Gustave (with a -e) was not Gustav Regler, the political commissar of the 12th Brigade, but a Parisian worker, who was appointed *responsable* for our English section, i.e. if we had a gripe or wanted something I would go to him and he would try to get something done about it. I have no idea who 'George' was.

It must be very strange to read those two separate accounts by your father and mother. And dovetailing them together might make a fascinating book. Have you thought of trying to get it published? Has Bill McGuire seen it? He might have some idea where to go if you do.

Once again, thank you so much for sending me this. I am not clear about whether you want it back or not. If there had been corrections to make on the m/s I would have sent it back but I didn't find any errors. But if you need it back let me know and I will send it.

With thanks and best wishes

[Signed]

Bernard Knox

Bernard Knox
13013 Scarlet Oak Drive
Darnestown
Maryland 20878

May 18 1992

Dear Charlotte Kurzke

There is no question of having to 'forgive' Jan for not knowing what was happening to me: he was busy getting the MG's back into the village and we were under fire.

Your description of him as a 'rather solitary man who tended to sit back and observe and contemplate much of the time' exactly fits the Jan I remember in Spain. In a bunch of very excitable types he always seemed philosophic and slightly amused.

I will forward the manuscript to Bill: I am sure he will be delighted to see it. And he may have some ideas about publication: he certainly has connections in that world.

One thing occurred to me as I read the MS. Jan mentions a sketch he made on one of the group – Steve Yates I think. He made several such sketches – one of John Cornford I remember. Is there any trace of them? They would make a remarkable addition to the book.

If is does get to the publishing stage I would be very glad to write a short piece in addition to your introduction – with some details about the unit we were in and Jan's part in it, etc. I do hope it finds a publisher – it is a unique first hand account of what is now a legendary past. One which many young people –as I know from questions I am asked – find fascinating.

Best wishes

Bernard Knox

Bernard Knox
13013 Scarlet Oak Drive
Darnestown
Maryland 20878

June 7 '92

Dear Charlotte Kurzke,

I think I would prefer to wait until you have got the material organised before I read any more of it. I am wondering what the shape of the book will be: if it is to include Jan's travels in Spain prior to the war there will have to be some skilful editing to make sure that it doesn't read like a lop-side family memoir. Unless (as may be the case) that material is clearly relevant and illuminates the later account of his service in the Brigade.

As for the sketches, he may very well have lost whatever he had done before he was wounded – the conditions in which we were operating were not really conducive to making or preserving such material and if his experience parallels mine, he arrived at the dressing station at Las Rozas with nothing on him but his clothes.

But do keep in touch. And of course, if I am to write an introduction, I will have to see the finished manuscript, whatever form it takes, before publication.

Best wishes

Bernard Knox

p.s. I shall be away from home (in Spain and France) from June 25 to July 17.

Bernard Knox
13013 Scarlet Oak Drive
Darnestown
Maryland 20878

August 9 1992

Dear Charlotte Kurzke,

I am sending the account of Jan's travels in Spain in 1933 off to Bill McGuire tomorrow (I have to go to the Post Office to mail it and today is Sunday). I am sorry to have taken so long to read it and to answer your letter. I came back from Europe to find a pile of work that had to be taken care of first.

I found the MS fascinating. I had no idea when I knew him that Jan had been in Spain before the war, still less that he had travelled the roads as a tramp. It is a most interesting tale, beautifully told, but it breaks off at the most fascinating point. (You are right about leaving the bull fight aside). What happened to Putz and the others? It's a tantalizing fade-out.

Well, perhaps your mother's account will help somehow to bind all this together. The photographs and documents you mention might also help.

Bill McG. will soon have the whole thing in his hands and can perhaps suggest what can be made of it.

Best wishes

Bernard Knox

August 12, 1993

Dear Charlotte:

Thank you for your long and very interesting letter of July 27. I think your solution to the problem of Jan's silence about your mother is correct: you need an introduction which will explain why the two narratives of the second half (the interwoven sections covering events after Jan was wounded) have the contradiction. Once that is made clear there should be no problem: in fact the story of her efforts to help him and devotion to him set side by side with his exclusion of her from his account of his life make for poignant reading. (I'm not being cynical and don't want to sound like a publisher (God forbid) but I did find her narrative very moving in that respect but was puzzled about the reason – once clear, I think it makes her story almost tragic – and absorbing.

What you need to do with her narrative before she finds Jan again is to cut out all the bureaucratic stuff that has little or nothing to do with her search for Jan (though keeping in very interesting items like Auden and, possibly, Claude Cockburn). Jan's part, I think, can stand as it is – except for the bull fight. You can mention Putz and our feeling that Jan went to Spain in hopes of finding her in your introduction, where you could also write about your mother and her background. I think it could be a fascinating book.

As for Jan's memory for conversations, I find your explanation convincing – you might put in something about that in the introduction. And also some background – his upbringing in Germany for example. I seem to remember that he was slightly deaf in one ear and told me that his father, an officer in the field artillery, took him when he was a baby to hear a salute fired by the battery on some state occasion, for which he blamed the later ear trouble. At any rate, you should include what you know or can find out about his background as well as doing the same for your mother.

So do persevere. I think you have something quite extra-ordinary here.

247

If you think it would help, I could write a short piece about my recollection of Jan.

All best wishes

Bernard

Bernard Knox
13013 Scarlet Oak Drive
Darnestown
Maryland 20878

February 27 1997

Dear Charlotte Kurzke:

Forgive me for leaving your letter so long unanswered; I have been very busy and also slowed up by a bad and lingering cold.

Of course you are welcome to use in the book anything I wrote to you. As for reading the MS I will be glad to do so but should warn you that I have other MSS ahead of it that I must read first as well as MSS of my own that I am working on. All I can promise is that I won't leave you in the dark as Hugh Thomas.

Unlike him, I don't have access to or influence with publishers, but at least I can give you a critical assessment of the book.

I hope the winter is releasing its grip: I know what a disaster an unseasonable English winter can be.

Best wishes

Bernard Knox

Bernard Knox
13013 Scarlet Oak Drive
Darnestown
Maryland 20878

July 7 1997

Dear Bill:

I have finally had a chance to read the Jan-Kate manuscript right through at one go instead of the piecemeal attacks on it that were all I could afford for a long time. I am very sorry to have taken so much time over it; the problem was not only a lot of exigent deadlines but also a long series of visits to doctors and clinics in search of a diagnosis of something that turned out to be, luckily, a minor and not a dangerous disturbance.

It is hard to imagine what a prospective publisher will make of this text. Jan's sections are all very well written and profit from the accuracy of his painter's eye. The only thing that will puzzle the reader is the fullness of the many long conversations he records. How can he have remembered all that? But the sections written by Kate, except for the first, the account of their holiday in Portugal before Jan went back to Spain, are too discursive; in the detailed description of office intrigues and meetings in Barcelona and the mundane details of the many long trips to Valencia, Almería, Murcia etc. the reader feels a constant urge to skip. These sections, I think, need to be cut so as to keep everything connected with her search for Jan and everything of interest in her account of meeting with various people (Auden, for example).

But the real difficulty most readers will face is something Charlotte remarks on in the preface, the total exclusion in Jan's account of Kate from his narrative – not only the meeting with him in Madrid before Boadilla which ended with the night they spent in a hotel (he substitutes a night in a hotel with a girl he picks up) but also of her many visits to him in hospital and even of her company on the train leaving Spain for France. Coupled with her devotion to him once found it presents a real problem both morally and artistically. For one thing, the reader cannot help feeling that if he is capable of *suppressio veri* in such a vital matter, he may also [be] capable of *suggestio falsi*.

Jan's account of his wanderings in Spain prior to the outbreak of the war I found very interesting, and it certainly gives a grim picture of the desperate penury of much of the Spanish countryside, a condition that fuelled the anarchist rage against the upper classes. But it stops abruptly, leaving the whole business of the girl up in the air. Perhaps a section ending before his meeting with his fellow-Germans could be kept as a prologue, so to speak, that explains his determination to go and fight for the Republic when the war starts.

I realize that this will not be very comforting news for Charlotte, who has worked so hard and well to pull these documents together. But I doubt that any publisher would consider it for very long in its present form. If Kate's sections could be skillfully cut, Jan's first section somehow rounded off and an introduction by Charlotte alerting the reader to the discrepancy between Jan's and Kate's accounts provided – pretty much what she has written already – I think it might have a chance.

Will you pass this rather discouraging letter on to her for me? I think it might seem less cruel coming to her through you, accompanied by whatever suggestions you yourself choose to make.

Best wishes

*Bernard*

*p.s. Shall I send the MS back to you? To Charlotte? Or is it a disposable copy?*

# Appendix 2: Searching for Putz

Putz was a nickname given to Margrethe Zimbal, who was born in 1916 in Breslau in East Silesia to an art teacher, Hans Zimbal and his wife Elisabeth. Putz met Walter Reuter, a photographer, by chance one day in 1932 when she was hitch-hiking near her home town, and they immediately formed a friendship. At that time, Walter was already in a relationship with Sulamith Silivia, who would later become his wife. He invited Putz to visit them in Berlin, where he introduced her to his communist friends, including the radical lawyer Hans Litten.[35]

Putz's father joined the Nazi party in 1933 and soon became an ardent devotee. In the meantime, with Hitler's rise to power and Litten's arrest, things were getting too hot in Berlin for Walter and Sulamith and they decided to head for the Swiss border. When Walter sent Putz a telegram to tell her of their intentions, she sent one back saying "I'm coming with you."[36]

They left Berlin on 14 March, 1933 and hitch-hiked their way across Europe, earning spare change by singing to the accompaniment of their guitars.[37] They arrived in Madrid in May 1933 and met up with fellow German photographer Otto Pless and his friend Mariano Rawicz, who helped to set up Walter as a freelance news photographer and offered the threesome temporary accommodation. They ended up staying for several months, before setting off to busk their way around Andalusia in late 1933 or early 1934. Rawicz recalls in his memoirs:

> All three wore navy-blue shirts and sandals on their bare feet. He was wearing short trousers and the women wore short skirts. It was the classic outfit favoured by the Wandervögel, an anarchist youth organisation which had been broken up and persecuted by the nazis. [...] It was the first time that I had come across anarchists at close quarters. There's no doubt that they were honest and well intentioned. But their scorn and hatred towards everything bourgeois and everything with a hint of authority, hierarchy and organisation made them suffer to a certain extent from the same defects and vices that they were trying to combat. The only decent, just and valid opinions were their own.[38]

Putz features in the Granada chapter of the first part of Jan's memoir, when Walter invites him to join them on their travels, on the one condition that he mustn't fall in love with her. This would have been in the late spring or early summer of 1934. As Bernard Knox notes in his correspondence, it's quite frustrating that the narrative breaks off there. It's reasonable to assume that a romance ensued (or at least an infatuation on Jan's part) in spite of his undertaking to Walter. Some promises are made to be broken.

The three companions are only mentioned in passing in the Cádiz chapter. It is possible that Jan may have written other chapters describing events before and after the Cádiz episode. His daughter Charlotte noted that his papers were a complete jumble when she received them from her brother, after Jan committed suicide in 1981,[39] so it is possible that there were more parts that were lost or discarded along the way; that of course is pure speculation. We have not come across any other sources that mention where Walter, Sulamith and Putz went or who they met between leaving Madrid and turning up in Málaga late in 1934, although there is at least one photograph of Jan with the two girls in Granada, probably taken by Walter (see page 63).

What is known from other sources is that after parting with Jan some time after the bull fight in Cádiz, Walter and the girls travelled on to Málaga (or Torremolinos), where Walter and Sulamith's son Jasmin was born on 18 October 1934.[40] Putz then departed for Mallorca with another German companion, Erwin Bresler. It is probable that by this time Jan would have moved on from Mallorca to England.

During their time in Mallorca, Putz found work in a bar in Cala Ratjada near the Western tip of the island.[41] The Wikiki had been owned and managed by Jack Bilbo, who claimed to be an ex-henchman of Al Capone, but by the time Putz and Erwin arrived he had sold it and moved on to Sitges where he set up another cocktail bar known as the SOS. By 1936 Putz and Erwin were also living in Sitges, and in his memoirs Bilbo mentions them both, using pseudonyms to disguise their identities.[42]

In Sitges, Erwin worked at the SOS and "they joined the JCI

and lived with KPD(O) members Else Homberger and Gerhard Henschke [...] and in August 1936 all four went as part of the POUM contingent in the campaign to retake Mallorca."[43] Bresler was killed in action in Porto Cristo on 16 August.

As described in detail by Mary Low in *Red Spanish Notebook*, after returning from Mallorca, Putz insisted on going to the front in Aragon.

"Two days after the return from Mallorca, Putz left for the Aragon front with four young Spanish boys. They all had packs on their backs and went away singing. They had only been at the front six hours when the boys were shot down in couples on either side of her, and she was left alone. Afterwards she wrote to us sometimes from the mountains, where she was acting as scout, creeping at night over the dark hills on the borders of no-man's land, not knowing how far from the enemy's advance posts she might be. Then she was back in Barcelona again, doing political work and attending the International Bureau."[44]

However, in Low's words, "she was not one to be long without a man," and while she was at the front a fellow militiaman fell in love with her, a German tailor named Walter Schwarz. He and Mary tried to persuade Putz to find a role in the rearguard, working in an office or as a nurse, but she insisted on returning to the front.[45] [46]

One day we were there in the café with her, when her old company, the *Bandera Puig* had been called back to the front. We could hear the trumpets blowing. Putz was swinging on her chair, sucking a straw, and her quiet face was inscrutable. We saw them come marching down the street, the dust rising and the red flag fluttering. They passed us.

Suddenly Putz jumped up and threw away her chair and ran after them all down the street, crying, "Wait for me, wait for me, I'm coming too! I'm coming."[47]

She was hit by a sniper on 22 October when on manoeuvres supporting the assault on Huesca, as she tried to rescue a wounded colleague under fire. She died of her wounds the following day.[48] Her body was brought back to Barcelona where it was placed on view at the local POUM headquarters in the Plaza del Teatro. There followed a parade along the Ramblas to the Plaza de Cataluña, attended by a huge crowd, including comrades from the POUM, together with representatives from the UGT, CNT, PSU and ERC, the International Red Cross, all the major police forces and a cavalry section of the POUM militia, as well as senior political figures including Bonet, Gironella, Geas and Puig Domenech.[49] In the words of her friend and comrade, Otilia Castellví, she was 'the prototype of the revolutionary woman [...] feminine but strong, brave and heroic, fighting until victory or death'.[50]

Simon Deefholts

# Notes

[1]William (Bill) McGuire (1917-2009): US writer, editor and scholar at Princeton University. He visited Kate and met Jan in the mid-1960s and tried unsuccessfully to find a publisher for their memoir of the Spanish Civil War. In the 1990s, with Bernard Knox, he tried again, also without success, using a new typescript produced by Charlotte Kurzke under the working title *The Good Comrade.*

[2] La Criolla was the most famous nightspot in Barcelona's Chinatown in the 1920s and 1930s, embracing an 'anything goes' culture of jazz, flamenco, cocaine and sexual libertarianism. For a fuller account of the club see *La Criolla – La puerta dorada del barrio chino* by Paco Villar, Comanegra, 2017.

[3] Walter Reuter (1906-2005): German photographer. He worked on the same newspaper as Jan in Berlin in the early 1930s. They met up again in 1934, both refugees in Spain, when Walter was travelling with his wife, Sulamith Siliava, and a young German girl named Margarethe Zembal (nicknamed "Putz"). After spending some time in a French concentration camp in 1939, he escaped to Morocco with his family, was captured by the French and sent to a Labour camp, and finally escaped again and emigrated with his family to Mexico (Source: *Walter Reuter, el fotógrafo alemán que retrató México*. El Mundo, March 27, 2005.)

[4] Margarethe Zembal (1916-1936): see Appendix 2 on page 253.

[5] Fatima was a false name used by Jan to protect the identity of Sulamith Siliava (1910-1954). She left Germany in 1933 with Walter Reuter and their friend, Margarethe Zembal (Putz). Their son Jasmin was born in 1934, while they were travelling in Andalucía. Sulamith left Spain with Jasmin in July 1936, while Walter stayed on in Madrid to document the war. They reunited in France in 1939, eventually escaping to Mexico in 1942. She committed suicide in 1954.

[6] For more detail on the months immediately preceding Jan's departure to Spain, see *Never More Alive: Inside the Spanish Republic*, by Kate Mangan, The Clapton Press, London, 2020, Chapter 1.

[7] John Cornford (1905-1936): Cambridge University graduate. Fought in

Aragón with POUM militia in August 1936, then returned to Spain with a group of friends including Bernard Knox and John Sommerfield.

[8] Bernard Knox (1914-2010): Englishman. Joined the IB shortly after receiving his BA from St John's College, Cambridge. One of John Cornford's close friends. Established contact with Jan and Kate's daughter, Charlotte Kurzke, in 1990 and tried to help her place the memoirs with a publisher.

[9] Chris Thornycroft (1915-2001): Went out to Spain fresh from Oxford University, where he had studied engineering. He later joined the Thaelmann Battalion where he fought alongside Esmond Romilly. (See Boadilla by Esmond Romilly, Hamish Hamilton, 1937, republished by The Clapton Press, 2018.

[10] The Jock referred to here is Robert Clarke (1901-?) from Bathgate in Scotland. The author names him as 'Jock Clark' on p.189. (Source: Richard Baxell.)

[11] John Sommerfield (1908-1991): One of Cornford's recruits. His memoir, *Volunteer in Spain*, (Lawrence & Wishart, 1937) was derided by George Orwell, who wrote: 'Seeing that the International Brigade is in some sense fighting for all of us [ ... ] it may seem ungracious to say that this book is a piece of sentimental tripe; but so it is.' (Source: *Collected Essays, Journalism and Letters*, vol. 1, ed. Sonia Orwell and Ian Angus (New York: Harcourt Brace, 1968), 276–278.) Jan Kurzke was also dismissive both of Sommerfield's version of events and of the man himself, whom he damned with faint praise. (Source: Letter from Jan Kurzke to Bill McGuire, 05 May 1965, private papers held by Charlotte Kurzke, printed in IBMT Newsletter Issue 35, 2-2013, p.19.) Cornford was more generous, describing Sommerfield (who was only 18 in 1936) as, 'tough and starting like me with no military training, has become a good soldier, and a good scrounger which is very important in a badly equipped army.' (Letter to Margot Heinemann, 8 Dec 1936, reproduced in *John Cornford, Understand the Weapon, Understand the Man*, edited by Jonathan Galassi, Carcanet Press, 1976, p.185).

[12] Frenchman from Marseilles; unidentified.

[13] Bernard Knox describes Marcel as 'a French character who was a

particular friend of mine; I sat next to him on the train from Paris to Marseille when we all started out.'

[14] H. Fred Jones (1906-1936): John Cornford described Fred as, 'a really good section leader; declassed bourgeois, ex-guardsman unemployed organiser, combination of adventurer and sincere Communist: but a really powerful person and could make his group work in a disciplined way in an army where there wasn't much discipline.' (Letter to Margot Heinemann, 8 Dec 1936, reproduced in *John Cornford, Understand the Weapon, Understand the Man*, edited by Jonathan Galassi, Carcanet Press, 1976, p.183). Sam Lesser, who also fought alongside Jones, married his widow, Nell, in 1943.

[15] Steve Yates (1895-1936): John Cornford described him as, 'an ex-corporal in the British army, expelled and imprisoned for incitement to mutiny [. . .] and a good bloke.' (Letters to Margot Heinemann, 21 Nov & 8 Dec 1936, op.cit. pp.183 & 186.)

[16] Jock Cunningham (1902-1969): Mutineer. Later became commander of the British Battalion. He saved Sam Lesser's life at Lopera (where John Cornford and Ralph Fox were killed) by heading out on his own into no man's land and dragging him back to the Government lines. Repatriated Aug 1937.

[17] Joe Hinks (19067-1943): Ex-British Army. Served in India. Later enlisted with the Red Army in China.

[18] George Sowersby (1912-?): Born in Edinburgh. Arrived Oct 1936 and repatriated Feb 1937. (Source: Richard Baxell).

[19] Pat's real name was Tommy Patten (1910-1936) from Co. Mayo. According to Bernard Knox, he was killed a few weeks after Aravaca.

[20] Hans: Unidentified.

[21] Edward Burke (1912-1937): Real name Edward Henry Burke Cooper. John Cornford described him as 'Edward Burke of the *Daily Worker*. Ex-actor, looks like a sap, always loses everything, but has a queer gift for understanding machinery . . .' (Letter to Margot Heinemann, 8 Dec 1936, op. cit. p.185)

[22] Alfredo (-1936): According to John Sommerfield, 'he was a French-Canadian with some Jewish ancestry, and had been a regular army officer and machine gun expert; he was tall, fresh-complexioned, with dark curly hair, very good looking, with a charming, rather worried manner. We liked him a lot.' (John Sommerfield, op.cit. p.47.)

[23] André Marty (1886-1956): Member of the French National Assembly intermittently from 1924 to 1955, secretary of the Comintern from 1935 to 1944. As political commissar of the International Brigades from 1936 until 1938, his ruthless pursuit of suspected fifth columnist earned him the sobriquet 'the butcher of Albacete'.

[24]General Kléber was the *nom de guerre* adopted by Manfred (Moses) Stern (1896-1954) for his role as commander of the XI International Brigade. He was a member of the GRU (Soviet intelligence agency). He later assumed command of the 45th Division of the Republican Infantry. He left Spain in 1938 when the International Brigade was disbanded.

[25] Griffin MacLaurin (1910-1936): One of Cornford's 'recruits', referred to by Bernard Knox as 'a Cambridge man like John and myself'. (Source: *Premature Antifascist,* The Antioch Review, Vol. 57, No. 2, Essays: Personal & Political, Spring, 1999, pp.133-149).

[26] Possibly Tommy Patton, who was killed at Boadilla (see Appendix: Letters from Bernard Knox, p. 242). Richard Baxell notes that the third man to go with Yates and Maclaurin was actually Robert Symes, who was also killed.

[27] This was John Sommerfield. He describes the moment in his own memoir: 'I woke suddenly, thinking it was my turn to go on sentry. There was almost complete silence. I looked at my watch, and it was just after twelve. So we hadn't gone after all, I thought, wondering why John hadn't called me, as I was supposed to relieve him at midnight. The silence was uncanny, no one breathed. I got up to look for John, stumbled over Joe's mattress, and found that there was no one on it. I stopped dead, listening, and heard nothing, nothing at all, not a breath, not a whisper of life. Complete, devastating silence surrounded me. I was alone.' John Sommerfield, op.cit. pp.147-8.

[28] This is a reference to the Edinburgh University student William David Beveridge Mackenzie (1916-?), the son of a Rear Admiral. He was

originally believed to have been killed, but was actually repatriated in December 1936. (Source: Richard Baxell.)

[29] 'Greta the blonde Swede' was actually Kajsa Hellin Rothman (1903-1969), who was born in Karlstad, Sweden. Virginia Cowles, an American journalist she worked for as an interpreter, described her as: 'a Swedish girl who dressed in men's clothes and wore her hair in a Greta Garbo bob. She had held jobs all over Europe ranging from governess to tourist guide, and had finally wound up in Barcelona as a marathon dancer. On the twelfth day of the dance, war broke out and she went to the front as a nurse. She spoke seven languages fluently and her talents finally had been employed by the Press Bureau, who appointed her as a semi-official interpreter for the foreign journalists.' (Source: *Looking for Trouble*, Viriginia Cowles, Faber & Faber, 1941, p.32.)

[30] In all probability *Chicote's*, an art deco American Bar at Gran Vía 12, a favourite pre-war haunt of the *señoritos*. Now something of a tourist haunt, operating under the name *Museo Chicote*.

[31] Probably John or Joseph Ernest Stevens (?-1937), an Australian living in London who was killed at Brunete. (Source: Richard Baxell.)

[32] Unlike the International Brigaders and Russian aviators, the US pilots in Spain were highly-paid mercenaries, earning far more than the International Brigaders' allowance of 10 pesetas a day. For a personal account of a US pilot's experiences in the Republican air force see *Some Still Live* by F.G. Tinker Jr, recently republished by The Clapton Press.

[33] The Palace Hotel was Madrid's first Grand Hotel, commissioned by King Alfonso XIII in 1912. Its central feature was a huge ballroom covered by a glass dome, which was used as a mass operating theatre when the hotel was converted into a hospital during the Siege of Madrid.

[34] Nansen Passports (so called after the Norwegian, Fridtjof Nansen, High Commissioner for Refugees at the League of Nations) were identity documents issued stateless individuals to enable them to travel across international borders. They were recognised by over 50 countries.

[35] Hans Litten (1903-1938) famously subpoenaed Adolf Hitler as a witness in the trial of four Storm Troopers on charges of grievous bodily

harm and was arrested in retaliation in the wake of the Reichstag fire. He committed suicide in February 1938 in Dachau concentration camp.

[36] *Retrato hablado de Walter Reuter*, Anon. Universidad Nacional Autónoma de México.

[37] *El viento limpia el alma*, Walter Reuter, Lunwerg Editores, Madrid, 2009.

[38] *Mariano Rawicz, Confesionario de papel: memorias de un inconformista*, Mariano Rawicz, Editorial Comares, 1997, pp.26-27 & 193.
[39] *The Good Comrade*, by Jan Kurzke & Kate Mangan, with an introduction and notes by Charlotte Kurzke, IISH Amsterdam.

[40] *Jas Reuter y El Colegio de México*, Martí Soler, *Otros Diálogos de El Colegio de México*, 27 March 2020. Soler was a colleague of Jas Reuter who had access to a personnel file containing Jasmin's birth certificate. Other anecdotal sources mention Walter and Sulamith settling in Torremolinos, just along the coast from Málaga.

[41] *Les cançons perdudes, la vida de una joven alemana de la columna Bayo*, Gabi Rodas, *Diario de Mallorca*, 12 April 2019.

[42] *I Can't Escape Adventure*, Jack Bilbo, Cresset Press, 1937, pp.212-213.

[43] *With the POUM International Volunteers on the Aragon Front* (1936-1937), Andy Durgan, Ebre 38 Revista Internacional de la Guerra Civil (1936-1939), Núm. 8, any 2018 p.131 et seq.

[44] *Red Spanish Notebook:The First Six Months of the Revolution and the Civil War*, Mary Low & Juan Breá, Martin Secker & Warburg, London, 1937, pp.175-179.

[45] Bernat Ortega, series of tweets dated 24 January 2020 (Twitter).

[46] Walter Schwarz was a tailor who had arrived in Barcelona in 1932 and became a prominent member of the POUM. (Source: Andy Durgan, op.cit.)

[47] Mary Low, op.cit. p.177.

[48] Mary Low, op.cit. p.178.

[49] *La Vanguardia*, 24 October 1936.

[50] *La Batalla*, 23 October 1936.

# Also available from The Clapton Press:

**NEVER MORE ALIVE:**
**INSIDE THE SPANISH REPUBLIC**
**by Kate Mangan with a preface by Paul Preston**

When her lover, the German refugee Jan Kurzke, made his way to Spain to join the International Brigades in October 1936, Kate Mangan went after him. She ended up working with Constancia de la Mora in the Republic's Press Office, where she met a host of characters including WH Auden, Stephen Spender, Ernest Hemingway, Robert Capa, Gerda Taro and many more. When Jan was seriously injured she visited him in hospital, helped him across the border to France and left him with friends in Paris so she could return to her job in Valencia.

This first edition includes a Preface by Paul Preston, an Afterword by Kate's daughter, Charlotte Kurzke, and a note on certain key Comintern agents in Spain by Dr Boris Volodarsky.

theclaptonpress.com

# Also available from The Clapton Press:

**FIRING A SHOT FOR FREEDOM: THE MEMOIRS OF FRIDA STEWART with a Foreword and Afterword by Angela Jackson**
Frida Stewart drove an ambulance to Murcia to help the Spanish Republic and visited the front in Madrid. During the Second World War she was arrested by the Gestapo in Paris and escaped from her internment camp with help from the French Resistance, returning to London where she worked with General de Gaulle. This is her previously unpublished memoir.

**BRITISH WOMEN AND THE SPANISH CIVIL WAR by Angela Jackson – 2020 Edition**
Angela Jackson's classic examination of the interaction between British women and the war in Spain, through their own oral and written narratives. Revised and updated for this new edition.

**BOADILLA by Esmond Romilly**
The nephew that Winston Churchill disowned describes his experiences fighting with the International Brigade to defend the Spanish Republic. Written on his honeymoon in France after he eloped with Jessica Mitford.

**MY HOUSE IN MALAGA by Sir Peter Chalmers Mitchell**
While most ex-pats fled to Gibraltar in 1936, Sir Peter stayed on to protect his house and servants from the rebels. He ended up in prison for sheltering Arthur Koestler from Franco's rabid head of propaganda, who had threatened to 'shoot him like a dog'.

**SPANISH PORTRAIT by Elizabeth Lake**
A brutally honest, semi-autobiographical novel set in San Sebastián and Madrid between 1934 and 1936, portraying a frantic love affair against a background of confusion and apprehension as Spain drifted inexorably towards civil war.

**SOME STILL LIVE by F.G. Tinker Jr.**
Frank Tinker was a US pilot who signed up with the Republican forces because he didn't like Mussolini. He was also attracted by the prospect of adventure and a generous pay cheque. This is an account of his experiences in Spain.

**theclaptonpress.com**